T0304815

The Tree That Bends

The Tree That Bends

How a flexible mind can help you thrive

Professor Ross White

QUERCUS

First published in Great Britain in 2024 by Quercus Editions Ltd

QUERCUS

Quercus Editions Ltd
Carmelite House
50 Victoria Embankment
London EC4Y 0DZ

An Hachette UK company

A CIP catalogue record for this book is available
from the British Library

HB ISBN 978 1 52942 999 2
TPB ISBN 978 1 52943 000 4
EBOOK ISBN 978 1 52943 002 8

1

Typeset in Minion by CC Book Production

Printed and bound in Great Britain by Clays Ltd, Elcograf S.p.A.

Papers used by Quercus are from well-managed forests and other responsible sources.

*Dedicated to the memory of Tom White –
an uncle, a mentor and a friend, who opened my eyes
to the importance of learning to thrive.*

Contents

PART III:
Interacting with the World Around Us

APPENDICES

Preface

In an ancient wood stands a majestic tree. This tree has known summer's blistering heat and winter's icy chill. It has endured times of drought and floods of unrelenting rain. It has been dappled by sunlight and engulfed by the darkness of a moonless night. It has stood serenely still in times of tranquillity and been buffeted by winds gusting violently. And still this tree stands, resolute and unbowed. When you look at the shadow cast by the tree, it will be strikingly familiar to you. It is your silhouette; you are that tree.

Introduction

Have you ever felt that you are not enough? Ever been plagued by thoughts that you need to do more? Ever responded by cranking up your level of commitment, only to notice the toll it takes on your wellbeing? You aren't alone. Across the globe, people are waking up to the reality that placing too much emphasis on performing better can leave us feeling worse. High-performance mantras such as 'No limits', 'All or nothing' and 'Suck it up' belie the fact that we aren't indestructible, and frantic efforts to control our emotions neglect the important functions they serve. Rigidity takes hold. We get lost in our heads, trying not to have certain thoughts; we avoid situations that provoke strong emotions; we become captive to familiar routines. All of this can serve to diminish our ability to thrive – our capacity to both perform well and feel well.

What if I were to tell you that there is a set of evidence-based skills you can learn that would help you thrive? Although we might not be able to stop stresses and strains, we can choose how we respond to them. We're conditioned to prize the idea of being 'relentless', yet the surprising truth is that we need to relent more, not less. To do so, we need to be psychologically flexible. Flexibility is not about bending to the will of others. Flexibility is about being attentive to the demands that situations place on us, navigating the competing motivations these situations evoke, and making choices that optimize our performance, our wellbeing, and the blend between the two.

The Tree That Bends has been written to help you shift the perspective you take on the landscape of your internal experiences – your thoughts, emotions and bodily sensations. The importance of flexibility in the way we relate to that 'scenery' is often overlooked, but the wisdom of it has been with us for some time. As the Zen proverb goes, 'Change how you see, see how you change.'

This book will help you to appreciate that feeling satisfied with life depends on how you relate to the thoughts you have about experiences, on your ability to understand emotions as indicators of what truly matters to you, and on your flexibility to make choices that honour what you hold dear. In short, this book provides a step-by-step guide to developing what I call a 'flexible mind' that will be pivotal in helping you thrive.

A quick word on the title: *The Tree That Bends* is a phrase that can be traced back to East Africa and the Tanzanian proverb: 'The wind does not break the tree that bends.' For millennia, trees have played an integral role in the story of human evolution. Whether it's the fruit they grow, the shelter they offer, the carbon they capture or the materials they provide, we have a lot to admire them for. Yet even the mightiest of oaks can be uprooted if it fails to flex in a gale. Considering that trees have been around for so much longer than we have, we have much to learn from them about what it takes to thrive.

In this book, I draw on my more than fifteen years of my experience as a clinical psychologist. A key strand of my work involves working with those in high-performance environments, particularly elite-level athletes such as international rugby players, Olympic and Commonwealth athletes, and players at English Premier League football academies, but also people working in the worlds of music, acting and business. I have provided mental health and wellbeing support to a variety of business executives working in *Fortune* 500 companies.

In the work that I do, I've had the privilege of listening to many courageous people sharing testimonies of their lives in elite and highly pressured environments. Through this work, I have seen these people experience the full gamut of emotions: I have shared in their moments of exhilarating success, consoled them in the depths of despair, supported them in coming to terms with the huge sacrifices they have made, and helped them to chart pathways forward when they face the uncertainty of life beyond their high-performance roles. Many of the people I have supported have endured years of striving to be tough, and they are now paying the price. Yet ironically, for some, it is not doing more of the tough stuff that is the scariest proposition; it is doing less of it. Such are the societal pressures that we live under, and the pervasive power of notions of toughness and grit.

What does high performance mean to you? It is a question you might ask of top sportspeople, business gurus, entertainers or politicians who easily fall into that category. Yet maybe we should be asking ourselves here, because the idea of 'high performance' – and high-performance psychology – has never been more relevant to our own lives. Being a high-performance individual is not an occupation, it's a disposition; it's not what we do, it is *how* we do what we do. Whether you are a principal in a school, a self-employed florist, a first responder or an accountant, **if you take pride in what you do and want to perform well in the varied roles and responsibilities you fulfil in life, then the term 'high performance' applies to you.** For me, high performance is a lens that magnifies the importance of looking after our wellbeing. In the absence of wellbeing, performance doesn't stay high, it nose-dives. Sustaining high performance requires us to authentically recognize both our motivations and our limitations.

I want to shatter the assumption that efforts to build excellence require us to make compromises in relation to our wellbeing. This assumption has stymied the psychology of human performance for far too long. Success and wellbeing are not a zero-sum game – achieving need not come at the expense of breathing. *The Tree That Bends* **has been written to empower the smarter, more flexible version of who we are. It is about breaking through without breaking you – taking care of yourself, so that you can continue to take care of business.** By developing a flexible mind, you can appreciate when you need to go fast, when you need to go slow, when you need to go hard, and when you need to go home. So, if you're feeling frustrated, thwarted, unmotivated, conflicted and/or unfulfilled in areas of your life, this book is for you. Equally, if you aren't having any of those feelings today, this book will be helpful preparation for the times when life's challenges ask important questions of you.

Through my work as a Professor of Clinical Psychology at Queen's University Belfast, I have become an international expert in understanding how the culture we live in shapes our understanding about mental health and wellbeing. I have collaborated with international agencies such as the World Health Organization and the United

Nations High Commissioner for Refugees to develop effective forms of support for people experiencing adversity. These experiences have taught me that, no matter where in the world people live, and no matter what cultures they exist in, we all share a deep-seated commitment to causes that matter to us – whether they be providing for our families, inspiring the next generation, developing excellence in particular skills, or caring for our environment. In *The Tree That Bends*, I will draw on all of this experience to help you thrive in pursuit of what you're passionate about, in the cultures within which you operate.

Throughout my career, I have used my clinical expertise to provide support to people experiencing crises that have struck at the heart of their sense of self. This has included anguished refugees trying to create new lives for themselves in countries far from home, tearful teenagers bullied because of their sexuality, disconsolate people struggling to cope with the harsh judgements that they are making about themselves, elite athletes coming to terms with their careers prematurely ending because of injury, and weary business executives trying to reconcile the huge personal sacrifices they have made, only to realize that it was someone else's dream they were chasing. A recurring theme across this work has been the sense of uncertainty, precariousness and despair that arises when people struggle to understand what their experiences mean for who they are and what they believe in.

For me, this is also a personal thing. I grew up in the small town of Moira, which sits in the heart of Northern Ireland. I might be biased, but I think the people from this part of the world are amongst the warmest, friendliest and most down-to-earth folk you could ever meet. This belies the fact that over the course of thirty years, and throughout my upbringing, political unrest and sectarian violence resulted in the murder of over 3,000 people. Unfortunately, I have witnessed at first hand the impact that rigid intransigence and a lack of flexibility can have on the lives of people and the communities they are part of. I have come to recognize that sticking religiously – pardon the pun – to old beliefs can profoundly stifle opportunities for people to come together to work for the collective good. There is space enough in this world for people to honour their own traditions while being respectful of the identities and traditions of others.

I have also witnessed the power of flexibility in action: how the strength and courage of people impacted by what are colloquially referred to as 'The Troubles' can make them powerful ambassadors for change through the words of forgiveness they share. Consider Gordon Wilson, who, when his daughter Marie was killed by a bomb in the town of Enniskillen in 1987, said, 'I miss my daughter, and we shall miss her, but I bear no ill will, I bear no grudge.' The transformative effect of developing flexibility in our response to the stories that we create about ourselves, and others, was apparent to me from an early age.

Flexibility (of the psychological kind) is the ability to be present in the here and now, and to tailor our behaviours to situational demands in service of doing what matters to us, even if difficult thoughts and emotions show up. It can be measured: a range of self-report questionnaires have been developed to assess flexibility (including the Psy-Flex, CompACT-10, MPFI, and AAQ-II), and specific neural pathways in the medial prefrontal cortex area of the brain have been implicated in flexibility. A review of research studies conducted with a range of populations, including students, people with physical health problems, people seeking psychological support and office workers, found that low levels of psychological flexibility are consistently associated with worse levels of wellbeing (defined as a measure of how we experience the quality of our own lives). Flexibility has been highlighted as an important factor for both the emotional wellbeing and the performance of high-performance individuals. For example, research studies conducted with athletes including basketball players, tennis players and footballers found that higher levels of flexibility are associated with lower levels of anxiety and depression, higher levels of life satisfaction, and improved sporting performance.

Over the last forty years, a talking therapy called Acceptance and Commitment Therapy* (ACT, pronounced as the word 'act') has been developed and refined with the aim of building flexibility. ACT is an innovative form of cognitive behavioural therapy that recognizes that the impact of challenging thoughts, emotions and sensations can be inadvertently increased by our efforts to avoid, suppress or control them. When we get trapped in cycles of struggling against our internal experiences (referred to as experiential avoidance) we have less opportunity to do the things that matter to us, and we can feel unfulfilled, discontented and lacking in vitality. ACT aims to build flexibility so that people can do what matters to them even though difficult thoughts, feelings and sensations might still occur. There is a growing body of research demonstrating the

---

* Also referred to as Acceptance and Commitment Training in high-performance contexts.

effectiveness of ACT for improving wellbeing and addressing a range of physical and mental health difficulties. For example, ACT has consistently been highlighted as an effective treatment for improving day-to-day functioning, quality of life, pain intensity and mood of people experiencing chronic pain caused by conditions such as arthritis, fibromyalgia or diabetic neuropathy. It does so by helping people to drop their struggle against thoughts, emotions and sensations that they can't prevent, thereby reducing the impact that those experiences have on the person's life.

ACT has been endorsed by national bodies such as the Society of Clinical Psychology (American Psychological Association, Division 12) in the US and the National Institute for Health and Care Excellence in the UK. Importantly, research has shown that ACT interventions can improve self-reported levels of flexibility, and that these changes in flexibility are related to improvements in the difficulties people experience. Furthermore, people who are not mental health experts can be trained to successfully deliver ACT interventions. In 2020, in the wake of the COVID-19 pandemic, the World Health Organization (WHO) disseminated a free-to-download self-help programme called *Doing What Matters in Times of Stress* that is based on ACT principles and techniques. In recent years, ACT has also been adapted to specifically support wellbeing and performance in sport, music and workplace settings.

Drawing on the principles of ACT, this book will help you develop a flexible mind so that, going back to the wisdom of the Tanzanian proverb, you can be more like 'the tree that bends'. The book is divided into three parts:

Part I: In the Thicket – This section sets the scene by exploring how striving needs to give way to thriving in our lives, and a flexible mind is the key to doing and feeling well.

Part II: What Trees Teach Us About Flexibility – This section explores how the aspects of a flexible mind can be developed. I'll relate our ability to be Anchored, Willing and Empowered (represented by the acronym AWE) to the roots, trunk and crown of a tree respectively.

Part III: Interacting with the World Around Us – In the same way that trees respond dynamically to their environment, this part looks at how a flexible mind helps us balance three distinct motivational modes – Get, Threat and Reset – so we can thrive in our changing environments.

Throughout the book, I draw on my experience as an expert practitioner, trainer and supervisor of ACT. I share insights gleaned from my work with clients to help you understand how a flexible mind will be helpful in your own life (names and other details relating to these case studies have been changed to protect anonymity and confidentiality). I reflect on my own life and the journey I have taken in developing a flexible mind. You will see that I also share stories about inspirational characters – some of whom you may be familiar with – to illustrate key points. Reflecting my own areas of interest and speciality, these stories are drawn unabashedly from the worlds of sport, business and entertainment, but viewed through the lens of my professional expertise. While these stories may or may not overlap with your own areas of interest, I hope that my reasons for sharing them will be both clear and helpful. Finally, in addition to my own expertise, I have drawn extensively on academic research and other evidential sources to inform this book. To avoid cluttering the pages with citations and footnotes, I have given further details about research evidence and sources in the Notes section (pp. 321–66).

This book is not a set of rules to be rigidly followed. As you might have guessed from the theme of flexibility, the first rule of a flexible mind is: 'Hold rules more lightly'. The second rule is . . . well, surplus to requirements, owing to the first rule! Another thing the book is *not* is a life hack – social media is replete with them. It is instead about better understanding the nature of life – the nature of your life. If you are only interested in quick fixes and/or expect other people to assume the responsibility for bringing about change in your life, this book is not for you. We all know what it takes to bring about changes in physical conditioning. Psychological conditioning is no different. The rewards will be worth the effort.

Finally, a word to the wise: this book is not a substitute for professional support. It is my sincere hope that applying the learning that it provides will help to reduce the need for professional support, but that cannot be guaranteed. Sometimes life circumstances conspire against us and we can struggle to cope. Let me be very clear: the only shame associated with seeking help is *not* seeking it. If you need it, please reach for it. Your mind may well try to convince you to do otherwise – minds do that. Through the course of this book, you will learn that your mind is not always the best source of advice! Your physician or general practitioner will be an important starting point for support. I have also listed some additional sources of support on p. 316.

INTRODUCTION

I am glad that *The Tree That Bends* has found you. I hope you enjoy the book as much as I have enjoyed writing it. Oh, and by reading this book, you're going to learn a lot about trees! Into the woods we must delve to better understand ourselves . . .

PART I

In the Thicket

CHAPTER 1

High Performance, High Price?

There's a pernicious message in society that we need to do more – not just in our work, but in how we live our lives. The promise seems to be that if we *do* more, we will feel like we *are* more – more worthy, more recognized, more respected, more whole. It's an empty promise. As the late writer Alan Watts once remarked, 'It's all retch and no vomit.' We never get *there*. Instead, we just end up being less *here*. And the travesty of it all is that we can end up colluding in our own exploitation at the hands of unscrupulous employers, manufacturers of new-fangled products, slick marketeers or omnipresent online retailers. Furthermore, while there is a growing imperative to implement anti-bullying programmes in schools, workplaces and sports organizations to protect us from other people's cruel and demeaning behaviour, our *inner bullies* continue to run amok. We constantly admonish ourselves for not doing enough. Even when we do achieve, it can create a burden of expectation that more *should* follow. A 'do as much as you can . . . and then do some more' approach to life has taken hold. And it's not just quantity, it's quality too. We are stalked by fears about doing things poorly. Indeed, we can become so focused on not screwing up that we start to lose touch with what we were trying to achieve in the first place. When the tennis player Naomi Osaka lost to Canadian Leylah Fernandez in the third round of the US Open tournament in September 2021, she lamented, 'When I win, I don't feel happy, I feel more like a relief, and then when I lose, I feel very sad.' The pursuit of achievement can become joyless irrespective of the outcome.

In this chapter, we will shine a spotlight on some of the key concepts related to the psychology of high performance and how these may be fuelling our culture of what I refer to as 'do more to be more'. In doing so, we'll address the following three questions:

1. What do the terms 'no limits', 'resilience', 'mental toughness' and 'grit' really mean?
2. What challenges might these concepts hold if you take a high-performance approach to your life?
3. What does 'thriving' look like, and what are its unique benefits?

The limits of 'no limits'

In recent years, talk of the 'no limits' mindset has become *de rigueur* in discussions relating to high performance. This is the idea that the challenges we face in life should be viewed as opportunities to unlock our latent potential. It's a compelling idea that has been popularized in books such as Dave Alred's *The Pressure Principle* and Anthony Lynch's *No Limits: How to Build an Unstoppable Mindset*. But 'no limits' is a bit of a misdirection. Alred, Lynch and others who extol the virtues of the 'no limits' mindset aren't pretending that there aren't any limits; instead, they are proposing that we should find ways of working *beyond* those limits.

The fact of the matter is, there are limits. Your body, your capabilities, your relationships, your sanity, as well as the time, energy and resources available to you: all of these have limits. There is a risk that in trying to push beyond the limits we face, we fail to appreciate why those limits exist in the first place. Before deciding whether you *should* aim to improve your lot, it's important to understand where that *should*ing comes from and where it might inadvertently take you.

In January 2024, Jürgen Klopp, the then-manager of Liverpool Football Club, stunned the footballing world by announcing that he was stepping down at the end of the 2023–24 Premier League season, despite being under contract until 2026, and despite the team being top of the league and still in the running for four major trophies. In announcing the decision, he said: 'I underestimated or judged it wrong because I thought my energy level was endless because it always was – and now it is not . . . You have to be the best version of yourself, especially for a club like Liverpool. I cannot do it on three wheels.' Similarly, a year before, in February 2023, the French footballer Raphaël Varane announced his retirement from international football at the comparatively young age of twenty-nine years – six weeks after helping his team reach the World Cup final. He told Canal+: 'I gave everything, physically and mentally. But the very highest level is like a washing machine, you play all the time and you never stop . . . I feel like I'm suffocating and that the player is gobbling up the man.' High-performance environments can have a ferocious appetite.

Our ability to go above and beyond our limits is seen as a sign of our 'resilience'. The word resilience comes from the Latin *resilire* – 'to bounce back' – yet, when applied to people, it can mean very different things. For example, 'resilience' can variously describe:

- our ability to continue unhindered in the face of challenge or change (so-called 'robust resilience')
- experiencing an initial disruption in our capabilities that quickly resolves (so-called 'rebound resilience')
- demonstrating enhanced capabilities in the face of challenge or change (this overlaps with the concept of 'post-traumatic growth' that was coined by American psychologists Richard Tedeschi and Lawrence Calhoun)

Whether unhindered, resolved or enhanced in the face of adversity, 'resilience' is a confusingly ambiguous term. These days, 'resilience' is liberally used to describe everything from people to organizations, communities, buildings and systems that prevail through times of stress and strain. Lamenting the ubiquity of the word, a 2015 article in the *New York Times* suggested that 'resilience' had become 'profoundly hollow'.

In popular culture, 'resilience' tends to be used to capture traits such as tenacity and perseverance when experiencing stress: the idea of bouncing back, no matter what. Yet, the laws of physics tell us that we cannot constantly 'bounce back'. Robert Hooke, the seventeenth-century physicist, carried out painstaking work observing how different weights (a form of force) affected the extension of springs. Hooke proposed a law stipulating that up to a particular point, known as the 'elastic limit', the spring would return to its usual shape when the force was removed. However, if the size of the force was repeatedly increased, eventually a point would be reached when the spring would extend beyond its elastic limit, Hooke's Law would cease to apply, and the shape of the material would be irreparably changed. If the force applied to the spring is increased still further, the material eventually reaches 'breaking point' and snaps. While Hooke's work continues to be influential in the field of engineering, the term 'breaking point' has also been adopted into discussions about human performance.

In modern life, we are constantly encouraged to extend ourselves more. If your business is impacted by a global pandemic, pivot; if the number of emails you receive daily is rising, respond more efficiently; if there aren't enough hours during the working week, work at the weekends. An important part of not exceeding our own breaking point is changing the default position away from this relentlessness. The influences we're subjected to, whether it's workplace cultures, social media feeds or even the criticism we direct at ourselves, all produce stresses. Unfortunately, we can't always control those influences or the situations in which we find ourselves. **But while we can't stop the stresses, we can choose how we respond.** As Viktor Frankl, an Austrian psychotherapist and survivor of the Nazi concentration camps of World War Two, wrote: 'Everything can be taken from a man but one thing: the last of the human freedoms—to choose one's attitude in any given set of circumstances, to choose one's own way.'

I believe the 'no limits' mindset needs to give way to a 'know limits' mindset: knowing what our limits are and making choices that help us to both feel and perform well. To help us ease away from breaking point, this will include choosing to relent *more*. Relent to the need for rest, relent to experiencing difficult emotions, relent to the realization that you are not going to get everything done, relent to your yearning for a life full of purpose and vitality. Relenting isn't about giving in or being weak; nor is it about kowtowing to unrealistic demands from others. It's about being flexible and pragmatic in how you invest your time and effort. Relenting, when the situation requires it, is playing it smart.

Choosing to relent more may well be met with stiff resistance from some quarters. Have you ever noticed that some people have occupations tailor-made for their personalities? The patient and methodical nature of Carol the teacher, the effortless compassion of Ahmed the nurse, the confident assertiveness of Tony the city trader . . . you'd be forgiven for thinking that their careers had picked them. Of course, we try to choose an occupation to which we are suited, but our occupations also shape us – some traits get rewarded, while others are discouraged. Selfless, relentless dedication is celebrated; anything short of that is labelled 'quiet quitting'. The flames of perfectionism burn even brighter when fuelled by praise and recognition. Enthusiasm and conscientiousness are inundated with fresh requests; it's the willing horse that gets all the work. Additional demands supplement, rather than supplant, existing ones. The new to-do list gets layered on top of the old one, like an ever-thickening, artery-furring, coronary-inducing club sandwich of busyness. And everything is fine until it isn't. George Ezra, the English singer-songwriter who has sold over 3.8 million albums at the time of writing, neatly captured the tension between working and keeping well when he said: 'It can be incredible and unsustainable.'

It's not that dedication, tenacity and the unflinching pursuit of excellence aren't potentially desirable and effective qualities in the work that we do – they *can* be. It's just that when we rely too heavily on these traits, other potentially important qualities, such as being cautious, curious, sceptical or unconventional, might get neglected. It's evolution marching to the beat of the working week – certain qualities get selected while others become extinct.

In the world of high performance, a mythology has developed that propagates this imbalance. Take David Goggins, a former Navy SEAL who now competes in ultra-distance athletic events as a runner, cyclist and triathlete. A successful author with a considerable following on his popular social media channels, Goggins always finishes his videos with his two-word catchphrase – 'Stay hard!' And who would argue with him? Well, I would. I think he needs to add the following qualification: 'when the situation requires it'. Context matters. Not every situation requires the same solution. There are times when a less hefty and forceful approach to life is required. But if the pursuit of high performance is the war that some suggest, caveats and nuance are the first casualties.

Pithiness is a virtue, but it can also be misleading. The so-called availability bias dictates that information that is easier to recall disproportionately shapes our understanding of concepts. Because less sexy qualities, which are no less pivotal to sustaining effort, don't feature in Goggins' videos or this week's *Daily Stoic* quotes, their importance risks being underplayed; 'Rest well!' or 'Seek support!' make for far less compelling catchphrases . . . While many qualities may contribute equally to high performance, it can seem like some of those qualities are *more equal* than others.

Tough grit

In particular, two concepts have been co-opted by the 'relentlessness is everything' agenda – mental toughness and grit. While the origins of these concepts can be traced to high-performance environments, they are touted as indispensable psychological assets for pursuing greatness in all walks of life.

In recent years, the concept of mental toughness has received growing attention in the worlds of sport, education, business and the military. Numerous self-help books, such as Damon Zahariades' 2020 *The Mental Toughness Handbook*, extol the virtues of mental toughness and provide instructions for how it might be achieved. This is a seductive sell. Intuitively, the idea of mental toughness seems appealing – the sporting archives are replete with images and stories of tenacious and resolute competitors who have triumphed, and bookshelves are chockfull with the stories of military operatives who had the temerity to survive against the odds. But getting a clear and consistent definition of mental toughness has proved difficult, and establishing its scientific legitimacy is even harder. In the early noughties, Peter Clough (a psychologist now based at Manchester Metropolitan University in the UK) and his colleagues proposed that mental toughness consists of the four Cs: Control [of emotions], Commitment, Challenge and Confidence. They introduced an assessment instrument called the Mental Toughness Questionnaire-48 (MTQ-48) to measure it. Yet, although the MTQ-48 has been widely used to assess mental toughness, Clough and his colleagues' conceptualization of mental toughness has been criticized and concerns have been raised about whether the questions in the questionnaire neatly tap into the four Cs.

A review of the research evidence by Andreas Stamatis (a researcher based at the State University of New York) and his colleagues that was published in 2020 sought to determine whether interventions that aim to increase 'mental toughness' in elite sport settings are actually doing an effective job. Across the twelve studies published between 2005 and 2019 that they examined, they found that increases in levels of mental toughness did occur during the delivery of these interventions. However, they noted that only a small number of 'gold standard' studies (randomized controlled trials) had been conducted, and they highlighted concerns about the quality of the research and the level of potential bias in the methodologies used.

Assessments and research aside, the term 'mental toughness' is itself potentially problematic. It is susceptible to a phenomenon known as the 'expectancy effect' – the possibility that we will alter our report of an experience so it aligns with what we think is expected of us. Imagine going into a training session tomorrow and a colleague, psychologist or coach invites you to complete a mental toughness assessment. What would your reaction be? Perhaps you would be intrigued to see how you might score. Maybe you would be curious about why you were being asked to complete the assessment, and what the score would be used for. It is also possible that you might be concerned at what a low score might say about you. You might well be worried about being labelled 'mentally sensitive' – or, worse still, 'mentally weak'. Indeed, James Bauman, a sports psychologist working at the University of Virginia, Charlottesville, USA, wrote an editorial in the *British Journal of Sports Medicine* warning that a pre-occupation with needing to be mentally tough in high-performance environments was preventing people from seeking help. This chimes with US Olympian figure skater Sasha Cohen saying: 'Athletes most likely don't get help for depression or mental health issues because they can't even admit that it's an issue ... You need to show the world that you are strong.' Daniel Gucciardi, a leading researcher in mental toughness based at Curtin University in Australia, takes the opposite view from Bauman. He suggests that focusing interventions on developing 'mental toughness' would be more likely to get those who might be put off by stigma surrounding 'mental health' through the door of the consulting room. But as a clinical psychologist, I am concerned about using mental toughness as a Trojan horse to support mental health and wellbeing, as it contributes to the harmful assumption that mental health issues are something to be ashamed of. **Ironically, being vulnerable often requires more courage than being tough.** And avoiding the vulnerability of asking for help – by adopting a 'tough it out' approach – can be the surest route to burnout.

In Damon Zahariades' *Mental Toughness Handbook*, emotions are cast as potential toxins and toughness is the antidote. He warns that what he refers to as 'negative emotions' (such as fear) can 'sabotage us' or 'prompt us to make terrible decisions, hide mistakes and feel like giving up'. The 'emotional mastery' element of mental toughness (similar to Peter Clough's focus on the 'control of emotions'), on the other hand, is presented as the solution: 'Mentally strong people have mastered their emotions'. In general, there is a sense that we should deal with the inside world of our thoughts and emotions with the same attitude that we might adopt with a competitor in the outside world. Emotional mastery is akin to trying to 'outmuscle' your own difficult thoughts and emotions. **But emotions are not our enemies. It's not emotions that sabotage us; it's the choices we make in response to them that can.** Rather than 'mastering' emotions, we would be better served understanding them and the important functions they serve. We'll focus more on emotions in the next chapter.

As a highly decorated soldier, Jocko Willink, a retired US Navy officer and Special Forces operative, draws on his personal experiences of tough situations in his writing and podcasts. He has published several books on leadership, including the *New York Times* number-one bestseller *Extreme Ownership: How U.S. Navy Seals Lead and Win*. In a 2019 podcast, in which he fielded questions from listeners, Willink provided the following answer to the question 'How do you build mental toughness and resilience?': 'Do some hard things. Do some mental and some physical challenges that require you to push yourself harder . . . If you want to be tough, be tougher. You don't need to meditate on it. Just be tougher. You already have it.'

The implicit assumption is, of course, that tough situations require us to get tough in response – tough with ourselves and tough with others. We've all heard the phrase, 'When the going gets tough, the tough get going.' But is it necessarily the case that to achieve a desirable outcome, our attitude must be a mirror image of the challenges we are facing? This is a question that Martin Luther King Jr addressed in the 1963 book *Strength to Love* when he wrote: 'Darkness cannot drive out darkness; only light can do that. Hate cannot drive out hate; only love can do that.' 'Toughness' in response to tough circumstances may not necessarily be the optimal option.

Although mental toughness is hyped as being crucially important for achieving our goals, we also need to pay attention to what is motivating us to work towards those goals in the first place. It's not just what we are doing that matters, it's why we are doing it. I believe that connecting with our purpose, rather than mental toughness, is the fundamental ingredient when it comes to doing challenging things. Willink himself draws heavily on a sense of purpose, though he may not credit it for his 'mental toughness'. When he was asked on the same podcast what he would have done had he not been in the military, he said:

> *If I wasn't [in the] military, if I couldn't have joined the military, I likely would have been probably a policeman or a firefighter. I think I have a pretty inherent sense of duty, some patriotic feeling to serve and, straight up, I also like some kind of level of danger, and I like to take some level of risks, and I feel good about those.*

Willink isn't just motivated to do tough things for the sake of it (whether it is as a soldier, firefighter or policeman); he's committed to choosing to do the tough things because they serve a higher purpose – he is motivated to serve others. Let me be clear: I have no doubt that Willink *is* tough – he would definitely kick my ass – but more importantly, Willink is living his life authentically. He is being true to what matters to him. While the 'just be tougher' mantra may work well for him, it works because it aligns with his sense of purpose. We will return to purpose in Part II of this book.

Like mental toughness, 'grit' is frequently touted as a key ingredient for high performance. The word 'grit' has been used for centuries to describe a firmness of mind and/or a plucky spirit. It was Angela Duckworth, a psychologist working at the University of Pennsylvania, who adopted the term to describe a particular personality trait. In her 2017 book *Grit: Why Passion and Resilience are the Secrets to Success*, Duckworth defines 'grit' as a combination of perseverance (i.e. continued effort) and passion (which resonates somewhat with purpose and is the ability to identify important long-term goals).

Although Duckworth makes a persuasive case for the important role that grit plays in educational and workplace achievement,
there has been pushback from sections of the scientific community
about the concept's credibility, how it is measured, and whether it
offers anything uniquely new. For example, in an article entitled
'Much ado about grit', Marcus Credé and colleagues based at Iowa
State University and the University of Alabama reviewed research
findings relating to grit. They concluded that programmes aimed
at enhancing grit may have little effect on performance and success. And the following year, in another article, Credé stated: 'many
of the core claims about grit have either been unexamined or are
directly contradicted by the accumulated empirical evidence'. A
recurring criticism of grit is that it is conceptually very similar to
the personality trait of conscientiousness – the ability to diligently
stick to tasks. Research has highlighted that there is indeed a very
strong statistical relationship between grit and conscientiousness. To
her credit, Duckworth and her colleagues have conceded that there
is overlap between the two, but she claims that long-term stamina
differentiates grit from the short-term intensity of conscientiousness.
Nonetheless, it has been suggested that the idea of grit is guilty of
the 'jangle-fallacy' – when two identical things are considered to be
different simply because they are labelled differently. Grit may well
be 'old wine in new bottles'.

Conscientiously sticking to the same tasks – in a 'gritty' kind of
way – could prove to be *counterproductive* for our performance or
wellbeing. Continually banging your head against a brick wall won't
make the wall disappear; nor will it do your head much good. In a
similar vein, Duckworth's theoretical model of grit has been criticized for prioritizing 'consistency' over 'adaptability'. Our purpose

and goals can evolve, our dreams can fade to lost causes, and our world can be turned on its head. Being adaptable (or flexible), not ceaselessly consistent, is crucial for prospering in the changing circumstances in which our lives unfold.

Distorted views on 'success'

If grit and mental toughness have their weaknesses, what qualities might be more important for successfully achieving high performance? Well, before we think more about this, we need to recognize the impact that a phenomenon known as 'survivorship bias' can have on our understanding of success. *Survivorship bias* occurs when we narrowly focus attention on successful people, organizations or technologies, and deduce that particular characteristics they possess have *caused* their success. Yet, if we were prepared to look at other examples of people, organizations or technologies who were unsuccessful, we might find that they share exactly the same characteristics, and that the victors' success may have actually been determined by other factors, or indeed by chance. Our understanding about success is being skewed by what we choose to focus on.

The work of mathematician Abraham Wald was pivotal in identifying the concept of survivorship bias and the problems it can cause. In 1943, at the height of World War Two, Wald was working as part of the Statistical Research Group (known as the SRG) at the University of Colombia. The US military were keen to engage members of the SRG to determine how they could better protect their warplanes as they conducted missions over Germany. Decisions to armour the aircraft fuselages had to be carefully considered, as the armour added weight to the planes and negatively impacted their performance. The data compiled by the US military indicated that most of the damage sustained by planes returning from bombing runs was to the wings and the tail of the aircraft.

The proposal made by the US military was that the tail and wings should be reinforced. But Wald's report, entitled 'A Method of Estimating Plane Vulnerability Based on Damage of Survivors', concluded the opposite. It was crystal clear, he declared, that the armour should be added to the areas where the data showed the damage to be lightest. Why? Wald realized that the reason why those areas – the engines and cockpit – seemed to be hit the least was because planes that had sustained damage in those areas were the ones that *hadn't* made it back to base. The data set was, quite literally, fatally flawed; it was the information that was *missing* that was of fundamental importance for making the best decision. The US military followed Wald's advice, and he and his colleagues are credited with saving many lives.

Here's another example of survivorship bias, this time from a barn in Ireland. There are estimated to be more than 160,000 farms spread across Northern Ireland and the Republic of Ireland combined. On all of those farms, you will find sheds or barns, and in some of those barns, you might be fortunate enough to stumble across a classic tractor like the Massey Ferguson 35. Production of the Massey Ferguson 35 in the UK and the USA stopped in 1964, so they are a dying breed. If you were to strike up a conversation with a farmer who still owns one, she might well give the chassis of her Massey Ferguson 35 an affectionate tap and nostalgically remark, 'They don't make 'em like that anymore.' The fact that the tractor has survived at least fifty-eight years seems to provide evidence of its superior build quality. But wait – how long did the other 388,381

THE TREE THAT BENDS

Massey Ferguson 35 tractors produced between 1956 and 1964 last before they went for scrap? Rather than build quality, it might well be the fondness that people in Ireland have for the little red tractor (Harry Ferguson, who developed it, was born in Ireland) that has led farmers there to hold on to their Massey Fergusons and take care of them as well as they have.

The message here is simple: be wary of stories about business entrepreneurs, actors, musicians, sports stars, special forces operatives or, indeed, tractors who are held up as prime examples of what it takes to succeed – particularly those who are highlighted as having taken irregular or unorthodox paths to success. Although plucky stories of the 'outsider made good' have compelling charm and appeal, we must be open to the possibility that many others exactly like them may have taken the same path with a different outcome. It's important to be attentive to the information that may not be immediately available to us as well as the information that is. Other people's stories can certainly be an inspiration, but you are the author of your own unique story. And an important part of that will be determining what 'success' means to you.

The idea that 'success' is closely aligned to the achievement of a particular goal or outcome – such as reaching a level of seniority within an organization, exceeding a sales target set by a manager, landing a place with a prestigious orchestra, achieving the qualifying standard for a major sporting championship or writing an international bestselling book – is increasingly under question. There is now recognition that success isn't just about outcomes; it's about the *processes* we engage in: our habits and routines, such as engaging in deliberate practice, reflecting on our performance, etc. Managers and coaches tell us that if we 'take care of the processes, the outcomes take care of themselves'. The author and speaker Simon Sinek has used the concentric rings of his 'Golden Circle analogy' to helpfully distinguish between the *why* (i.e. our purpose), the *how* (i.e. our processes) and the *what* (i.e. our product) of the activities we engage in. But I believe that there's another vital element – the question of *which* (i.e. our proclivity):

- *Which* attitudes, thoughts and emotions tend to show up when we engage in our processes?
- *Which* options are we willing to consider in our efforts to blend wellbeing with achievement?
- *Which* response is most appropriate in the current situation for fostering the life we wish to live?

Asking 'which?' draws attention to the important distinction between our processes and our *experience* of those processes. For example, we could be mingling in a room full of people, yet feel completely alone; we could be demonstrating incredible prowess on the sports field, yet be convinced we're an imposter; or we could be leading team meetings, yet be rapidly approaching burnout. Our experiences are shaped by the thoughts, emotions and sensations that arise as we engage in our processes. As you will learn in subsequent parts of this book, we can become better skilled at noticing those elements of our experience and exercise choice in how we respond to them. The flexibility of 'which?' allows us to broaden our understanding of 'success' to move beyond narrowly focusing on outcomes and processes, and towards focusing on the quality of our experiences, so that we can foreground retaining a sense of vitality and being present and engaged as important indicators of success. This is, in essence, what it means to *thrive*.

Thriving

Imagine that you're suddenly unexpectedly flush – say, you've just won the jackpot on a game show. Let's imagine that you can invest £10,000 of your winnings to have a very good chance of being world-class in your chosen field. After careful consideration, you decide you'll go for it. Now let's imagine that you can invest an additional amount of money to maintain high levels of emotional wellbeing while pursuing that world-class status. Would you be willing to pay more or less than the £10,000 you had already spent? How much is your wellbeing worth compared to achieving world-class status?

Of course, money isn't the only thing we can invest – there's also our time. Let's substitute the currency in the paragraph above for hours. The Swedish psychologist Anders Ericsson and his colleagues found that, on average, 10,000 hours of deliberate, challenging practice are required to become an expert violinist. Malcolm Gladwell popularized this finding in his bestselling 2008 book *Outliers*, coining the '10,000-hour rule' for success – what was true for violinists, Gladwell contentiously proposed, was true for all. Engaging in deliberate practice for four hours a day, five days a week, over a ten-year period would get you your 10,000 hours (10,400 hours, to be precise!). It's no small effort. But the '10,000-hour rule' doesn't allow for the additional time required to keep us physically and emotionally well in pursuit of that expertise. Take a moment to convert the money you were willing to invest in your emotional wellbeing into hours. How might those hours also be budgeted on a weekly basis across a ten-year period? That's the time you could be meeting with friends, walking in the countryside, supporting family members, meditating, reading poetry, listening to music, going to therapy, getting a massage, learning the ukulele, taking ice baths, knitting, exploring the great outdoors, resting, surfing, journaling, doing Pilates, eating good food, sleeping well, being kind to yourself, caring for others, etc. This is the stuff of vitality and wellbeing.

Is there a golden ratio for how much time we should allocate to our emotional wellbeing compared to performance? Well, that's the £64,000 question! While research has identified that the optimal work performance of office workers requires a ratio of around 3:1 for productive work time vs time to relax during office hours, this does not capture how the workers allocated time away from work. The likelihood is that one size will not fit all, and the ratio will need to flex depending on who we are and what we are doing. What is clear, though, is if you're not investing time in your wellbeing, it's not the stock market that will crash, it's you. And it's our reluctance to let go of what's not working for us that sows the seeds for the crash.

The concept of *thriving* is a central focus of this book. There are two pillars of thriving – our ability to function well *and* maintaining good levels of psychological wellbeing. As Rong Su, a psychologist now based at the University of Iowa, puts it: '[T]o thrive in life is not only marked by a feeling of happiness, or a sense of accomplishment, or having supportive and rewarding relationships, but is a collection of all these aspects.' Based on their research, Su and her team developed self-report questionnaires to measure thriving (including the Brief Inventory of Thriving), which have been used to good effect across a range of different cultural contexts.

More recently, psychologist Daniel Brown, who is based at the University of Portsmouth, and his colleagues have explored the concept of thriving in sport. They define thriving as athletes simultaneously experiencing good levels of psychological wellbeing *and* achieving their performance goals. Wellbeing in this sense is more than just transient feelings of joy and pleasure; it reflects what Aristotle referred to as a *eudaimonia* – a form of happiness that reflects an authentic and virtuous approach to living a 'good life' incorporating the full range of human emotions. There is growing recognition that high levels of wellbeing are important, although not sufficient, for maintaining good sporting performances. As one of the athletes they interviewed in their research said: 'being in a good mental state is really important . . . if you're a happy athlete and you're enjoying what you're doing, then you're generally going to do well. If you're overthinking everything and stressing about stuff, then that's when it's going to start going downhill.'

Brown and his colleagues have highlighted that our ability to thrive is determined by an interaction between what they term 'personal enablers' (e.g. our qualities, attitudes and behaviours) and 'contextual enablers' that relate to the characteristics of the environments in which we find ourselves (e.g. the availability of family support, workplace culture, etc.). In essence, our ability to thrive is built on the interactions that we have with the world around us; it's about knowing our limits and working within them so we can maintain our efforts to do what matters to us and enjoy good levels of vitality as we do it. Unlike concepts like resilience or post-traumatic growth, thriving is not restricted to being understood as a response to stressful experiences. Thriving applies as much to the opportunities that arise in life as it does to challenges.

In recent years, the concept of thriving has been embraced by sporting bodies. For example, in 2018, the then-English Institute for Sport (now the UK Sports Institute), which provides scientific, technological and medical support to UK Olympic and Paralympic athletes, launched an initiative called Project Thrive. The aim of the project was 'to facilitate the creation of psychologically underpinned and sustainable high-performance environments that develop the person as well as the performer to thrive'. It coincided with UK Sport (the body that funds UK Olympic and Paralympic sports) evolving its strategic vision for the Tokyo Olympic Games cycle and beyond from the tough and gritty 'No compromise', which proved divisive, to one that would help athletes 'Win well' and 'Grow a thriving sporting system'. Thriving's twin focus on performance and wellbeing is now a core element of the vision of UK athletics.

And it's not just sport: the concept of thriving is impacting the business world, too. Sir John Kirwan, the former New Zealand All Blacks rugby player, has spearheaded the development of an online platform called Groov that has thriving at its core. Groov is used by organizations across the globe to promote wellbeing at work by helping employees to integrate mental health practices into their workdays. Kirwan's commitment to thriving comes from lessons learned during his own experience of depression. In an interview with fellow retired rugby player Alan Quinlan on the *How's the Head?* podcast, Kirwan said: 'One of the dumbest things people ever told me was that a zebra doesn't change its stripes. That is bullshit, because I have changed my stripes. I made a decision to change myself, I worked incredibly hard on my mental health and went from surviving to thriving.' In Part II of this book, you'll learn how developing a flexible mind can help you change your stripes, so that you too can thrive.

For too long, 'pushing through' has been the default position for achieving success. While grit and mental toughness have exerted a powerful influence on the psychology of high performance, and indeed have permeated popular culture, concerns have been raised about their scientific legitimacy. And what are we perceiving 'success' to be, anyway? Our understanding of what contributes to success can be distorted by survivorship bias. Furthermore, a mechanistic focus on processes and outcomes ignores the human experience that sits at the heart of them. Being conscientious, being tough, and doing hard things may well help us along the road to success, but it's important to travel *well*. Thriving incorporates a dual focus on both performing and feeling well, wherever we are on the journey.

High Performance, High Price? – Summary Points

- The idea that success can only be achieved at a heavy personal cost is deeply ingrained in high-performance cultures.
- Performance psychology concepts such as mental toughness and grit fail to acknowledge the need to be responsive to changing circumstances, and the important role that emotions can play in communicating what matters to us.
- It's not our emotions that sabotage us, it's the choices that we make in response to them that can.
- In addition to the *why* (purpose), the *how* (process) and the *what* (product), we need to think about the *which* (proclivity), and how this can impact on our experience.
- Thriving is a concept that focuses on optimizing our performance without compromising our wellbeing.

CHAPTER 2

Flexibility: From LAG to AWE

In 1872, Charles Darwin, in his book *The Expression of the Emotions in Man and Animals*, proposed that humans are born to experience emotions, which serve important functions and have evolved through time. More than 150 years later, that observation still holds true. We all experience emotions, and we all respond to those emotions in particular ways. We can cast them as inconvenient and troublesome distractions, experiences that we risk 'getting swept up in' or 'overwhelmed by', or we can recognize the opportunities they provide: a chance for us to understand what's important in life so that we can make choices accordingly. In this chapter, we'll explore two different ways of responding to our emotions – one characterized by *rigidity*, one by *flexibility*. Over the course of the chapter, you'll receive answers to the following questions:

- What functions do emotions serve?
- How might trying to control or suppress emotions create difficulties in your life?
- How can you respond to your emotions in a way that helps you thrive?

Emotions: Friend or foe?

A technical definition of emotions suggests they are a 'multicomponent response (subjective, physiological, neural, cognitive) to the presentation of a stimulus or event'. Neuroscientists have pinpointed specific parts of the brain that are central to the experience of emotions – chiefly the two amygdalae that sit deep within the brain. The almond-shaped amygdalae (the name is, in fact, derived from the Greek word for 'almond') serve as a data-processing system that triggers the release of chemical messengers into the body, including hormones such as adrenaline and cortisol. These hormones set in motion a chain of physiological reactions that can influence how we respond to the circumstances in which we find ourselves. Joel Minden, clinical psychologist and author of the book *Show Your Anxiety Who's Boss*, uses the acronym STUF to capture the network of responses that an emotion encapsulates:

S   Sensations within our bodies, e.g. butterflies in the tummy
T   Thoughts that tend to focus on characteristic themes depending on the emotion, e.g. worry thoughts in anxiety
U   Urges to react in particular ways, e.g. flee a situation
F   'Feeling labels' that we assign to the experience, e.g. 'excitement'

Research has found that emotions can also be infectious. The term 'emotional contagion' refers to how emotional reactions can spread between people via facial expressions, vocal expression and body language.

But as well as being responses, emotions also offer us information – *if* we choose to look for it. The Stoic philosophers of ancient Greece suggested that if you could notice the initial stirrings of an emotional reaction, you would be well placed to do something constructive about it. This was the idea that Daniel Goleman popularized in his bestselling book *Emotional Intelligence*. Goleman defines emotional intelligence (EI) as 'the capacity for recognizing our own feelings and those of others, for motivating ourselves, and for managing emotions well in ourselves and in our relationships'. As such, emotional intelligence plays a pivotal role in determining how our day-to-day experiences unfold and the impact those experiences have on us. Indeed, a review of research evidence that collated findings from twenty-five separate studies into EI found that higher levels of EI were consistently linked to higher levels of wellbeing.

The concept of EI overlaps with what has been termed 'emotional granularity' – our ability to recognize, differentiate between and appropriately label different types and intensities of emotions. Emotional granularity is important because it allows us to talk about emotions more clearly and respond to them more effectively. In 1980, in an attempt to classify and order our emotional responses, the US psychologist Robert Plutchik introduced his 'Wheel of Emotions' (see the diagram overleaf). He proposed that there are eight primary emotions – anger, fear, sadness, disgust, surprise, anticipation, trust and joy – and that these primary emotions can combine to give rise to secondary and tertiary emotions. For example, sadness and surprise can combine to give rise to disappointment, while anticipation and joy can combine to create optimism. Plutchik organized the wheel so that contrasting emotions face each other – sadness sits opposite joy, and fear is opposite anger. Also, different points on the same spokes of the wheel capture different intensities of the emotion. For example, if you look at the spoke located at the nine o'clock point on the wheel, you can see that rage is an extreme version of anger, whereas annoyance is a milder form. (For those interested in gauging their own emotional granularity, I've outlined Plutchik's primary emotions in the Appendix on p. 292.)

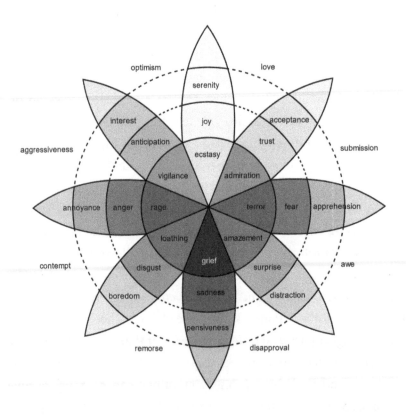

Plutchik's wheel also illustrates that emotions – primary or otherwise – rarely occur in isolation. Depending on the situation we're in, a range of different emotions can show up. In a sense, it's like a carousel ride at a fairground – at any point in time, multiple horses of emotion can be either rising or falling. Sadness, for example – the emotional state that occurs when something or someone important has been lost to us – might coexist with anger, which we might feel when we perceive an injustice has occurred.

One of my first experiences of deep sadness in childhood was when our pet Labrador, Kim, died. Kim had been a faithful companion to me and my sisters when we were growing up. I was devastated by her loss and the Kim-shaped hole that it left behind; it seemed cruel and unfair that a dog so lovable had been taken from us. This pain and upset will be familiar to anyone who has lost a pet. And even if, with the passing of time, we might consider taking care of a new pet, memories of the loss we experienced might cause us to hesitate: having emerged from the rawness of grief, we fear putting ourselves in a position to have our hearts broken once again. Yet in his poem 'On Joy and Sorrow' celebrated Lebanese-American poet Kahlil Gibran explains that sadness and joy are irrevocably bound: 'When you are sorrowful look again in your heart, and you shall see that in truth you are weeping for that which has been your delight.' The sadness I experienced when Kim died was commensurable to the joy she brought to my life. The brighter a candle shines, the darker the shadow it casts. Yet, it is also true that only by being willing to risk experiencing sadness once again can we also experience the joy that caring for someone, or something, can bring. These two emotions, joy and sadness, are unavoidably yoked together. I am glad that, with time, I was able to understand the message that the sadness of Kim's passing conveyed – if I hadn't, Bobby (our Cavalier King Charles spaniel) wouldn't be by my side as I write! When we try to avoid experiencing challenging emotions, we risk denying ourselves the opportunity to have other emotional experiences too.

Emotions are messengers

From exhilarating highs to the depths of despair (and everything in between), our moods wax and wane. If your moods were a media-streaming service, there may well be times when you would want to cancel the subscription – too much horror and drama, and not enough comedy. But what if our emotions are less like some Dread-flix streaming service, and more like a public address system communicating important information to us? To help my clients recognize the functions that emotions can serve, I coined the acronym TEAM – Treat Emotions As Messengers. For example, going back to Plutchik's wheel, you might identify yourself as feeling joy, and recognize this as a message that celebration is in order. A feeling of fear is often a very clear message that our safety is in jeopardy and we need to be very wary. The sensation of disgust might also be sending you a warning signal – perhaps that a food is rotten and should be avoided!

When we avoid or deny our emotions, it can lead to difficulties; it's like choosing to ignore a fire alarm as the house burns down around us. Of course, no system is without its faults. Fire alarms can prove to be false alarms – burned toast, anyone? – and our emotions are no different: they are imperfect. A range of factors can distort and skew our emotional experiences – alcohol and drugs, tiredness, chronic stress, misperceiving situations, hormonal changes, mental health difficulties and neurological disorders can all play a part. We can find ourselves feeling fearful in the absence of any clear and obvious threat, amped up when we really ought to be calm, or dreadfully sad for reasons that escape us. And we can judge ourselves for the erratic and unpredictable nature of our emotions. But just like berating the fire alarm for going off won't make it stop, getting annoyed or frustrated with emotions doesn't help; that's just more emotions being piled on top of the existing ones.

LAG

In Chapter 1, we discussed how modern life can encourage us to push the override button and press on through difficulties, but when our lives become more about denying or fighting against our emotions rather than working with them, we can start to lag. LAG is the three-letter acronym that I use to capture the state of rigid, stilted emotional – and, ultimately, behavioural – inertia that can adversely impact our ability to thrive.

- **L** stands for 'Lost' – lost to time and place, inside our heads, detached from what is happening around us, ruminating about the past, or worrying about the future.
- **A** stands for 'Avoidant' – buying into the mind's stories that we won't be able to cope with certain emotions and avoiding situations that provoke strong emotions.
- **G** stands for 'Grinding' – grinding out familiar routines according to the same old rules, even when these cease to move us towards what matters to us.

LAG can lead us to feeling disconnected, discontented and unfulfilled; it can lead to us living life small. To avoid experiencing challenging emotions, our minds create rigid rules that restrict how we act: 'I can't speak in front of other people because I'm worried it will go horribly wrong', 'I am not confident enough to take on a leadership role', 'I can't take on a new business venture, because of the fear that it will fail'. Rules of this kind can take hold insidiously over time, and their impact can be profound – we stop trying new things. And this, in turn, can make us feel unmotivated, our goals seeming distant or unattainable. Perversely, more emotions, ranging from frustration to despondency, may show up when we realize that our 'go-to' strategies for dealing with challenges are no longer cutting it. All of this takes its toll. Research has found that LAG – also referred to as 'experiential avoidance' – is a major contributor to mental health difficulties, distress, lower levels of wellbeing and poorer life functioning. Evidence is also emerging that suggests that bodily markers such as the electrical conductivity of our skin, the variability of our heart rates, and activity in our facial muscles can be used to identify those who have elevated levels of LAG. So, it's not just our minds that experience LAG, it's our bodies too.

The breeding ground for LAG can vary from person to person. For some, it can be a significant traumatic incident, while for others it can be a series of seemingly less significant events. The net result is the same: we get stuck in a loop of avoidant behaviours that diminishes our ability to thrive.

Let me give you an example from my own experience:

Hitting the road

It's a wet and windy Saturday night early in 1994. My father is driving a teenage me up to a nightclub not too far from my hometown. The Byrds' version of the song 'Turn, Turn, Turn' is playing in the car during the journey.

Arriving at the venue, I hop out of the car, and rush through the wind and rain to meet my friends. The evening goes well, and everyone has a good time. A friend kindly offers to give me and two others a lift home – an offer that we gladly accept. The breezy atmosphere in the car is a sharp contrast to the wildness of the wind that whips rain against the windscreen. Towards the end of our journey, the driver steers the car into a right-hand bend in the road, and as she does so, a sudden, strong gust catches the back of the car. The tyres lose traction, and the car starts to hydroplane in a clockwise direction over the road's surface. The pirouette has begun, and we are powerless to stop it. Our fortunes are in the laps of the gods.

From my rear passenger seat, I grab the headrest in front of me and pull myself to the centre of the car to look out the windscreen just as we complete a 180-degree rotation. I know that this must be happening incredibly quickly, but time is moving very slowly. Everything seems silent. Deadly silent. One single question flashes into my mind: *Is there a car coming behind us?* In that one moment, nothing else matters, only the answer to that single question. If there is a car coming, then we are dead. Mercifully, there are no cars travelling behind us. We continue to spin.

Turn, turn, turn . . .

The car is now on the hard shoulder of the carriageway, which

45

serves as a run-off area where motorists can stop in case of emergencies. We're not stopping. The front tyres of the car catch on something. The world turns upside down as the car flips. The car is now skidding on its roof down the hard shoulder, the silence shattered by the horrendous scraping and screeching of metal grating on the road's surface. Foolishly, I hadn't fastened my seatbelt, so I am being flung tumble-dryer-style around the back of the car. I come to rest on the roof, perilously close to the now-windowless rear door as the car continues to slide. Cold, damp air rushes in. The very real thought crystalises in my mind: *I am going to be dragged out of the car at any second. I am going to die.*

I fall out through the shattered back window of the car on to the rain-soaked ground. As soon as I hit the road, I instantly bounce back up on to my feet – just like a circus performer would do in one of those 'Ta-daaaa!' moments. In stunned disbelief, I run my hands over myself to check that I am not an apparition, that I am still in my body. I look at the upturned car. It is rotating slowly on the same spot – a disturbed and distorted not-so-merry-go-round.

Turn, turn, turn . . .

Miraculously, no one is killed. We sustain some knocks, but there are no broken bones. I have badly cut hands (where I had protected my face from the glass). When I finally get home, I am greeted by my mum, who has been worried sick. Still caked in mud and blood, I climb into bed. I struggle to get to sleep for a long, long time. One thought keeps revolving around in my head: *I should be dead.*

Did this experience trigger some moment of insight or trans-formation? No, the truth is it didn't. The car had been on the road to Moira, not Damascus. No epiphany. And yet, in the days, weeks and months that followed, I struggled to process what had happened. I lost direction and found it difficult to apply myself academically. Prior to the accident, my family had been encouraging me to gain entry to a medical school and become a doctor, but my brush with mortality meant that a profession so concerned with life and death suddenly felt like someone else's dream.

Following the accident, I became very anxious about the idea of being in control of a car. Driving lessons became endurance tests. I would get tense and the driving instructors (note the plural – I got through several of them!) would become exasperated – it was all white knuckles and red mist. Could I have benefited from some psychological support at that time? Yes, almost certainly. But I didn't understand what difference it could make, nor was I prepared to admit that I needed 'that' kind of help. I would muddle through. I passively chose not to confront the issues. Instead, I decided that driving a car wasn't for me, and I gave up on trying to pass my driving test.

LAG had set in.

Why do we get stuck?

What stops us from trying something different? Have you ever got halfway through a TV show or a film that hasn't exactly lit up your world and found yourself thinking, *Well, I've got this far with it, I might as well keep going*? Maybe you've bought a car that has experienced repeated mechanical problems; you should really sell it, but the small fortune you've just handed over to the mechanic for the latest round of repairs makes you hang on to it. The 'sunk-cost fallacy', which was originally proposed by economist Richard Thaler, dictates that we can be reluctant to change tack in an endeavour in which we have invested heavily – even when it isn't delivering for us or is incurring considerable costs. Our careers and relationships are not immune from the sunk-cost fallacy. We can be dogged in persisting with lost causes, and reluctant to change to new ones.

An added complication is that we don't yet know what we might to grow to love – the Mongolian throat-singer you've yet to hear, the beach you've yet to visit, the ice-cream flavour you've yet to taste, the exercise regime you've yet to try, the soulmate you've yet to meet, the Netflix series you've yet to watch, the book about trees bending you've yet to finish. Although the future guards its secrets jealously, our past whispers seductively that it already knows the answer. We conclude that the best way forward is to continue along the path that we have been travelling on. And we confine ourselves to being one-trick ponies, rather than horses that can win on many courses. Clichés and maxims that we use in everyday language compound the problem by engendering a spirit of conservatism: devils we know and devils we don't, what's not broken not needing fixing . . . And then there's the line (and it pains me to write this): 'That's how we've always done things around here.' All these phrases serve to maintain what I'll call 'historical validity': the tendency to restrict potential options to only those that have worked in the past. No other alternatives are considered. But if you look too much to the past, you end up walking backwards into the present, blind to the opportunities that lie in front of you.

How a flexible mind can set you free

Flexibility (or developing a 'flexible mind' as I refer to it in my work with clients) will help counteract LAG by supporting you in relating to thoughts and emotions in ways that will allow you to transform rather than conform. Just as physical flexibility allows us to be supple and pliable to meet the demands of physical exertion, improving our range of motion and reducing the risk of injury, a flexible mind allows us to be agile in responding to our emotions, thoughts and sensations so that we can both perform and feel well.

As you learn more about what a flexible mind is, it's important to understand what it *isn't*. It is not shelving your plans to paint the hall when a friend arrives at your front door and asks if you mind taking their dog for the afternoon. Flexibility isn't about being amenable or accommodating. In fact, developing a flexible mind might well require us to be less, not more, obliging to demands placed on us by others – that hallway isn't going to paint itself! Nor is flexibility simply finding more ways to do things that make us feel good. It's about being prepared to open your front door to a metaphorical wolf – a wolf that represents challenging emotions such as fear, sadness and anxiety – so that you can be freed from the constraints that avoiding those emotions place on you. We all like to think that we are flexible in how we respond to life's ups and downs. But rigidity is the norm: we lose sight of what matters to us; we relate to difficult thoughts and emotions as things to be avoided, resisted or controlled; we get bound up in old routines that are no longer serving us; we get absorbed in our inner selves and miss important opportunities available in the world around us. A flexible mind challenges these attitudes.

Optimal choices

Choice, according to the author and psychotherapist James Hollis, 'is what defines and validates a life'. A flexible mind allows us to make *optimal* choices. The word 'optimal' comes from the Latin *optimus*, meaning 'best', and first entered the English language at the end of the nineteenth century, when it was used in the study of biology to describe favourable circumstances – especially under particular restrictions. The 'particular restrictions' part is important here. As I highlighted earlier, context matters. A flexible mind is not one particular mindset, but the ability to flexibly deploy different mindsets as our circumstances require. Changes in our environments present unique challenges that require unique responses – flexibility is about being open and responsive to the situations in which we find ourselves so that we can make choices that optimize our performance, wellbeing and the blend between the two.

And just to be clear, you are not going to get every choice 'right'. We can all get stuck in cycles of self-recrimination about choices that we have made, but flexibility teaches us that that there will always be new choices to make. It's not about becoming fixated on yesterday's choices; it's about optimizing the choices we can make today.

We hear a lot about the importance of building better habits, and are told that better habits lead to better results. Many years of working with people operating in high-performance environments has taught me that this can certainly be the case; we can all use habits to fulfil our potential, whatever our chosen field might be. But choosing to slavishly stick to routines is not always a recipe for success. Habits should never usurp the purpose they are intended to serve; the tail ends up wagging the dog when they do. Habits, too, need to flex. A flexible mind allows us to optimize our choice of behaviours to the situations and challenges we face. Habits are blind – it's flexibility that sees.

The flexible mind also understands that we are not the sum of our emotional reactions. You might consider yourself a 'glass half-full person', imbued with a sense of optimism, or maybe you're more of a pessimist – a 'glass half-empty person'. But what if you could connect, and I mean deeply connect, with a third possibility? What if you are simply the *glass* – a glass that exists irrespective of its contents or its level of fullness? You are the container into which your experiences (and the thoughts and feelings about those experiences) are poured. Thoughts and emotions – like the contents of a glass – come and go; we, like the glass, endure. We are the *context* of our inner experiences, not the content of those experiences.

The idea that we are a *host* to our inner experiences is not a particularly new one. In his poem 'The Guest House', the thirteenth-century Persian poet Rumi noted:

This being human is a guest house.
Every morning a new arrival.
A joy, a depression, a meanness,
some momentary awareness comes
as an unexpected visitor.

Now, it might be that some of those visitors turn out to be false prophets heralding woes that never arrive. You might recognize this in your own life. Yes, we are impacted by problems that do occur, but we are also troubled by problems that never occur. While shifting the focus from 'content' to 'context' won't manifest a problem-free existence, it can reduce the impact that problems – both experienced and imagined – have on your life. It is possible to recognize the difference between your guest house and its unexpected visitors; the difference between you and the thoughts and emotions you experience; the difference between trying to change emotions, thoughts and sensations, and changing the relationship you have with those experiences.

Think of a flexible mind as psychological ju-jitsu. In recent years, ju-jitsu (particularly the Brazilian variant of the martial art) has been integrated to remarkable effect into the skillset of competitors participating in mixed martial arts competitions such as the Ultimate Fighting Championship. Ju-jitsu literally translates as the 'yielding art'. The 'yielding' element of the practice should not be mistaken for weakness or surrendering. Instead, ju-jitsu is about harnessing and recycling the momentum that is directed towards you from your opponent and using it to your own ends. In the same way, developing a flexible mind is about smartly using the emotional energy that situations create. This will help you to roll with the punches that life throws, and to capture that energy so that you can sustain your commitment to your core purpose and the causes that matter to you. That's what I mean by 'changing the relationship' you have with thoughts, emotions and sensations – rather than struggling against them, you can embrace and capitalize on the opportunities for learning and transformation that they provide. The world is waiting for you, waiting and wondering how you'll be when you meet it. Will you be rigid and resistant, or will you be open and responsive? Will you try in vain to outrun challenging thoughts and feelings, or can you bring them along the road with you?

AWEsomeness

In my work with clients, I highlight that flexibility is about being AWEsome. Why? Because AWE is the three-letter acronym I use to capture three key aspects of a flexible mind:

A stands for 'Anchored' – fully situated in time and place, and able to recognize that our thoughts and emotions are momentary experiences that come and go.

W stands for 'Willing' – able to accept our mind's story-generating tendencies, and being prepared to turn towards rather than away from the emotions associated with those stories.

E stands for 'Empowered' – able to act in accordance with their purpose and personal values.

These three aspects of a flexible mind, which we'll be exploring in more detail in Part II, are the polar opposites of the LAG that characterises a rigid mind.

- Being Anchored is the opposite of being Lost in our inner experience.
- Being Willing is the opposite of Avoiding situations that provoke strong emotions.

- Being Empowered is the opposite of Grinding our way through the same old routines.

The choices we are confronted with provide opportunities to exercise AWE. Will we choose willingness or reluctance, showing up or shutting down, being true and seeing it through or feeling scared and being deterred? It's the AWE of flexibility that helps us to choose to move *towards* what truly matters to us, rather than *away* from challenging emotions, thoughts and sensations. Flexibility is not merely the sum of its constituent parts – it is the multiplication of them. The 'flexibility formula' states that: *Flexibility = Anchored × Willing × Empowered*. Flexibility needs at least some of each of its three constituent parts to be present; the greater the amounts of each, the more flexible a mind will be.

At this point in the chapter, I want to follow up on my story of my own experience of LAG, and how I was able to engage in some psychological ju-jitsu of my own to transform it to AWE.

Yelling silently in New Zealand

'Ready to go, bro?'.

I'm not sure if it's a question or an order. It's a beautiful day in July 2003, and I am in Queenstown, New Zealand. My eyes remained fixed on the aptly named Remarkables – the mountain range that creates a stunning snow-capped backdrop to the town. The mountain tops are pristinely reflected in the still waters of Lake Wakatipu, which hugs the town to its southern edge. In a couple of days, we're scheduled to ski in the Remarkables. Depending, of course, on how the next few minutes pan out`. . .

FLEXIBILITY: FROM LAG TO AWE

I am standing on a wooden platform that the A J Hackett Bungee Company have christened 'The Ledge'. Although the drop from the platform is officially 47 metres, it looks like much more. The effect is accentuated by the fact that The Ledge is located beside the Skyline gondola station, 400 metres above Queenstown. Trust me when I say that 47 metres looks and feels like 447 metres.

Looking the guy who has just strapped me in straight in the eye, I reply with a less-than-convincing, 'I guess so.' He smiles a smile he has smiled a thousand times before. I wave over at my friends Chris and Roisin, who are standing at a viewing point directly across from The Ledge – a wave that is being recorded on the camcorder that Chris holds in his hand. My impending plunge will be captured for posterity, and Chris is doubtless providing a riveting commentary.

I shuffle towards the edge of the ledge. Every sinew in my body is screaming in unison, imploring me not to do it. I take a moment to gather myself. You may have previously done a bungee jump, or you may have that still to do, but I am sure that you will know what those agonizingly long seconds of contemplation feel like; whether it's performing in front of a crowd, having a difficult conversation with a colleague, jumping out of an aeroplane, or counting down from ten as the anaesthetist holds your hand`. . . your mind can do somersaults. Mine is doing Olympic-sized somersaults.

Fear has risen, dark and cold. The risk of injury or death looms large on the horizon. Why on earth would I do this? The fact that the guy from A J Hackett has gone to all the effort of getting me ready certainly isn't reason enough. Nor is the 'no refund' policy. In truth, the motivation has been growing for ten years – the ten years that have passed since the car crash. I am on The Ledge not merely to jump off a platform; I am on The Ledge to jump *into* the fear that has gripped me for so many years. I am ready and willing to transform rather than conform.

Unleashing an almighty yell, I jump. As I plummet towards the ground, I realize that I have fully exhausted my yell. I am now yelling silently, and I am still falling. Mercifully, the bungee rope does its job, kicking in with a jolt and springing me back from the ground below. Unlike some bungee jumps, which lower you gently to the ground to release you afterwards, people who jump from The Ledge are winched back up. Halfway up, the winch stops suddenly. My 'bro' shouts down in his thick New Zealand accent, 'There's a technical difficulty. . .' I will later learn that this was done for comic effect, but in the meantime, it leaves me dangling tenuously and precariously. In those vulnerable moments before the winch starts again, I take in the view once more. The mountains and the lake are as stunningly beautiful as before, but my outlook has shifted.

Two months later, I return home from my travels and set my sights on righting a historical wrong. It is time for me to get my driving test – it is long overdue. I am determined to get on to a training programme to become a clinical psychologist, and being able to drive is part of the essential criteria to accessing the training. After taking some lessons, I book a driving test, which is scheduled for 14 January 2004.

As I sit in the car in the moments prior to the test, I notice the waves of anxiety growing, and the feelings of fear amplifying: fear of what being alone and in sole control of a car might bring; fear of a third failure in the driving test. As I sit alone in the car watching the examiner walking towards me, I close my eyes and return once again to The Ledge. The anxiety and fear I experienced didn't stop me then, and it isn't going to stop me now. I can feel the fear and do it anyway.

Driving examiner: 'Ready to go?'

Me: 'Yes.'

Forty minutes later, the driving examiner issues those immortal words: 'I am pleased to inform you that you have passed your driving test.' I yell a silent scream of delight. Flexibility has got me into the driving seat.

Emotions are experiences that we are hardwired to have, and yet we often find ourselves trying to avoid or get rid of them. When we relate to our emotions as obstacles in our way, or something that needs to be mastered, their impact can be intensified rather than diminished: they end up dictating how we react. Rigidity sets in – we get *lost* in our internal world, we *avoid* situations that provoke challenging emotions, and we *grind* out the same old patterns of behaviour – LAG. Developing a flexible mind offers another way, one that allows us to adapt our responses to the contexts in which we find ourselves so that we might thrive. A flexible mind is characterized by us being Anchored in time and place, and noticing that thoughts and emotions come and go, being Willing to have difficult thoughts and emotions without being dictated to by them, and being Empowered to act in line with our purpose and personal values – AWE.

Maybe you feel that your mind is sufficiently flexible already? Maybe you're right – maybe you never get so preoccupied by your thoughts that you stop noticing what's happening around you; maybe you never try to suppress or avoid challenging emotions that accompany those thoughts; maybe you never waver in your commitment to doing what it takes because of troubling thoughts and emotions. If that's the case, bravo: you're a tenth-dan black belt in the art of flexibility. If you're a lesser mortal, however, then opportunities exist to build the AWE of a more flexible mind. Besides, even a tenth-dan black belt in ju-jitsu will be the first to concede that there is always more to learn. In the next part of the book, we'll be looking at evidence-based techniques you can use to action AWE in your own life.

Flexibility: From LAG to AWE – Summary Points

- We are not our emotions – we are the context in which these experiences occur.
- Emotions come in various forms and can serve as important messengers.
- Efforts to suppress or avoid emotions can be counterproductive – when we shoot the messenger, we tend to miss the message.
- Research has indicated that the rigidity of being *lost* in time and place, *avoidant* of inner experiences and *grinding* out old habits (LAG) is linked to a range of psychological difficulties.
- Flexibility, which is characterized by being Anchored, Willing and Empowered (AWE), helps us to be present, make space for difficult thoughts and emotions, and still do what matters.
- Flexibility is enabled through the choices we make.

FLEX

In drawing Part I of the book to a close, and to give you a taste of what Part II will bring, I invite you to send a flex message to yourself and to the world. You can do this if and when you notice that you are feeling stressed or under pressure, and you notice that your thoughts and emotions might be getting the better of you. Begin by slowly spelling out the following to yourself:

F . . . L . . . E . . . X marks the spot.

Saying the letters F, L and E allows you the time and opportunity to bring your awareness to the X that marks the spot. And what exactly does the X mark? It marks the opportunity to say the following four statements to yourself:

- *'I am here.'*
- *'I am holding my thoughts and feelings.'*
- *'I will commit to doing what matters.'*
- *'I will take care of myself so I can continue to care of business.'*

These four short sentences gift you a sense of the power of a flexible mind and how it can help you to thrive.

PART II

What Trees Teach Us
About Flexibility

In 1859, the English philosopher John Stuart Mill wrote that human nature is 'a tree, which requires to grow and develop itself on all sides, according to the tendency of the inward forces which make it a living thing'. Throughout the history of civilization on the island of Ireland, the Celtic Tree of Life (or Crann Bethadh) has been an important symbol. Its interconnected roots, trunk and crown captured the links believed to exist between the heavens, the earth and the mystical realm of the 'otherworld'. It symbolizes qualities of wisdom, endurance and longevity. In this section of the book, we will explore how the roots, trunk and crown of your metaphorical tree represent your ability to be Anchored, Willing and Empowered respectively.

CHAPTER 3

Anchored

There's an old proverb that says: 'When the roots are deep, there is no need to fear the wind.' The roots of a tree form a sprawling underground network. Their combined length can be hundreds of miles. There are hundreds of thousands of root endings, each forming an entrance ramp on to a subterranean highway transporting the water and nutrients from the soil that the tree needs to grow. Importantly, the roots also anchor the tree into the ground, providing it with support and stability. In this chapter, we will explore how those roots provide a helpful metaphor for the Anchored aspect of flexibility. To be Anchored, we must be grounded – deeply connected to the present moment and the places in which our lives unfold, and able to recognize that our awareness is the conduit through which our thoughts and feelings (the essential nutrients of our experience) flow. In this chapter, you'll learn about what you can do to feel more Anchored in the here and now. Specifically, we'll be answering three questions that are pertinent to being Anchored:

- Why is it so difficult to be present?
- What skills and capacities are important for helping you to be Anchored?
- What practical steps can you take to develop those skills and capacities?

Where are you? When are you?

It's happened more times than you might want to admit. You've wished, for good or ill, to be somewhere else. To be transported away from a difficult conversation with an irate colleague, the post-mortem following a poor performance, the long queue of gridlocked traffic, or the seat next to the toilet on a long-distance coach trip. Or maybe you've longed to be transported *to* a particular place – the shores of Lake Tahoe, maybe, or ensconced at a winery in the Tuscan hills, or nestled beside a loved one who's faraway. Let's call these 'teleportation goals' – the desire to be somewhere other than where you are. But when you mentally check out of your present location, you stop noticing what's happening around you. Leonardo da Vinci said that a typical human 'looks without seeing, listens without hearing, touches without feeling, eats without tasting, moves without physical awareness, inhales without awareness of odour or fragrance, and talks without thinking.' That's a lot of sensory experience to be missing out on.

Your mind is a spinning blue police box whirring through space and time. And like Dr Who's TARDIS, your mind is much more voluminous than one might expect when looking from the outside in. Inside, there is room for countless scenarios relating to the past or future to play out – a litany of ifs, buts and maybes that can ambush your attention and your ability to be present. You can end up living your life in time zones radically different from the one you are in.

The reality is, however, that the present moment is the only place where we can exercise choice and agency. **The only time that truly matters is now.** Pete Carroll, the Super Bowl-winning former head coach of the Seattle Seahawks, said: 'When we're at our best, there isn't a future and there isn't a past, you're just there in the moment.' But how much time are we spending actually thinking about what's happening now? Research suggests that we have around 6,000 thoughts during the waking hours of each day. Was that – pardon the pun – more or less than you thought? While a sizeable portion of those thoughts will be linked to the tasks we undertake throughout the day, many will not be. Research conducted by the psychologists Matt Killingsworth and Daniel Gilbert, which tracked the moment-by-moment contents of people's thoughts, concluded that we spend almost half (46.9 per cent) of our waking hours thinking about what *isn't* happening around us. Yes, you read that correctly – almost half the time. So, when we're not fully here, where exactly are we? We're 'mind-wandering'. That's the term used to describe the state of experiencing thoughts that aren't tied to the situations in which we find ourselves. Mind-wandering may well serve important functions, like helping us to plan for future scenarios or engage in creative thinking. It might also be a way for us to counteract feelings of boredom or avoid having to confront challenging feelings such as anxiety or fear. But mind-wandering has its drawbacks. It is associated with poor performance in various educational activities, and reduced vigilance to what is happening in the world around us (this is referred to as 'perceptual decoupling'). And that can bring problems – if your head is in the clouds when you're crossing a road, your body might not be long in catching up with it. Mind-wandering can also impact on our moods; Killingsworth and Gilbert's research provided evidence that mind-wandering causes lower levels of happiness.

Mind-wandering is associated with shifts in our *attention*. Attention allows us to maintain alertness to concentrate on what we are doing, switch focus between different tasks when we need to, and shut out potential distractions. It can be helpful to distinguish between two different forms of attention – endogenous and exogenous. Endogenous attention is goal-driven. It occurs when we deliberately focus on aspects of our experiences for a particular purpose – such as following instructions to set up a smart phone that we have purchased, or wiring an electrical plug. Exogenous attention is stimulus-driven. It kicks in when our focus gets drawn involuntarily to aspects of our experiences, such as a flash of lightning or roll of thunder if we are out for a walk. Both endogenous and exogenous attention can be either focused on our internal world or externally focused on the world around us.

I like to picture the two different directions that our attention can go in as being like Liverpool's famous Liver Birds. As birds go, Bella and Bertie are big. They stand at 18 feet tall, and they have a wingspan of 24 feet. Instead of feathers, however, their wings are made of copper. In 1911 they were mounted on top of the then-newly built headquarters of the Royal Liver Group in the Pier Head area of Liverpool, England. Bella looks out over the waterfront towards the sea, keeping a watchful eye over the sailors. Bertie faces the opposite direction, looking inland over the city. He is charged with protecting the residents of Liverpool. The story goes that if the two Liver Birds were ever to set eyes on each other, it would spell disaster – both of them wouldn't be doing their job.

Like Bella and Bertie, our attention is a sentinel that can look two ways – it can monitor the landscape around us, tracking what is happening in our immediate physical environment, or it can focus on the landscape within us: our thoughts, memories, feelings and bodily sensations. Outward exogenous attention can be activated by something like a burglar alarm going off in your home, while inward exogenous attention could be stirred by unwanted thoughts about messing up intruding on your thinking. An example of using outward endogenous attention is choosing to continue to read the words written on this page. Inward endogenous attention would be activated if you chose to close your eyes and recall some of the key points from the previous chapter instead. Clearly, there are a multitude of events occurring externally or internally, voluntarily or involuntarily, that can compete for our attention.

This competition for our attention has important implications for our ability to perform tasks efficiently and effectively. Attention serves as an important gateway into our working memory, which we use to hold relevant information in mind to solve problems and navigate the world around us. Attention does the collecting, working memory does the curating. Our attention is a finite resource – it has limited bandwidth and there are lots of bits of information competing for potential download. It's claimed that, on average, we shift our attention 1,840 times per day. But shifts in attention come at a cost. The 'switch-cost effect' emerged from observations that our performance is slower and more prone to errors when switching to a new task rather than repeating an existing task. On the other hand, if we spend too long focusing on a single task, our ability to remain alert declines – a phenomenon called 'vigilance decrement'. Attention can be fickle.

Digital distraction

As if it's not already hard enough to focus, marketers and advertisers have developed techniques to steal our attention. They know that our attention is drawn to what is recognizable ('familiar'), very noticeable ('salient') and/or related to the outcomes we are seeking to achieve ('goal-driven'). This helps explain why experiences as diverse as an advert that references our name, seeing blue flashing lights, or the promise of a better life, have the potential to capture our attention. Importantly, there will be times when we fail to notice that our attention has been stolen; we lack awareness of where our awareness has gone.

There is a popular belief that digital technologies such as smart phones and other mobile devices are causing a crisis in attention – the global population has been beset by what I'll call 'Attention Deficit Cyberactivity Disorder' (not a real condition). However, concerns about an attentional apocalypse predate the introduction of smart phones by at least 1,700 years! Records from the fourth century CE reveal that monks living in what is now Türkiye struggled to focus their attention on prayer and other pious duties. Prominent scholars of the time linked these difficulties to *acedia* (from the Greek word *akēdeia*, meaning 'to lack care') – a state of despondent dejection to which monks seemed to be susceptible. And what did people suspect as a cause of *acedia*? Books! Yes, books were the cutting-edge technology of medieval times suspected of eroding monks' attention.

Through the ages, it's the new *kit* on the block that gets all the attention for stealing attention.

Although an absence of long-term studies means that we can't be certain that our attention spans have declined in recent years, a recent survey of the UK population found that nearly half of us (49 per cent) felt that our attention span was shorter now than it used to be. A whopping 73 per cent of people agreed that we are living through a time when competition for our attention is non-stop – only 6 per cent disagreed. Software developers leverage a range of persuasive techniques, based on decades of research in the fields of behavioural and cognitive psychology, to hook us in and sustain our interaction with technology. Notice how the 'autoplay' feature on Netflix has us watching a third episode of *Better Call Saul* in a row – another fifteen minutes won't hurt, will it? 'Cookies' generated by our online activity allow web-browsers to learn about our preferences, and push content tailored to those preferences our way. So, when we interact with digital technologies, we are not only signing our attention's death warrant, but also hastening the arrival of the executioner. Digital technologies have paved the way for the emergence of a slew of problematic habits, including online gambling and porn addictions. One of the most pernicious impacts of precision-guided forms of digital distraction is that we can end up committing less attention to what truly matters to us – our friends, family, work, dreams and ambitions. Research has linked increased smart phone and social media use with increased mental health difficulties in young people. A study that recruited nearly 30,000 young adults from across the globe also demonstrated that those who had received their first smart phone at a younger age had lower levels of mental health and wellbeing than did those who received it later in their development – the effect was particularly pronounced in female participants.

But digital technologies can't simply be dismissed as a curse. They are also a cure. Sixty per cent of the people who participated in the UK survey agreed with the statement: 'Having multiple forms of instant information at my fingertips helps me find solutions to problems I face at work, in my personal life, or elsewhere.' The Big Tech genie is out of the bottle, and has made itself so indispensable that not everyone will be keen to squeeze it back in. And there are benefits to routinely interacting with digital technologies: Netflix entertains us; Zwift helps us become fitter. A range of AI-powered apps such as Kuki and Replika have even been developed to provide us with avatar-based companionship and advice. Whether these chatbots are safe for widespread use or are as effective as the 'real thing' continues to be debated. Technology itself can also be harnessed to help *maintain* our attention. Rather than being devoured by the tiger of technology, we can ride on its back. We can use computer programmes such as Freedom to block access to the internet and the myriad opportunities for procrastination that it provides for set periods of time. Technology isn't the cause of our difficulties with attention, but our lack of awareness of how we use technology can be. Becoming more aware of how our attention operates can help stop the rot and help us become more Anchored in the present.

Digital technologies actually provide a helpful metaphor for understanding how we can be uprooted from the present moment. Let's imagine you have a smart device – we'll call it a 'u-Phone' – that allows you to scroll through your moment-by-moment experiences, just like you would scroll through posts on a social media feed. You swipe past aspects of your experience that don't seem interesting or important, choosing instead to linger on what sparks your curiosity – *That person over there looks like my cousin Alex. I wonder how Alex is settling into life living in London? Maybe I could visit him there sometime* . . . Your attention has moved off at a tangent, and you are less connected to the moment-by-moment 'feed' of what is happening around you. Or perhaps an aspect of your experience leaves you feeling irked: a colleague expressing a view you don't agree with in a meeting, or another driver cutting you off on your commute home. You're not going to like every aspect of your experience, just as you don't 'like' every post on a social media feed. Although there is the option of shifting your attention on to something else, instead you get absorbed in the thoughts and feelings the situation provokes, and memories of other irksome experiences start to stir. The internal 'doomscrolling' proceeds at pace . . .

This metaphor illustrates the fickle and meandering nature of our attention. We can be drawn to certain elements of what we notice, and this can trigger a host of thoughts and feelings, which serve to hijack our attention. But there is an additional layer to the metaphor that can help us to take a wider perspective on the nature of attention. We can broaden our awareness to notice the design of the u-Phone device on which the social media app is running. The u-Phone is separate to the social media feed – it's the hardware, while the app is the software. We can choose to engage with other apps on our smart phones – maps, the compass, the torch, the camera function, etc. – which allow us to better explore and appreciate our current surroundings. This aspect of the metaphor allows us to recognize how we can expand our attention beyond particular thoughts and feelings, and use our five senses to be more inquisitive about our present-moment experiences. We are not the contents of our thoughts and feelings; we are the hardware on which the processes of thinking, feeling and sensing operate.

Attention needs to vary

Attention can seem like a bundle of contradictions. Focused attention can enhance performance, but *too much* focus degrades both attention and performance. Switching attention between tasks is part of daily life, but *too much* switching attention makes it difficult to get any single task done. Allowing our awareness to wander has its benefits, but it also has its costs. Attention has enabled us to develop astounding technologies, but these technologies return the favour by commandeering our attention. Gloria Mark's excellent book, *Attention Span: Finding Focus for a Fulfilling Life*, helps to explain the chimera-like nature of attention by pointing out that attention is dynamic, not static; it needs to vary according to the contexts in which we find ourselves and the demands we face. It is designed to cycle flexibly between periods of intense focus, the completion of routine tasks, and a state of mind-wandering. Problems emerge if we get stuck in one attentional state: when we are deeply focused on finalizing the strategy for an upcoming event, we forget that the departure time for the afternoon school run was ten minutes ago; when we daydream too much about an upcoming holiday, we struggle to complete the report that management needs to sign off before we leave; when we spend too much time playing *Candy Crush Saga*, we miss out on dreaming up the next sensational online gaming craze.

We can opt to be more intentional about how we deploy our

attention. For example, we can purposefully schedule time for focused work and time to relax so that our minds can wander. Attention can be a choice – our choice. Recognizing this choice is a key aspect of getting rooted back into the present moment. Learning to deploy finite amounts of attention in sustainable ways is also key. Otherwise, we end up like moths to a light bulb – fluttering ourselves into a state of exhaustion.

I learned a lot about the rhythms of my own attention through writing this book. *The Tree That Bends* has received lots of my attention – but that attention has waxed and waned. For me, late mornings are the most productive time. There have been occasions when attention has been in short supply – if I'm tired, juggling different commitments, or being interrupted by my dog Bobby protesting about the window cleaner assailing our home. At times, I've noticed my inclination to stubbornly persevere with the writing long after my focused attention has left the building. But tenacity is not the cure for ailing attention. The clock spins forward, while the cursor on the screen remains steadfastly stuck in the same position – a blinking protest at the lack of progress. Some sentences have felt like life sentences . . .

But an important part of getting things right is knowing where we might be going wrong. Aristotle said: 'Knowing yourself is the beginning of all wisdom.' I began to see the motionless blinking cursor as a cue for me to do something else – chat with my wife, take a walk, wrestle with Bobby, strum some guitar chords, or check what was happening on social media. The time when our minds are telling us we are not allowed to change tack is the perfect moment to show it that we can. A surgeon client of my mine, reflecting on lessons learned from the demanding procedures he undertakes with patients, said: 'If it's hard somewhere, go somewhere else.' That's not about quitting the procedure, it's about taking a breath and changing the angle of attack. It's about being pragmatic rather than dogmatic, and recognizing the rhythm of our attention so that we can deploy it in sustainable ways.

Equally, there have been times during the writing of this book when the words have flowed, and I've been on a roll. But this has presented challenges of its own – the urge to keep going has risked tipping my attention into the red zone. The flexible move I'm most proud of developing in the writing of this book is the ability to step away from the writing process when it is going well. As difficult as that can be, it leaves me feeling enthusiastic about returning to it. When it comes to focused attention, less can mean more.

Now that we have learned more about the nature of our attention and established why it can be so difficult to be present, let's turn that attention to the second key question for this chapter: What skills and capacities are important for helping us to be Anchored? We'll begin by exploring the concept of meta-awareness – the capacity to notice where our attention is currently focused.

Meta-awareness

Thinking back to Bella and Bertie, meta-awareness (also referred to as the 'observing self' or meta-cognition) is akin to taking a bird's-eye view of the demands that our moment-by-moment experiences are placing on our attention. When a bird takes flight, it *separates* from the surface on which it stands, *elevates* its position using forces of thrust and lift, and *navigates* by scanning the environment and adjusting its direction accordingly. These processes of *separating*, *elevating* and *navigating* are central to the process of meta-awareness. We must:

- **Separate** – Unhook from experiences we may have been tangled up with.
- **Elevate** – Take a wider perspective on the range of different elements that make up our current experiences.
- **Navigate** – Reorientate our attention according to what is optimal in that context.

Although levels of meta-awareness vary from person to person, the good news is there are things we can do to enhance it.

Research studies have demonstrated that mindfulness meditation can lead to improvements in meta-awareness. Mindfulness meditation is one of many different types of meditation – for example, there is also transcendental meditation and zazen meditation. When participating in mindfulness meditation (also referred to as 'formal mindfulness practices'), we are instructed to rest our awareness on rhythmical events such as our breath or the ticking of a clock. This helps to anchor our awareness in the here and now. The expectation is not to have our awareness constantly on our breath or the clock; instead, it's about noticing when our awareness has wandered *away* from them, so we can gently bring it back. That's the stuff of meta-awareness. Formal mindfulness practices can vary in duration depending on our level of experience and the circumstances we are in. In addition to mindfulness meditation, we can also engage in what are referred to as 'informal mindfulness practices'. For example, we can select an activity that we routinely do – such as brushing our teeth, making a cup of coffee, going for a stroll, or refuelling the car – and rather than drifting into autopilot as we would normally do, we can instead try to bring our full conscious awareness to the task. Inevitably, our attention will wander to other things, or be hooked by judgements that might arise about the task, but when that happens, it's a case of noticing and refocusing.

The aim of both formal and informal mindfulness practices is to build our capacity to be more mindful. Being more mindful means having the ability to pay attention to our present-moment experiences with an attitude of detached curiosity. Mindfulness practices are the techniques; being more mindful is the quality they engender. Developing meta-awareness, and the opportunities it provides to track our attention, is crucial for helping us to be more mindful throughout the day. In addition to improving meta-awareness, mindfulness meditation has also been linked to improvements in our ability to sustain attention for longer, improved bodily awareness, and an increased capacity to recognize our thoughts as the mental representations they are rather than necessarily accurate representations of reality.

Importantly, research has shown that practising mindfulness meditation can also have positive impacts on a variety of physical and mental health challenges, ranging from physical pain and hypertension to anxiety and depression. Studies conducted in high-performance environments have shown that mindfulness meditation can support both performance and mental wellbeing – the two pillars of thriving. Yet it's important to understand that the primary goal of practising mindfulness meditation is neither performance nor wellbeing, but just *being*. John Kabat-Zinn, who has done more than most to popularize mindfulness meditation in the West, emphasizes that: 'Meditation is the only intentional, systematic human activity, which at the bottom is about not trying to improve yourself or get anywhere else, but simply to realize where you already are.'

The roots of a tree aren't a temporary measure; they grow more extensive with each passing day. This allows the tree to stay anchored as it matures. Similarly, our efforts to stay Anchored require ongoing commitment and dedication. I believe that scheduling time into our diaries to regularly engage in formal and informal mindfulness practices is the single greatest step we can take in becoming more grounded into the present. If you are interested in learning more about how you can practise mindfulness meditation, I recommend checking out Amishi Jha's book *Peak Mind: Find Your Focus, Own Your Attention, Invest 12 Minutes a Day*. Apps such as Smiling Mind and Headspace can also provide advice and guidance – yes, digital technologies can help you get Anchored! If you do choose to practise mindfulness meditation, you would be in good company. Author and businesswoman Arianna Huffington, three-time Super Bowl-winning MVP Patrick Mahomes, Northern Irish golfer Rory McIlroy and tennis star Serena Williams are just a few of those who have spoken about the benefits that practising mindfulness meditation has brought to their lives.

A few years ago, I worked with an international footballer who was struggling with elevated levels of anxiety on and off the pitch. He had moved to the UK from abroad with his wife and young family, and was excited about embarking on a new start in a new country. However, this excitement was dampened by the arrival of COVID-19 in early 2020. The restrictions on social contact meant that his wife was unable to meet new people and establish herself in the new community in which they were living. My client felt like he had 'cashed in a lot of chips' by moving the family to this new location, and he was worried that the move was not going to be a happy one for them. This worry was compounded when he experienced a training injury that ruled him out of playing for several weeks. Suddenly, he became acutely aware of the competition for places in the team that he had joined. Although he recovered well from the injury, he struggled to maintain his attention when he returned to training, and the coaches expressed concerns to him that he seemed withdrawn and distant. My discussions with this client provided an opportunity to explore his worries further. These focused on two key themes – the first being his concerns that his family would continue to struggle with a relocation for which he felt responsible, and the second being his fears about getting injured again and not being able to establish himself in the team. As we spoke, it became clear that the client was engaging in a considerable amount of mental time-travel: revisiting the past, wondering whether moving to the UK was the right decision, and drifting to gloomy thoughts about a catastrophic future. Helping him to be more Anchored in the present moment was identified as an important strand of our work.

Over the course of our work together, I supported him in practising mindfulness meditation, both during our sessions and in the time between sessions. He made good progress in this and the other elements of the work we did together. In our last session, we were reflecting on key learning points. He spoke enthusiastically about the benefits of mindfulness and the insights that he had gained from it. 'You can get lost in your thoughts, then you end up judging yourself for getting lost, and then you end up even more lost. That was a key learning point for me,' he said. That's meta-awareness in action. The client had developed his ability to notice when his attention had drifted to unhelpful thoughts about the past or the future, and he was able to separate, elevate and navigate his attention back to the present. By developing your meta-awareness, you too will be more likely to find yourself in the present and less likely to get lost in mental time-travel.

Mindfulness meditation has its critics, however. It can leave people feeling underwhelmed, disappointed or even unsettled. Some of the backlash that mindfulness meditation has received is because of the unreasonable expectations placed upon it. Mindfulness practices are not a panacea, nor will they be instantly transformative. Beware those who say, 'I tried that mindfulness once. It didn't work.' They are missing the point. As we have noted, mindfulness meditation requires practice. Our ability to be more mindful is a muscle that needs to be developed over time. Nor are mindfulness practices something to turn to only at times of crisis. That would be like delaying the sewing of a parachute until a plane's engine has spluttered into disquieting mid-flight silence – 'Now, where did I leave that needle and thread?' Concerns have also been expressed that the promotion of mindfulness meditation is being used as a diversionary tactic. In his book *McMindfulness: How Mindfulness Became the New Capitalist Spirituality*, Ronald Purser takes aim at various parties – including corporations, schools and government agencies – for co-opting mindfulness as a way of situating the source and alleviation of people's suffering in their minds rather than the societal injustices and social inequalities they face. Purser is concerned that mindfulness is being used to placate people who should otherwise be agitating for societal change. But does improving one's awareness of present-moment experiences through mindfulness necessarily conflict with enhancing one's social awareness and responsibility? Not necessarily. In a review of *McMindfulness*, the journalist Jonnie

Wolf quoted philosopher Amia Srinivasan's belief that we can 'be guided by both a concern for appreciating the world as it is, and making the world as it ought to be'.

For some people, it's the term 'mindfulness', rather than what it actually entails, that can pose challenges – the term can seem non-descript or confusing. But labels shouldn't get in the way of what the practice is intended to offer. If the word 'mindfulness' lands awkwardly for you, think of it as 'exercising your attention muscle', 'strengthening your meta-awareness', or 'practising your noticing skills'.

Anchoring yourself in the here and now

Remember I defined mindfulness as paying attention to present-moment experiences with an attitude of detached curiosity? Even in the absence of formal or informal mindfulness practices, curiosity is an attitude that helps us to explore the here and now with a spirit of openness. Curiosity ignites our senses, which serve to illuminate the world around us. Allow me to demonstrate. Take a few moments to be curious about the place where you are currently situated, even if it is familiar to you.

- **Be curious about what you can see.** Pick three objects and describe their shape and colour to yourself.
- **Now notice three things that are in contact with your body.** What sensations of temperature, pressure or texture are there in the contact between your body and these objects?

- **Next, listen to the different sounds you might be able to hear.** Where are those sounds originating from? How loud are they? If it's quiet, be curious about whether there is any variation in the sound of that silence.
- **When you're finished, think of some 'Anchoring statements' that might serve as a shorthand way of cueing you to be more present.** Examples that my clients use include, 'Be here now', 'Be where your feet are', 'Now is all we have', 'Be Anchored', 'Be grounded' and 'Notice and refocus'. Equally, you can come up with your own. Consider setting alerts on your phone to remind you to use the Anchoring statements. You can do it – right here, right now.

Anchoring statements worked for Dan Carter in high-pressure moments. Carter is rugby royalty. Before retiring from the sport, he was capped 112 times by the New Zealand All Blacks, was named the International Rugby Board Player of the Year on a record-equalling three occasions, and won the Rugby World Cup twice. He is the record point-scorer in international rugby. Just under 90 per cent of the points Carter scored for the All Blacks came from successfully kicking conversions and penalties – when the spotlight was solely on him. In the seconds before kicking at goal, there was plenty of scope for his attention to mentally time-travel to past failures and feared future outcomes, but instead Carter had strategies he could use to keep himself Anchored. He spoke about these in a podcast interview:

When I was kicking a goal in front of 80,000 people . . . you know, the last thing I want to be thinking at the back of my run-up is, like, 'Oh my God, 80,000 people are watching me, what if I miss? I can't miss. I've just missed the last two. What if I miss three in a row?'. So . . . I needed to go external . . . I'd start pushing my toes in the ends of my boots – into the ground for a couple of seconds. OK, cool, I can feel the grass at the ends of my toes. OK, now I tell myself, 'OK, breathe,' and then all of a sudden, for five seconds, I haven't thought about missing the kick, or all the people that are watching me. So, I'd go back to my routine – breathe, visualize the ball going through. That was something that would really help me get back on track, and just reminding myself to just live in the now.

Like roots burrowing into the earth, Carter's toes – and the use of the Anchoring statement 'OK, breathe' – helped him to stay present. You, like me, may never have won a Rugby World Cup or kicked a penalty in front of 80,000 people, but bringing curiosity to your present-moment experiences may well help you to make the most of today's opportunities.

Being present isn't always pleasant

Often, being present in the moment is more an act of surrender than an attempt at conquest. 'Surrender' in this sense doesn't mean giving in; instead, it's the willingness to notice the thoughts, feelings and sensations that may be present without struggling to resist, banish or control them. This is a point that George Mumford, a mindfulness practitioner and performance coach who has worked with the Los Angeles Lakers, Chicago Bulls and New York Knicks NBA teams, understands well. In a *New York Times* article entitled 'Be Here Now: How to Exercise Mindfully', Mumford is quoted as saying: 'You're not trying to make things happen, you're allowing them to happen.'

Anchoring yourself in the here and now can involve turning towards thoughts, sensations and emotions from which we'd rather turn away. Dark thoughts, stultifying boredom, searing pain – mindful awareness isn't always a bed of roses. It takes courage. The intention of mindfulness practices is not to make us think or feel differently, it's to help us *notice* differently – to notice present-moment experiences, the judgements our minds make about them, and the urges that arise in relation to them. This helps us to be more aware of what is influencing the choices we make in the here and now. **Wisdom is not constituted by what we think, but our ability to notice what we think**. Notice how moving from 'I can't do this' to 'I am noticing that I think I can't do this' might introduce more flexibility in how you choose to respond.

The band Metallica know a thing or two about dark thoughts and searing pain. They formed in Los Angeles, CA, in 1981, when singer/guitarist James Hetfield responded to an invitation for musicians to join a band that drummer Lars Ulrich had placed in a classified ads newspaper. Metallica's first album, released two years later, was called *Kill 'Em All*, which the record label judged to be less nefarious than what the band originally wanted to call it – don't ask. Over the last forty-plus years, they have released chart-topping albums (125 million sold to date) and played to sell-out crowds in theatres and arenas. But Metallica's meteoric success has been tempered by times of tragedy and struggle. On 27 September 1986, the band's tour bus skidded off a road in Sweden, and their bass player Cliff Burton was killed. In the years that followed, the band members grappled with grief and the stresses and strains that life in the limelight can bring.

James Hetfield has spoken candidly about his own personal battles, including several stints in rehab for alcohol addiction. In an article published in the *New Yorker* in November 2022, Hetfield talked about how being more Anchored in the present moment has helped him:

> *You're not feeling shameful about past stuff, you're not future tripping in fear about what's coming up next. You're right there, and you're doing exactly what you need to do . . . I think everyone searches for that sense of presence. I searched for it in the wrong medicines for a long time. I just wanted to turn my head off. That worked, until it didn't work.*

Rather than relying on potentially destructive methods aimed at numbing out pain and discomfort, Anchoring into the present can help us to 'sit with it' as an aspect of a broader range of experiences. It's a sign of the times that when Metallica headlined the Lollapalooza festival in Chicago in July 2022, one of the band's tour trailers was labelled 'Yoga'. It seems the former hellraisers are embracing a new, flexible approach to life on the road.

Arrival fallacy and mis-wanting

We have a pernicious tendency to devalue the present moment in anticipation of an imagined better future. So-called 'When . . . then' traps (e.g. 'When I get a long-term contract, then I'll be happier') have been identified as an important threat to us being more present. The 'now' is perpetually judged to be inferior to how things could potentially be; the present is a humdrum staging post on the journey to some longed-for destination. Let me be clear: there's nothing wrong with identifying clearly defined goals and working hard to achieve them, it's just that this needn't come at the cost of being fully present now. And why is it that when we achieve an amazing outcome, we often feel underwhelmed?

Research has shown that we tend to overestimate the levels of happiness that positive outcomes can bring. In his 2007 book *Happier: Learn the Secrets to Daily Joy and Lasting Fulfilment*, Tal Ben-Shahar coined the term 'arrival fallacy' to capture how achieving our goals doesn't necessarily bring sustained happiness. Longed-for achievements can feel like a damp squib. And there's no time for the squib to dry out, either – we've been warned from an early age about the perils of 'resting on our laurels'. Rather than celebrating what's been achieved, we're encouraged to build towards what's next. We are well versed in what the poet John Astin refers to as the 'the ancient legend that tells us this is not enough'. During an interview in 2005, Tom Brady, the then-New England Patriot NFL team's star quarterback, was asked which of his three Super Bowl winner's rings was his best. His response? 'The next one. The next one is the best.' He won four more over the sixteen years that followed. Despite his incredible success, Brady struggled to step away from his sport – retiring, unretiring and then re-retiring. We can be hugely successful, and still struggle to find contentment.

Daniel Gilbert and his colleague Timothy Wilson coined the term 'mis-wanting' to capture how we mistakenly prioritize certain goals in the erroneous belief that they will make us feel a particular way in the future. The risk of experiencing the arrival fallacy is intensified if we mis-want; the goals we have been working towards haven't been the right ones. We can achieve everything that we wanted, only to find out it wasn't what we wanted after all. The experience of the arrival fallacy can lead to feelings of dissatisfaction and bouts of self-recrimination: *What's wrong with me? Why can't I enjoy what I've achieved? When will I ever be satisfied?* Lou Holtz, the former Notre Dame football coach, proposed that we should instead ask ourselves the following question: 'What's important now?' (represented by the acronym WIN). He emphasized the importance of remaining focused on the present. WIN-ing encourages us to focus not just on *what* we do in the present, but also on *how* we do it – the qualities we embody in how we interact with ourselves, others and the world around us.

Savouring

According to the American psychologist and author Rick Hanson, our brains are 'like Velcro for negative experiences, but Teflon for positive ones'. Research has indicated that when it comes to life events, bad events tend to register more than the good – a phenomenon known as 'negativity bias'. You know this already: the flat tyre that complicates the journey to a family wedding; a tense exchange with a colleague that overshadows an 'away day'; the one critical review that undermines the five positive ones . . . Memories of difficult times linger like the smell of last night's takeaway, while the sweet scent of success dissolves quicker than candyfloss in the rain. We need to take extra care to ensure that the good moments stick. The process of *savouring* is crucial for amping up the good. Just like the roots of the tree absorb vital nutrients from the soil, we must absorb the nourishing aspects of our present-moment experiences. Rather than narrowly adopting a 'When . . . then' attitude in our lives, we need to embrace a 'Now . . . allow' approach: *now* that we have achieved a moment of success, we can *allow* ourselves the opportunity to celebrate it.

Although definitions of savouring vary, they tend to feature two components: noticing pleasant experiences, and enhancing those pleasant experiences. Our capacity to savour can be measured using scales such as the Savouring Beliefs Inventory, which invites us to express how much we disagree with statements such as, 'For me, once a fun time is over and gone, it's best not to think about it.' Savouring 'landmark' moments in our lives, like graduating from college, setting a personal best, getting married, receiving a promotion or becoming a parent, is thought to help with solidifying our memories of those events. The bias towards recalling the bad is offset by a specific emphasis on remembering the good. This may be one reason why savouring is associated with increased levels of life satisfaction and positive psychological functioning. Making the effort to savour has also been shown to increase how often people subsequently report life events as being pleasurable; seeing the good seeds more of the good. Let me be clear: savouring is not about trying to control our feelings by clinging to pleasant emotions; it's about allowing us to fully experience pleasant emotions when they do occur.

The innate temperament with which we are born, and the interactions we have with caregivers when we are growing up, influence our ability to savour. Indeed, research has shown that parents' patterns of savouring predict how well their offspring savour, both as children and adolescents. But savouring is a skill that we can practise and strengthen. There are two types of savouring that we can cultivate – reactive and proactive. Reactive savouring is something we can do in response to unexpected pleasant experiences, such as receiving praise from a colleague. Proactive savouring occurs when we deliberately organize activities and absorb the anticipation of the pleasure, as well as the pleasure that is experienced when it comes.

Boosting your capacity to savour will help you to stay Anchored in the here and now and mitigate the impact of the arrival fallacy. The following three-step process will help you to savour more:

1. **Focus your attention on your experiences** – Toggle your awareness between the events happening around you, and the thoughts, feelings and sensations that accompany those events. Notice urges to multitask or get hooked by distractions, and instead see if you can maintain your focus for just a few seconds longer.

2. **Catch 'killjoy thoughts' in flight** – If you notice thoughts that seek to dampen down your joy, undermine achievements or move you on to the 'next thing', know that you don't have to comply with them. Imagine instead embracing those thoughts in a warm, celebratory hug.

3. **Don't keep it all inside** – Many of us were raised to be alert to the risk of appearing arrogant or complacent, but try to move past this and embrace your successes. Communicate your good feelings with others, and share moments of joy with those who matter in your life.

This last step – sharing your joy – may not come easily to you. Our culture is awash with cautionary messages about the risk of appearing arrogant or complacent. It makes me think of a scene from *Star Wars: A New Hope*, when Luke Skywalker shoots down his first TIE fighter. He excitedly exclaims, 'I got 'em!', only for his compatriot Han Solo to respond, 'Great, kid. Don't get cocky!' (and this from a character who wasn't exactly shy about extolling his own virtues!). To be clear, savouring is not an act of indulgence, it's an act of awareness. We can take time to appreciate the waxy feel of lush green laurels without succumbing to resting on them.

It can be hard for us to be fully present in the here and now, as our minds (not to mention digital distractions) clamour to project us through time and space. But just as the roots of a tree help anchor it to the ground in which it grows, we too must find ways of getting Anchored in the present moment. This is not to say that the past and future are not important. They patently are. To believe that the past and future do not matter would risk invalidating the journeys we have undertaken and those that lie ahead. But letting them take prime position in our mental landscape can only detract from the opportunities we have to make a difference in the one time and place where we actually *can* make a difference: now. While mindfulness meditation and connecting with our five-sense experiences can help us improve our ability to be present, we also need to be conscious of our negativity bias and the risk of underplaying our achievements. We need to be purposeful in savouring the good times when they occur. Being present requires us to be courageous – particularly when times are tough. This is a theme we will explore further in the next chapter, as we move on to the next aspect of flexibility's AWE – being Willing.

Anchored – Summary Points

- We can struggle to be fully present in the moments in which we live our lives.
- Around half the time that we are awake, our attention has wandered away from what is happening around us.
- To work optimally, our attention needs to balance periods of intense focus with the completion of routine tasks, and we also need opportunities to let our minds wander.
- Meta-awareness – the ability to be aware of how our attention is currently deployed – is a key skill for helping us to be Anchored in the present.
- Practising mindfulness enhances our meta-awareness and ability to be Anchored.
- The process of savouring helps us to relish moments of success in a world that seems intent on moving us on to the next big thing.

CHAPTER 4

Willing

The trunk of a tree is made up of different layers. The aptly named heartwood sits at the centre of the tree and acts as a supporting pillar. The trunk's ability to flex in the face of the wind prevents the tree from breaking. Importantly, trees that are exposed to wind are stronger than those that are not. Through a process called thigmomorphogenesis, the swaying of a tree in the wind stimulates the formation of reaction wood, that bolsters the trunk against the strain. The sapwood part of the trunk acts as a pipeline, transporting water and minerals through the tree. In this chapter, we will explore how the trunk of a tree provides a metaphor for the Willing aspect of flexibility. Like the reaction wood that forms there, we must be willing to *absorb* the stresses and strains of life so that we can thrive. And just as sapwood doesn't grip on too tightly to the material it transports, we must be willing to *let go* of the stories that our minds create that may be hindering our ability to excel and feel well. In this chapter, we will develop both your willingness to recognize your mind's story-generating tendencies, and your willingness to work with, rather than against, the emotions that can show up with those stories. In doing so, we'll consider the following three questions relating to the being Willing aspect of a flexible mind:

1. What impact does trying to suppress, avoid or control thoughts, emotions and sensations have on your life?
2. What does a willingness to be open and curious about these experiences offer instead?
3. How can you develop your ability to be Willing?

To boldly go . . . where the wind blows

Bertrand Piccard is a Swiss psychiatrist. Through his work, he guides patients to explore their emotions so that they can discover more about themselves. But Bertrand Piccard himself is also an explorer and discoverer. In fact, he comes from a long line of explorers. In 1931, his grandfather, Auguste Piccard, used a hydrogen balloon to travel to the highest altitude achieved to that point in time (15,781 metres). In doing so, Auguste and his co-pilot became the first people to enter the Earth's stratosphere. Not to be outdone, Bertrand's father, Jacques, made it his business to be the first person to travel to the deepest part of the ocean – a feat he achieved in 1960, when he reached the bottom of the Mariana Trench, some 10,916 metres below sea level. It is rumoured that Gene Roddenberry, creator of *Star Trek*, was so impressed with the Piccards that he named the lead character of *Star Trek: Next Generation* 'Jean-Luc Picard' (only one 'c' in the surname) in their honour.

While his grandfather had gone up, and his father had gone down, the only place left for Bertrand to go was around. And that's exactly what he did. In 1999, Piccard and his British co-pilot Brian Jones completed the first continuous circumnavigation of the globe in a hot-air balloon. The pair travelled over 40,000 kilometres in nineteen days and twenty-one hours in the *Breitling Orbiter 3* balloon without using any fuel for forward motion – an incredible feat. Piccard and Jones were congratulated on their achievement by none other than the late Queen Elizabeth II, who said: 'The news of your splendid achievement has delighted us all.'

Hot-air balloons don't have a steering wheel. The only way to change direction is to gain or lose altitude and hitch a ride on winds that are moving in the direction in which you want the balloon to go. Two meteorologists, Luc Trullemans and Pierre Eckert, were pivotal to Piccard and Jones's success. They worked meticulously to map out a route for the *Breitling Orbiter 3* so that it could negotiate changing weather conditions and alter its altitude to find the winds that were blowing it in the right direction. Balloonists, like trees, don't get to decide how strongly and in what direction the wind blows. Instead, balloonists and trees alike must find ways of working *with* rather than *against* the wind. In an interview with the *New Yorker*, Piccard reflected on this approach of relinquishing control and accepting the uncertainty it brings as he said: '. . . acceptance is a decision you take. You accept to go with the wind. You accept to go into the unknown.'

I'd like to invite you to do the same.

The uncontrollables

We will all experience turbulent times in our lives: commitments will be broken, opportunities will go begging, we will lose people we love, and our health will falter. Despite our wish to be able to control how our lives unfold, circumstances will conspire against us. Faced with this intrinsic uncertainty, those trying to channel their lives towards high performance are often encouraged to focus their energy on what *is* under their control. Depending on what we're interested in, the 'controllables' can vary, from the duration and intensity of CrossFit training sessions and the tactics we employ in the acquisition of businesses, to the footwear we use on the running track, and the mentors we choose to work with in developing our skillset. But catchy as that 'Control the controllables' tagline is, it begs three key questions:

1. **What happens when the veil of control is ripped away?**
   – What happens when an injury interrupts the CrossFit regime, the competition nullify your tactics, Nike Alphafly trainers are banned from competition, or the coach decides to retire?

2. **What do we do about all the *un*controllables?** The stuff we can potentially control is merely the tip of a hulkingly big iceberg. You don't need to be the captain of the (Belfast-built!) RMS *Titanic* to know that it's what lurks beneath the surface that can pose the greatest problems.

3. **How do we manage the emotions that arise when we are confronted with what we cannot control?** The price we may pay for being conscientious and committed is that we might struggle to manage the emotional impact of circumstances that are outside our control. Jonny Wilkinson, the World Cup-winning former England rugby star, once put it plainly: 'All the uncontrollables in life just destroyed me.'

'Control the controllables' is a magician's trick, intended to divert attention away from the breathtaking enormity of everything we can't control. But it perpetuates the myth that what is outside our control should be ignored, for fear it will overwhelm us. While 'What if . . . ?' planning might help with anticipating and navigating some scenarios, the list of factors outside our immediate control is infinite: other people's behaviour, the past, the future, freak weather events, gridlocked traffic, disease outbreaks, wars, the Dow Jones index . . . There's only so much planning we can do. The really frustrating thing about unforeseen circumstances is that they are aren't foreseeable!

One of my favourite memes features a photograph of a person sitting on a beach watching the sun set with a drink in their hand. The slogan simply reads: 'Relax, nothing is under control.' That's not an inducement to relinquish responsibilities or accountability; it's an invitation for you to recognize the *limits* of your responsibilities and accountability. Sure, prepare and plan as best you can, but the real magic happens when we willingly face the feelings of fear, uncertainty and powerlessness that can arise when the unexpected occurs. **When we try to avoid feelings about not being in control, we end up being controlled by those feelings.** In my clinical practice, I see clients who experience problematic levels of obsessiveness and perfectionism because they have ramped up control in certain areas of life (at work and/or at home) to compensate for their inability to cope with what they cannot control. I support them in letting go of the 'control agenda' by developing their willingness to explore the emotions that the 'uncontrollables' provoke with an attitude of openness and curiosity. This is a key step in developing the flexibility we need to thrive.

PDFs

PDFs cause huge problems in our lives – they drain our attentional resources, sap our energy and prevent us from doing the things that we really want to do. No, I'm not talking about the billions of Portable Document Format files that are uploaded and downloaded on our devices every day – we'd be lost without those. I'm referring instead to an altogether more destructive form of PDF – *Persistently Denied Feelings*. These are the emotions we try to evade and supress because they seem inconvenient, self-indulgent or too much to handle; we may see them as a source of embarrassment or a sign of weakness. They could be feelings of guilt, shame, anger, sadness, fear or regret, or feelings of joy, hope, pride, love or excitement. PDFs come in all kinds of shapes and sizes. What unifies them all is our desire to put a lid on them.

Constraining our emotions can bring short-term benefits in certain situations – for example, not reacting angrily when others are trying to provoke us can help us to remain on task. However, problems emerge when evading or suppressing an emotion (or emotions) is adopted as a blanket strategy regardless of the context in which it occurs. I can't emphasize enough that our emotions are messengers that can serve important functions, mobilizing us to respond to unfolding events. For example, experiencing anger can be a signal that our rights have been infringed or disrespected, and can highlight a need to lay down a boundary or assert our own needs.

Distraction is a strategy that is frequently used to evade difficult emotions. There may well be occasions when using our imagination to retreat to our 'happy place' (visualizing a real or fantastical place that engenders feeling of joy or tranquillity) can help us through periods of acute stress or upset – for example, imagining lying on a Caribbean beach while reclining in a dentist's chair. But it's important to recognize that when we are in our happy place, we are *there*, we are not *here*. Our attention switches away from monitoring the situation we are in, and our ability to respond appropriately is diminished. What works in the dentist's chair may not work so well in a job interview.

Like the shoring up of coastal defences to protect against an encroaching tide, suppression and distraction are effortful, time-consuming work and bring no guarantee of success – if you're dead set on making sure you don't feel anxious, watch what shows up! And if our attempts to suppress emotions fail, we might be seduced by other methods – alcohol and substance abuse, gambling and other compulsions spring to mind – that can ultimately have a corrosive effect on our wellbeing and relationships. This can have dire consequences for our ability to thrive. The ultimate cost of suppressing our emotions is that we start to live life small. Ironically, we limit the choices we make for fear of experiencing certain emotions. But in doing so, we cut ourselves off from the very things that these emotions are alerting us to – the stuff that really matters. Life loses its vitality. As the American author John Augustus Shedd once remarked: 'A ship in harbor is safe, but that is not what ships are built for.' If we are willing to download our PDFs – to see them without fleeing from them, to feel them without reeling from them – we open ourselves to a life that is full of vitality. This gives rise to a sense of *equanimity* in which we can be open to our emotional experiences without being unduly disturbed by them. **We all have emotions; emotions don't have us.**

Often in life, it's times of crisis that serve to underscore the extent to which we've been denying important emotions – a period of ill health, the breakdown of a relationship, a disappointment at work. Here, I want to reflect on a time of struggle I experienced myself, and how finding the willingness to confront difficult emotions that I'd persistently denied provided me with opportunities for a breakthrough.

Unravelling in Seville

In June 2017, I travelled to Seville in Andalusia, Spain, to attend an academic conference. The association hosting the event had been organizing annual world conferences of this kind since 2004. As a repeat attender, I had been able to get to know colleagues from across the world who also attended regularly. Over the years, many of these colleagues had become good friends. So, both professionally and personally, attending the conference in Seville felt like an opportunity too important to miss.

The months running up to June 2017 had been particularly busy with work-related travel. I had travelled to Japan in March and to Uganda in May to learn more about mental health in those countries and to build research collaborations. Plans were also well advanced for an upcoming trip to Ghana the month following the conference in Seville. While I recognized how incredibly fortunate I was to travel so extensively with work, I was coming apart at the seams.

For many years, I had struggled with a problem that I had refused to acknowledge or confront. The truth of the matter was I had become addicted to work. 'Do more' and 'Don't say "No" to a request' were all-too-familiar reframes that dictated how I worked. Knowing what I know now, I recognize that the compulsion to immerse myself in my work was due to longstanding concerns that I wasn't enough – concerns that will doubtless be familiar to many. My sense of self-worth was dependent on the approval of others, and the way I learned to cope was to prove to others that I could do more. I might not be the smartest or the most talented person, but I could prove my worth by working hard – at school, at university, in the gym and at work.

Dedicating myself to work seemed to keep nagging insecurities at bay. But it was a hamster's wheel that I couldn't get off, and it was incurring considerable costs. A failure to invest energy in other areas of my life had ended relationships and squeezed the time I spent with friends and family. When I arrived in Seville that summer, I felt exhausted, and the conviction that I had nothing left to give was growing bigger and bigger. Support from friends and family felt like a line of credit that had run dry. Doubt and indecision seemed to be enveloping me in a smothering cloud that would steal the breath from my chest. The world felt cold and lonely, as if I was a million miles from any living soul – including my own.

Although Seville is a wonderful city, I was going to see precious little of it on this trip. I was overcommitted – contributing five presentations across the conference programme, and co-facilitating a two-day pre-conference workshop. I remember that it was stiflingly hot during the conference – the daytime temperature sat consistently at around 40°C. But the heat had been steadily rising for me over the last twelve months. In 2016, I had moved from Glasgow to Liverpool with my then-partner. It was taking time to settle in the new city, and me being away so much certainly wasn't helping. It was a point of friction between us, and I seemed wholly unprepared to acknowledge that it was something I could do anything about. I had hoped that the move to Liverpool would help bring us together, but it was pulling us apart.

I managed to get through the various conference commitments and made it to the final day – 25 June 2017. Although I had caught up with some colleagues during the conference, time for socializing had been scarce. At any rate, I had become sick of the sound of my own voice, and doubted whether anyone would want to listen to me anyway. In the hotel lobby, I bumped into Rosco Kasujja. Rosco lives and works in Kampala, Uganda. I had been fortunate enough to collaborate with him over the previous seven years. He's a great colleague, and a fantastic friend. The thousands of miles between Uganda and the UK mean that we don't get to spend time together that much. Seville was an opportunity to do exactly that, but it was an opportunity that had been missed. The sadness I felt hit me hard. This was a microcosm of my life – too busy to connect with the people who mattered to me. We hugged and collapsed on to a large circular pouffe in the hotel lobby, both of us lying back and staring at the ceiling. As is the case with good friends, Rosco and I didn't need to say a lot to each other for a lot to be communicated. We chatted where we lay – two still figures amongst the frenzied busyness of the hotel lobby. I shared with him how I was feeling, and he listened. And it was in my sharing and his listening that I realized that things needed to change.

It became apparent that amidst all the travel and work commitments, I had lost sight of who I was. I am no poet, but I went to my hotel room and found myself writing a poem to try to get outside what I was feeling inside. And penning those lines of poetry, and turning towards the emotions I was feeling, finally helped me to accept that I needed help with the low mood that I was experiencing.

Jennifer Nardozzi, a psychologist friend of mine who was also in Seville, had been sharing with me for some time how helpful psychological therapy had been for her, and how beneficial she thought it would be for me. While a small number of Clinical Psychology training programmes in the UK require their trainees to complete personal therapy during training, this was not the case where I trained. I had delivered lots of therapy in my career, but I had never received it. The PDF that I had to confront was the vulnerability of recognizing that the helper may need help. For lots of us, there may come a time when the nature of our struggles means we need to get the support of a trained professional, and that time had come for me.

It was not long after Seville that I commenced a course of therapy that has been incredibly valuable for me. It helped me to understand the factors that have contributed to my workaholic tendencies. I realized that, for years, I had been trying to subdue doubts and concerns about myself by managing how I came across to others. A consequence of this was I was presenting a version of myself to others rather than my full authentic self. That version of me craved affirmation, and the more encouragement it got, the more it wanted. I feared that if others were to see me 'warts and all', they would reject me. I was keeping other people at arm's length, and it was exhausting.

The first stage of finding a way through was being willing to embrace my own imperfections. Shining a light into the shadowy, unloved parts of my personality wasn't without its challenges, but it was transformative. By learning to lean in to my doubts and concerns, rather than trying to suppress them, I can now respond more flexibly when they occur. As a result, I have made great progress in recent years towards redressing the balance between my work and my life away from work. Sometimes, breaking down provides opportunities for breaking through.

Why the 'control agenda' doesn't work for thoughts

In 2021, Google launched the Pixel 6 phone. TV adverts broadcast in the UK to promote the phone made much of the 'Magic Eraser' function, which, for the first time, allowed users to circle parts of photos so that they could be removed – the annoying things that mess up images, like powerlines, pesky seagulls, passing traffic and . . . people. Whether it's an unwanted photobomber, an ex-partner or someone whose smile wasn't quite right, they can be removed – *circle, click, ta-da!* The tagline in the advert made me chuckle: 'It's perfect. Just like your memories, and how you want to remember them.' If only our thoughts and memories were that simple. Our thoughts, like our emotions, can be stubbornly resistant to our efforts to control or erase them. Allow me to demonstrate that by inviting you to play a little game with me. It's a simple game. All you need to do is follow my instructions. Ready?

Don't think about a tree bending in the wind. And, whatever you do, don't think about a tree with no leaves bending in the wind.

Whoops, you lose.

While this game might seem trivial, the same effect applies to more troublesome and unwanted thoughts that intrude into our consciousness. For example, commanding yourself not to think about the recurring thoughts about a recent time when you messed up would be equally futile. The so-called 'rebound effect', which was first noted by the late American psychologist Daniel Wegner, dictates that the harder we try to suppress thoughts, the more we end up experiencing them. Research has consistently shown that the wish to not have a thought is the surest way to have it. And yet, what advice do we give friends, family, colleagues and ourselves? 'Don't worry' ... 'Don't think so negatively' ... 'Stop comparing yourself to others'... 'Don't think of failing'... While well intended, this advice can create further problems. Not only does it risk paradoxically increasing the occurrence of those thoughts, but it also propagates a belief that these experiences are defective and should be avoided. That's a lot of experience being 'cancelled' right there. A better approach would be to acknowledge and validate the feelings, and then discuss what support might be needed, e.g. 'I am sorry that you feel worried, what do you think might be at the heart of that? What would be most helpful now?'

The flexible mind approach does not label thoughts and emotions as 'positive' or 'negative'. When we label thoughts and emotions as 'negative', we create a pretext for trying to expunge them from our experience without understanding why they might be there in the first place, or exploring the opportunities for growth they might provide. These inner experiences can serve important functions in the situations in which they arise. You wouldn't label your fingers and toes as 'positive' or 'negative', even though you might experience pain or discomfort in those parts of your body. So, too, with emotions. Research led by Emily C. Willroth, a psychologist based at Washington University in St Louis, has shown that people who make negative judgements about emotions such as sadness, anxiety or anger (i.e. evaluating them as bad, harmful or inappropriate) have uniquely low levels of psychological health – not just now, but into the future, too. That's not to say that the thoughts and emotions you experience in your life aren't difficult or challenging. As I have shared in this chapter, I know from my own life that they absolutely can be. Instead, it's about instilling a willingness to turn towards challenging and difficult emotions, rather than away from them. While we may not *want* emotions, the willingness to *have* emotions is an integral part of living with vitality. Put simply, a willingness to experience hurt and pain is the price of admission to living a full life.

Facing your emotions – the POPLAR technique

To develop your willingness to be open and curious about your own emotions, the next time you experience challenging or difficult feelings, work through the following steps, represented by the acronym POPLAR:

Pick up on the fact that the situation has provoked a strong emotional reaction in you.

Observe the most prominent emotion – is it anger, fear, shame, guilt, panic or something else?

Pinpoint your immediate urges to react. For example, depending on the circumstances, you might be tempted to quit, remove yourself from the situation, send a strongly worded email, placate the other people present, etc. See if you can allow the urges to be there without reacting to them.

Locate where in your body you are *feeling* the prominent emotion – is it in your chest, abdomen, head or somewhere else?

Assign physical properties to the felt experience of the emotion. If it had a colour, what colour would it be? If it had a weight, would it be? If it had a texture, what would it have?

Recognize that you can hold the emotion in that moment, the next moment, and even the moment after that . . . and that you can choose to respond in a way that is consistent with how you want to be in the world.

Consider doubling down on your willingness to be open to that prominent emotion by writing it on a piece of paper and placing it in your wallet or purse – in a location where you will see it from time to time. Wherever you go, you've chosen to bring your emotions with you. I have used this approach with many clients, some of whom have been experiencing intense emotional reactions. It takes a bit of practice, but clients find it very helpful. A point that I emphasize to my clients is that, at the end of the six steps, they are still free to follow through with the initial urge they had to react. It is their choice, and it is important that they are empowered to make it. My experience has shown that they very rarely go with that option, however. You, like them, can be willing to have strong emotions and yet not let those emotions dictate how you respond.

It was the best of times, it was the worst of times . . .

Lydia Thompson uses her speed to steal rugby matches from the opposition. She has been capped fifty-eight times by the England Women's Rugby (Red Roses) team, and has scored forty-seven tries.

Lydia has experienced many highs and lows across her career. She missed out on England winning the Rugby World Cup in 2014 due to injury, but was nominated for the World Rugby Player of the Year award in 2017. She played in the final of the 2017 Rugby World Cup, which the Red Roses lost to New Zealand. Five years later, she was part of the Red Roses team that faced New Zealand again in the 2022 World Cup final.

Lydia has spoken publicly about how developing a flexible mind by working with an Acceptance and Commitment Therapy trainer has helped her manage highs and lows, both in sport and in life. Speaking in an interview published days before the 2022 World Cup final, she highlighted how important developing a willingness to embrace doubt and self-criticism had been for her:

> *I am really not a confident person . . . you think at one point in your life you are going to sus it and you are going to have a solution and you are going to feel good enough . . . I think I have started to learn more that 'I am not good enough' is part of me and that's the driver for a lot . . . As much as it would be nice not to have the self-doubt and that little critic inside you, I have realized [it's] because of that I am where I am today.*

As it turned out, Lydia needed to draw on that flexibility at a catastrophic point in her career. On 12 November 2022, in the eighteenth minute of the World Cup final, with a crowd of over 42,000 fans watching at Eden Park in Auckland, New Zealand, Lydia was sent off for a dangerous tackle on New Zealand's Portia Woodman. She explained to me what happened:

I'd done a lot of homework, I and knew that [Portia is] a fantastic finisher. And in my head, in that split second, I had already decided that she was going to go for the line. So, I went to make a tackle to try and hit her into touch, but she had decelerated, and I hadn't adapted my tackle technique to get lower. In that split second, I had made the decision to tackle, which proved to be the wrong one. From then, it almost felt like I was outside my body. It still makes me feel sick when I think about it.

The two players clashed heads, and Portia was knocked unconscious.

I still find it really emotional [to think about], because I never like injuring another player . . . Our doctor was amazing and was straight on to it . . . And I knew it wasn't going to go well for me. I had never given away a card before.

At the point Lydia was sent off, England had been winning the game 14–0, but Lydia's card changed the course of the game. They would now have to play for at least a further hour with only fourteen players compared to New Zealand's fifteen. Lydia described the sense of dismayed bewilderment that she experienced after leaving the field of play.

When the red card happened, I was just so numb. I think my body almost shut down. It was like I wasn't there anymore. I just sat on the bench, and there was a part of me that wanted to just run off. But I couldn't. I was stuck. I think I was in shock.

It was just really hard. I couldn't watch the game. I wasn't able to engage with it . . .

Despite being a player short, the Red Roses continued to lead the game until the final eight minutes, when New Zealand's Ayesha Leti-I'iga scored a try to take the score to 34–31 in their favour. Although they battled valiantly, there was no way back for the England team.

And then the whistle went, and we'd lost. And I think that's when it hit me, and I just cried . . . I cried because it hurt so much . . . Once the whistle goes, there's nothing more that can be done. We'd lost. I felt so guilty and ashamed . . . I've obviously made many mistakes and had embarrassing moments, but none that have been so out there, so public and so costly.

When I saw Portia come on the pitch, I did feel relieved that she was walking, and she was OK . . . Being able to apologize to her at the end of the game was really important, because I felt so awful for taking the final away from her. As much as I didn't play the rest of the game, she didn't either. I felt like I'd completely let everyone down. It was my fault.

I'd made England's day that much harder and ruined our chances of winning. I'd cost them the World Cup and injured another player. I was blaming myself for the whole incident. I was really angry at myself and wished I could change it, but I couldn't . . .

In the weeks that followed, Lydia described being surprised by how kind and supportive other people were, and how she struggled to accept their kindness:

I couldn't understand how people could even look at me, let alone hug me or be kind to me. And other players came up and said, 'I've had similar things happen to me,' and they were really vulnerable with their own stories . . . So that was amazing, that people were normalizing it and just being so kind, because I felt like a criminal.

During that time, despite a strong urge to hide away, Lydia demonstrated the willingness to keep showing up. She maintained contact with other people and faced the challenging emotions that surfaced:

I still saw people. I still went out, even though part of me didn't want to. I knew it was important not to hide. That helped . . . Knowing that I was still part of this team helped . . . As much as I am part of this team, I need this team for me as well.

I was in so much pain . . . I think if I'd tried to suppress that and pushed that down and not acknowledged it, I think I would still be processing it, but because I just let it go, I just felt everything. And I think that really did help.

Lydia was clear that having a flexible mind doesn't provide immunity from adversity. Instead, it guides us in how we respond to adversity. Just as a tree forms reaction wood in response to the stresses and strains it experiences, Lydia's willingness to turn towards her pain provided opportunities for growth:

It would [be] lovely if [having] Acceptance and Commitment Training [means] you don't need to feel pain [Lydia holds her right fist in front of her as if holding a shield], but I felt so much pain ... I had daily choice points where I could choose to just disappear, to not engage. I didn't want to feel. I didn't want to have to go through it. I wanted to hide from it, and it's just that feeling of shame just really hurt ... But I've got to a point where I am grateful for the experience. If I could take it back, I would. But it has happened, and it has taught me a lot about myself. It's taught me a lot about how beautiful the community I live in is, and how kind people are ... You can have the worst kind of thing [happen] and still come out the other end ...

It's now a couple of months on ... I've engaged in the Six Nations campaign [Lydia was selected for England's Six Nations squad in the spring of 2023]. *I wouldn't have believed you [immediately after the 2022 Rugby World Cup final] if you'd said that's what I'd be doing right now ... [in my head] I'd retired from rugby and never wanted to face pain again. I never wanted to make a mistake on a rugby pitch again, and I guess by engaging with rugby, I risk doing that again.*

I asked Lydia what makes taking that risk worthwhile.

I'm still on the journey of exploring that ... I'm holding on to knowing that I will grow from this. This pain could hopefully help me be a better parent – if I get to be a parent ... You know your kids are going to make mistakes, and you will want to protect them as much as you can from that. But that is part of the risk of living, and hopefully I can be the support for them and show unconditional love and be a guide for them. No one wants to make mistakes. But they do happen. And yes, hopefully, there will be moments in the future when I can pull on this pain.

It was also clear that Lydia's willingness to be vulnerable with those she trusted was helping her benefit from the support and mentorship that they could provide.

My coach at Worcester [Rugby Club], Jo Yapp, is on her own journey as a director of rugby ... She was an incredible rugby player. She's had her own setbacks and challenges in sport, and now as a coach ... She's helping me grow, and I think that if I hadn't been open, [if] I hadn't been vulnerable, if I hadn't asked for help, I wouldn't have that relationship with her now, where I can turn to her and say, 'Jo, can we have a chat?'

Lydia Thompson was willing to lean in to the pain she had experienced, and to take the learning opportunities that it provided. It's not just tree trunks that flex in storms – it's Red Roses too.

Noticing our own stories

In essence, we experience everything at least twice: there's the event itself, and there's the story we construct about it. Stories are powerful. They can inspire, motivate and persuade. But stories can also antagonise, demoralize and inflame, corroding the relationships we have – not just with others, but with ourselves. Our minds are prolific producers of fiction – who we *think* we are, what we *think* we can do, what we *think* we cannot do. And even little fictions can cause big problems. Like fake news on social media streams, the stories our minds produce can hijack our attention: *I'm not good enough ... No one cares about me ... I'm too long in the tooth to try something new* . . . Thoughts can be headlines that hook us, and when they do, they influence how we act. The stories our minds create can serve to constrain the choices we make.

While our thoughts can focus on certain aspects of our experiences, it's important to recognize that they are separate from those experiences. Allow me to demonstrate. If you're willing and able to do so, place your right hand on your chest, roughly over the area where your heart is located. Now allow the following thought to form in your mind: *My heart is beating.* Let the thought crystallize in your awareness for a moment or two. If your mind wanders off, notice that it has wandered, and bring your attention back to the thought: *My heart is beating.* Recognize that the thought is indeed correct.

OK, now consider this question – and it's not a trick question: Is that thought pumping blood around your body? Or is that being done by something else? The thought exists separately from the thing that the thought is about – even if the thought is correct. Now, recall a thought you had about the state of your life during a time of considerable stress – for example, the break-up of a relationship or a crisis in your career. I am not asking you to contest the correctness of that '*My life is falling apart*' thought. Instead, I'm asking you to recognize that it's a headline that exists separately from the stressful experience.

Like news headlines, our thoughts can be based on unreliable sources or may be susceptible to bias and spin. Just as news outlets like CNN or the BBC adopt editorial policies relating to the content and style of their reporting, the stories generated by our minds can centre on familiar themes. This can serve us well when the themes are matched to the demands we face – the '*I need to be tenacious and uncompromising*' story can play well on the rugby pitch or in the boardroom. The credibility of that story is accepted faster than the terms and conditions for accessing free Wi-Fi. But sometimes stories are broadcast in situations where they may be less useful – the '*I need to be tenacious and uncompromising*' story doesn't work nearly as well at home. Context matters. We need to be discerning consumers of our minds' reporting. Our willingness to recognize the stories we get stuck with is an important first step in responding to them more flexibly.

My experience as a clinical psychologist has taught me that there can be certain recurring themes in the stories we get stuck with. These include thoughts about: our abilities (e.g. *I don't have what it takes*); other people's abilities (e.g. *My colleagues seem so much more confident than me*); what other people think (e.g. *People think I'm incompetent*); life rules (e.g. *I must never quit*); current circumstances (e.g. *I don't have access to the support I need);* future outcomes (e.g. *I'm going to fail*); past regrets (e.g. *I made the wrong choice*); guilt and responsibility (e.g. *I should have done more*); or a lack of meaning (e.g. *I'm not sure all these sacrifices have been worthwhile*). If you've noticed a few of these themes cropping up in your thoughts, don't be concerned. **You are not the problem; the problem is buying into thoughts that you might be the problem.**

The roving reporter

One way of getting unstuck from your thoughts is to imagine that you are a reporter broadcasting live from the scene of those thoughts, speaking to camera and relaying a concise summary of events into a microphone: *We interrupt this paragraph to bring you a breaking news story. Let's pass now to our reporter at the scene . . . At 12.36pm precisely, the thought occurred that I need to keep working until I get this paragraph finished. Ross White, reporting live from his study.*

The '*I need to keep working*' thought will doubtless be familiar to you. Imagining that you can 'report' that kind of thought will help shift your relationship with it. A reporter is distinct from the reports they file, and they are not themselves obliged to respond directly to the events on which they are reporting. Similarly, we are not obliged to respond directly to the thoughts that we have. Reporters also move on to the next story – they are willing to let old stories pass, so that they can be open and receptive to new contexts and the stories that these will give rise to. In the same way, we have to be vigilant to the possibility that we can get stuck with the same old stories, and that these might be inhibiting our ability to thrive here and now. Reporters conveying their stories – like the sapwood transporting a tree's water – serve as a metaphor for how we are the conduit in which our thoughts occur; they will come and they will go, and we need to be willing to allow them to flow.

This 'roving reporter' approach – an example of what is referred to as a 'cognitive defusion technique' – makes use of the meta-awareness we discussed in the previous chapter to draw a separation between us and the content of our thoughts. In addition to thoughts, however, we can also 'report' emotions and bodily sensations that we notice showing up in our experience rather than getting swept away by them: *An update on our earlier news bulletin – this paragraph was finished after lunch, and I'm feeling well-nourished and happy about that.*

Shelve (not 12) rules for life

When we buy in to our mind's stories about what we can and can't do, we get stuck in what is euphemistically called our 'comfort zone'.

In truth, our comfort zone is actually our *conforming zone* – we conform to rigid rules that lead us to live our lives small. There are numerous books and podcasts that proffer advice on how we can establish new rules in our lives – at the time of writing this chapter, the book *12 Rules for Life: An Antidote to Chaos* by the Canadian psychologist Jordan B. Peterson has sold more than ten million copies. There is clearly an appetite for implementing new rules. Rules create an illusion that life is under control. However, less focus has been given to what we should do with the rules we already have that are causing problems in our lives – the '*I shouldn't voice my opinions in front of others*', '*I must be relentless in pursuit of my goals*', '*I can't rely on others*', '*I need to implement more and more rules*' rules.

I would argue that, in order to grow, we need *fewer* rules, not more. It is our willingness to break the rules hindering our progress that transports us from the conforming zone to what I call the 'transforming zone'. This will, of course, take courage. Although it can bring rich rewards, transformation is a process that can be fraught with doubt and uncertainty. But as the poem 'Fear' (variously attributed to Kahlil Gibran or an Indian philosopher named Osho) puts it:

The river needs to take the risk of entering the ocean,
because only then will fear disappear,
because that's where the river will know,
it's not about disappearing into the ocean,
but of becoming the ocean.

Honing the ability to notice our mind's stories, and developing a willingness to break rules we may have set about avoiding emotions, can help us to see our fears as the 'paper tigers' they are – attention grabbing but lacking the ability to bite. The late, great NBA star Kobe Bryant made this point brilliantly in an interview with the author and podcast host Jay Shetty:

I've seen players – even myself, you know, when I was younger – being consumed by a particular fear, and to the point when you're saying, 'OK, nah it's not good to feel fear, I shouldn't be nervous in this situation right now,' and it does nothing but grow. Versus stepping back and saying, 'Yeah, I am nervous about this situation. Yeah, I am fearful about this situation. Well, what am I afraid of?' And then you kind of unpack it, and then it gives you the ability to look at it for really what it is – nothing more than your imagination running its course.

Strategic self-talk

Over the course of this chapter, we have seen that the mental chatter our minds produce – whether they are stories about our experiences or rules to which we should adhere – can exert a powerful influence on how we feel and how we behave. But the tables can be turned. We can be purposeful and intentional in how we use these words and this language. The key question is: Are you willing to be the author of your own life?

On 12 February 2015, the British tennis player Andy Murray won his second-round match in the Rotterdam Open tennis tournament by defeating the Canadian Vasek Pospisil. Collecting his kitbag, Murray made his way off court to the warm applause of the crowd

– but he didn't take everything with him. He left behind a page of handwritten notes. Two days later, the Dutch broadcaster and journalist Wilfred Genee revealed the contents of these notes to the world when he posted a photograph of that page on the social media platform X (then known as Twitter). It was a list of ten motivational statements that included instructions such as: 'Be good to yourself', 'Stick to the baseline as much as possible', 'Focus on each point and the process', 'Try to be the one dictating' and 'Be intense with your legs'. This page of notes provided clear evidence that Murray and his team were using an approach called 'strategic self-talk' to support his performance.

There are two types of strategic self-talk. *Motivational* strategic self-talk is intended to build a focused and determined mindset. Paul O'Connell, the talismanic former captain of the Ireland rugby team, has spoken publicly about how he and his teammates used motivational self-talk to keep them Anchored in the present moment and guard against the risk of mental time-travel (see p. 83 for other examples of Anchoring statements). 'Win the moment in front of your face' was the mantra they used as a way of not getting derailed by the errors, or indeed the small victories, that occurred during matches. Then there's *instructional* strategic self-talk, which aims to optimize the execution of skills. These instructions can relate to attention (e.g. 'Focus on each point and the process'), technique (e.g. 'Be intense with your legs'), strategy (e.g. 'Try to be the one dictating'), and/or the bodily position and feel (e.g. 'Stick to the baseline as much as possible'). Unlike 'rules' that broadly dictate what we can and cannot do, strategic self-talk is intended as a cue to retain an awareness of how we wish to act in specific situations.

Research conducted with athletes involved in a wide range of sports, including skiing, cycling and darts, has shown that both instructional and motivational strategic self-talk can improve performance. Instructional strategic self-talk was shown to be better for improving performance on fine motor skills, like golf-putting. It was effective regardless of the level of experience of the athlete, whether the self-talk was spoken aloud or expressed inwardly, and whether the message was generated by the athlete, a coach or a psychologist. However, it seems that your high-school English teacher was right all along – grammar matters! A research study demonstrated that self-talk expressed using second-person pronouns (e.g. 'You can do this') – as Andy Murray's was – is more effective at improving performance than first-person self-talk (e.g. 'I can do this'). It may be that using second-person pronouns will make your self-talk more persuasive because it resonates with the direction and encouragement you may have received from others during your life – a bit like being your own coach. Using second- or third-person pronouns may also help us to adopt the 'bird's-eye view' of meta-awareness we discussed in the previous chapter. A piece of instructional strategic self-talk that captures this chapter's focus could be: 'Like the trunk of a tree, you can be flexible in how you respond to turbulent times.' Sometimes, a short instruction or reminder can keep you on track: 'Be more tree.'

Life will always have its stresses and strains – a life devoid of them would diminish rather than increase our capacity to thrive. Much of what we experience is beyond our immediate control, and our reaction to what we can't control will play an important role in shaping our lives. We can respond to feelings of anxiety about the 'uncontrollables' by ramping up our efforts to control other aspects of our lives, or we can develop the willingness to lean in to our difficult thoughts, feelings and sensations so that a broader range of responses is available to us. Noticing the stories that our minds generate about our lives is an important part of this. Rather than being trapped in stories that dampen and demoralize us, we can use self-talk to author stories that steer and cheer us to do what matters to us most. In the next chapter, we will explore doing what matters in more detail when we turn our attention to the final aspect of AWE – being Empowered.

Willing: Summary Points

- Attempts to control, eliminate or evade difficult thoughts and emotions can be frustratingly ineffective and incur costs to our time, energy and attention.
- Being willing to find ways of working with rather than against thoughts and emotions is an important aspect of developing a flexible mind.
- A willingness to experience hurt and pain is the price of admission to living a full life.
- The stories our minds create about who we are place constraints on who we can be.
- By freeing ourselves from unhelpful rules, we can switch from the *conforming zone* to the *transforming zone*.
- Strategic self-talk can help us to build the willingness to embrace difficult thoughts and emotions.

CHAPTER 5

Empowered

A tree requires energy to function, and its 'crown', which incorporates the branches and leaves, acts as its engine. Leaves are crucial for gathering energy from the sunlight and exchanging gases that allow trees to prosper through the process of photosynthesis. For every square yard of forest, there's an estimated 27 square yards of leaf surface available to catch the sun's energy. The branches of a tree project the leaves upward and outward to harvest that energy. Through a process called positive phototropism, which is stimulated by the action of hormones called auxins, the branches grow assuredly towards the sunlight. The crown of the tree provides a helpful metaphor for the third and final component of flexibility – being Empowered.

Finding your energy source

In this chapter, we will be focusing on the aspect of flexibility that mobilizes you to do more of the things that matter to you. To better understand what helps you to be Empowered, we'll be exploring the following three questions:

1. What energizes you?
2. How can you transform that energy into how you act?
3. How can you ensure that you get optimal returns from those actions?

The first question is about *purpose*, the second about *personal values*, and the third relates to *pragmatic action*: what I refer to as 'the three Ps' of being Empowered. Purpose speaks to our life intentions and the difference that we wish to make to the world. Personal values are the qualities that we, as individuals, choose to prioritize as we move through the world. And pragmatic action is about the practical steps we can take in line with our purpose.

How do purpose, pragmatic action and personal values relate to the crown of a tree? Well, the energy that the sun provides to the tree's leaves is akin to the impetus and momentum that our sense of purpose grants us – purpose is like sunlight. Just as a tree's branches bud and grow incrementally in pursuit of the sun's light as it tracks across the sky, we can take pragmatic actions that allow us to progress towards our purpose – pragmatic action is like the buds branching out in increments towards the sun. The fact that not all branches will bear fruit is analogous to how not all our actions will lead to tangible outcomes – but when they do, our accomplishments are like the tree's fruit. Branches display different characteristics (e.g. straight, angular, nimble or robust) depending on where they are positioned on the tree and the conditions they encounter. Likewise, our personal values become evident in how we undertake pragmatic action – personal values are like the unique qualities that branches show as they grow.

Your purpose and your personal values are ongoing evolving

commitments that you can carry with you through life. If, like the late Nelson Mandela, peace and reconciliation is an important aspect of your sense of purpose, then embodying personal values such as warmth, respect and empathy in your interactions with others will be important on an ongoing basis. If, like Greta Thunberg, you are passionate about combatting climate change and its impact on the environment, then being tenacious, persuasive and politically astute will be helpful personal values to guide you on your journey. Or maybe, like Naomi Osaka, you're energized by wanting to promote improved understanding about the importance of mental wellbeing as a key purpose? If that's the case, then being open, courageous and committed will be important personal values for you as you move through life. There will always be new causes at which your purpose can be directed – people to inspire, species to protect, myths to be broken. And there will always be more opportunities to demonstrate personal values that help us to embody the change that we want to see in the world. In this sense, purpose and personal values are orientations rather than destinations – while they guide us on our journey, they never signal an endpoint to that journey. Reassuringly, no matter how far we drift from our purpose and/or personal values, there will always opportunities to turn towards them once again.

A purposeful life

Appreciating the importance of purpose in our lives is no fad – 'Mac & Cheese' flavoured ice cream it is not! Since civilization's early dawn, our ancestors pondered the purpose to our lives: to go forth and multiply, to live in harmony with nature, to pursue pleasure, to fight injustice, to acquire wisdom, to atone for the sins of a previous life, to treat others as we would hope to be treated . . . From the philosophies of ancient Greece, Taoism, indigenous belief systems such as *buen vivir* or *ubuntu*, and other spiritual or religious teachings, to the ideals of the Enlightenment or the views of twentieth-century political idealogues, the purpose of life has been keenly debated. One of the twentieth century's most influential texts on purpose is Viktor Frankl's *Man's Search for Meaning*. Born in 1905 into a Jewish family in Vienna, Frankl and his family were forcibly detained in Nazi concentration camps, where they endured barbaric treatment. Tragically, Frankl's father, mother and wife all died in the camps. In the first part of his memoir, which was published in 1946, Frankl reflects in agonizing detail on what he and so many others experienced. Trying to find meaning amidst the depravity was pivotal. 'Woe to him who saw no more sense in his life, no aim, no purpose, and therefore no point in carrying on,' he writes. Purpose was not just a lifeforce; it was a lifeline. For Frankl, the horrendous experiences that people can encounter don't diminish the importance of purpose – they *accentuate* it.

And what is 'purpose'? The American psychologist William Damon and his colleagues defined it as 'a stable and generalized intention to accomplish something that is at once meaningful to the self and of consequence to the world beyond the self'. Purpose allows us to see our lives as journeys where we can appreciate where we have been, where we are now, and where we long to go. Examples of questionnaire statements that tap in to purpose include: 'I have aims in my life that are worth striving for,' and 'I have certain life goals that compel me to keep going' (both items are from the Multidimensional Existential Meaning Scale). Purpose puts pep in our step – generating vitality and motivation to move towards what's important to us. It doesn't push, it propels – and it helps us to stay well. A high level of purpose is predictive of increased physical wellbeing (including lower mortality rates), a reduction in the onset of health difficulties, an improved ability to be resilient in response to adversity, the delayed onset of a host of health problems, and a willingness to engage in health-promoting behaviours. Furthermore, when we dedicate more time to our purpose, we experience increases in self-esteem and pleasant emotions.

My work has taught me that purpose serves three crucial functions:

1. **Purpose *motivates*** – It guides our behaviours towards what truly matters, e.g. inspiring others, embarking on adventures or fighting inequity.
2. **Purpose *vindicates*** – It helps to justify the sacrifices we make, including the opportunities we pass up, the time we spend away from our family, etc. As Friedrich Nietzsche famously remarked: 'He who has a why to live for, can bear almost any how.'
3. **Purpose *illuminates*** – It helps us understand that experiencing challenging emotions is an inevitable consequence of caring deeply about something.

This third point is worth emphasizing. Our emotions can be flag-bearers signalling that purpose is close at hand – the buzz of anticipation, the joy that progress brings, feelings of thwarted frustration, the crushing sadness of falling short, the dread of losing it all . . .

It would be tempting to recoil away from the sense of vulnerability, uncertainty and precariousness that shows up when we care deeply about something. Don't. **The willingness to lean in to challenging emotions paves the way to our purpose.** If we are hardwired to have those emotions, why not have them doing what matters to us? Recall from the previous chapter that Lydia Thompson said of her Rugby World Cup final heartache:

> *I'm holding on to knowing that I will grow from this. This pain could hopefully help me be a better parent – if I get to be a parent . . . You know your kids are going to make mistakes and you will want to protect them as much as you can from that. But that is part of the risk of living, and hopefully I can be the support for them and show unconditional love and be a guide for them.*

Being a guide to others, so that they might develop and grow through the pain they experience, is clearly an important purpose for Lydia. I have no doubt that she will go on to do wonderful things when she chooses to retire from rugby. Her willingness to take risks and get out on to the skinny branches will stand her in good stead.

Conventional wisdom suggests that we need to 'find our why' – the overarching sense of purpose that drives our actions. But **purpose is not *found*, it is *formed*.** The seeds of our purpose are already planted in the contributions we make to the world around us. Maybe you're a competitor, maybe you help others fulfil their potential, maybe you're an 'ideas person', maybe you're an animal-welfare advocate, or maybe you're committed to developing excellence in your craft.

The scion shoots of purpose will emerge from what brings vitality and enthusiasm to your day. But purpose needs to be cultivated – we need to invest time and effort to support its growth.

The author of the *Harvard Business Review Guide to Crafting Your Purpose*, John Coleman, highlights three important points about purpose:

1. Purpose is cultivated by investing time and effort in what matters to us.
2. Purpose isn't a single thing. Various aspects of our lives, including work, recreation, friends and/or family, provide opportunities for cultivating purpose.
3. Purpose isn't static – it can dynamically evolve as our lives progress.

Some important prompts that have been shown to help with cultivating purpose include:

- thinking about the social roles and responsibilities we are drawn to in life, e.g. becoming a mentor, parent, teammate or pet-owner
- reflecting on spiritual, religious and/or political beliefs that may help connect our experiences to something bigger than ourselves
- getting greater clarity on our sense of self and the type of personal values that matter to us
- considering our vocation and the aspects of our work that we may find enriching and rewarding

The sense of work-related purpose mentioned in the final point is sometimes referred to as a *calling*. Of course, your vocation may not be a 'calling'. Instead, it can provide income and security to help you to cultivate purpose in other areas of your life.

A day on purpose

I have developed an approach that I call 'A Day on Purpose' to help my clients cultivate their sense of purpose. Let's try that now. Imagine that you have a day free of doing the stuff you don't want to do, without any of those humdrum chores that steal time from your day and offer little in return. You can choose instead to do things that you feel passionate about: things that could even be in the service of something bigger than you alone. For example, some people might want to swim with dolphins, go climbing in the mountains, volunteer for a charity, or sculpt objects using clay. Take a moment to consider the following questions:

- How would you choose to spend that day?
- What matters enough for you to spend it *that* way?
- What difference, if any, would you hope that doing that might make?
- How would you know that it had been a day well spent?
- How would you feel at the end of that day?
- If you could have more of those kinds of feelings in your life, would you want them?
- Now take a moment to think about how you might do more of that stuff – even 1 per cent more – in your average week. **What one concrete action could you take in the coming week to help you to do that?**

That final point is important. We need to be *purposeful* in scheduling time to nurture our purpose. **Contentment will be hard to find if what we do is different to what we know to be important.**

It might not come as a surprise to hear that, for me, a key part of my purpose is supporting others to build their own sense of purpose. The work that I do with clients focuses a great deal on that. Another purpose that I am passionate about is communicating psychological concepts to a general audience in plain, easy-to-understand ways. The monthly '5 to Thrive' newsletter that I publish and the writing of this book chime with that purpose.

The events of 2018 were crucial in helping me to clarify my sense of purpose. I'll explain more about that now.

Goin' home

The course of therapy I embarked on when I returned from Seville helped me to open doors to past experiences that had been walled off in my mind. Accepting who I truly was meant that I was less preoccupied with who I ought to be. This was pivotal in helping me to reconnect with my own sense of purpose.

My struggles to settle into my new life in Liverpool had amplified a yearning to feel more deeply connected to a place and its community. In what seemed like the blink of an eye, I had been away from Northern Ireland for fifteen years, living first in Scotland and then England. And as great a city as Liverpool is, it had never felt like home. Northern Ireland was calling me back. My family were there, as were many close friends with whom I had stayed in touch through the years. My father and an uncle had recently experienced significant health scares, and I wanted to be more available to them. I was also aware of the Northern Irish 'brain-drain' that can serve to diminish opportunities for growth and development in the country. I wanted to give something back to the place that – for better and for worse – had shaped me. I realized I wanted to support people in Northern Ireland to find their purpose and fulfil their potential. It's a funny thing, but we can travel long distances only to discover that where we want to be is right back where we started.

Strong intention, light attachment

We can be flexible in how we choose to build our purpose. Depending on the situation, the same purpose can be served through a variety of different actions, not all of them dramatic. For instance, keeping a journal of daily reflections can serve the purpose of personal development, but so too can reading a book, attending an online seminar, or talking openly with a trusted friend. We only need to look at the multitude of different lengths, widths and shapes that a tree's branches assume to see how flexible a tree is in pursuit of its energy. No two branches are the same, yet they share the same function – to get the leaves to the light. And although purpose is a renewable source of power, we must still handle it with care. Greek mythology warns of the perils of flying too close to the sun. Just as Icarus fell from the sky, we too must be vigilant of the risk of burnout that can come from pursuing our purpose too keenly. When we're doing what matters, it can feel as though nothing else matters, but we need to take care of ourselves so that we can continue to care deeply about our purpose.

Purpose is intended to boost flexibility, not thwart it. So, while we can be strong with our intentions, we must also guard against the risk of becoming rigidly attached to doing things a particular way or arriving at a particular outcome – sometimes **serving our purpose is about strong intention but light attachment**. When we notice ourselves fixating on doing something in a particular way, or getting overzealous about achieving a particular feat, it can be helpful to remind ourselves of the transient nature of our existence and the impermanence of our accomplishments. I like to remind myself of what Tyler Durden says in the movie *Fight Club*: that we're 'polishing the brass on the *Titanic*; it's all going down'. No matter how hard we polish the brass, rearrange the deckchairs or try to boil the ocean, there's always going to be an iceberg out there with our names on it. None of us are getting out of this life alive. But rather than being an abject lesson in the futility of life, I see this as an invitation to enjoy the journey while we can, without taking ourselves or our achievements too seriously. Appreciating that our time on this Earth is fleeting can bring freedom rather than despair. So, when you commit to doing things, and no matter how passionate your purpose, it's worth remembering that you're always polishing the brass. The best you can do is commit to making it shine brightly.

Personal values are adverbs, not adverts

'Values' are everywhere these days. Whether it's the organization you work for, the online retailer you shop with, or the dental practice you hesitate to attend, a clear articulation of principles guiding behaviour is essential. And that can be a very good thing. After all, values help set expectations and provide impetus to act in particular ways.

Take 'Communication, respect, integrity and excellence' – as values go, it's not a bad list. You might think that this is the cultural DNA of an uber-successful educational institution, elite military unit or sporting team. In fact, these were the values of the Enron Corporation – the former energy company whose unscrupulous and deceptive accounting practices resulted in what was described as the 'corporate crime of the century'. In August 2000, the value of Enron's share price had peaked at a lofty $90.75. But in December 2021, when concerns grew about misrepresented earnings and hidden debt, the value of the share price plummeted to $0.25. The company was forced to file for bankruptcy. Its $63.4 billion of assets made it the largest corporate bankruptcy in US history to that point. More than 20,000 employees lost their jobs, and $2 billion of pension plans were wiped out. The narrator of the Oscar-nominated documentary *Enron: The Smartest Guys in the Room* noted that, in reality, Enron had 'contempt for any values except one – making money'. When it comes to values, talk can be cheap, and a lot of people can be left short-changed.

So yes, the articulation of values (particularly corporate values) can amount to a cynical exercise in sloganism – socially desirable self-affirmations typed into a (soon to be forgotten) Microsoft Word document, or buzz phrases emblazoned (in a large, elegant font) over an image of a Norwegian fjord that's hung on an office wall. But personal values aren't adverts, they are *adverbs* – the qualities that we bring to *how* we do things in the present moment. For example, we can do things compassionately, assertively, collaboratively, diligently, efficiently, skilfully or patiently – all examples of qualities that we might choose as personal values. When we get values off our walls and into our lives, the difference it brings to our sense of authenticity and vitality is palpable.

Clarifying personal values

As with purpose, the importance of personal values has been alluded to across time and cultures. Greek antiquity had the four classical virtues of prudence, justice, fortitude and temperance; Buddhism has the four Brahma-viharas of benevolence, compassion, empathetic joy and equanimity; and Christianity has the seven heavenly virtues: chastity, temperance, charity, diligence, kindness, patience and humility. Today, a mix of societal, cultural, spiritual, organizational and/or familial factors can vie to influence the qualities that we might feel we ought to personal value. To develop and maintain the Empowered aspect of a flexible mind, however, we must be free to choose the personal values that resonate most strongly with us. And there can be great variety in the personal values that each of us choose to prioritize in the different domains of our lives. If I was to send you an email listing my personal values, you might read it, scratch your head, and say to yourself, *Well, that's an inane list of qualities that neither excites nor inspires me.* And that would be OK. That's the magic of personal values; we each have our own.

The process of clarifying our values is about identifying the qualities that we want to shine through when we are being the most authentic version of ourselves. So, how does the clarification of values happen? Fortunately, there are a range of approaches that can help. While the temptation might be to shine the spotlight inward – to search one's own soul – clarification often comes from shining the spotlight outwards, on to those with whom we interact regularly. What do you admire about the way your friends, family members and colleagues conduct themselves? Is it their ability to personify generosity, patience, honesty, dedication, thoughtfulness, humour, empathy, or some other quality perhaps? **What we admire in others can serve as a guide to what we might choose to become.**

We can also admire people whom we haven't met and may not ever meet, such as athletes, musicians, authors, comedians, scientists, historical figures, thought leaders or social media influencers. What impresses you about how they conduct themselves? We must listen when other people's personal values speak to us. And then there are fantastical characters from books, games, movies or TV programmes. Whether it's *Guardians of the Galaxy, Calamity Jane, The Lord of the Rings, Star Wars, Jane Eyre, The Lion King* or *The Shawshank Redemption,* there will be characters whom you admire for the qualities they endorse. I must confess that I drew inspiration from the character of Thomas Shelby from the BBC production *Peaky Blinders* when delivering the groom's speech at my wedding – not for his tortured ruthlessness, but for his ability behave calmly and coolly when under pressure. The speech went well, and nobody got hurt!

If trying to draw inspiration from others isn't doing the trick, there are plenty of values card-sorting tasks and online tools that allow you to express your preferences for different values. Questionnaires such as the Valuing Questionnaire have been developed that measure the extent to which we are living in line with our values. Research has shown that believing our behaviours are more in keeping with our values is associated with higher levels of wellbeing and lower levels of depression, anxiety and stress.

I use the following process with my clients: the 'Birthday Speech exercise'. I hope it will be help you with clarifying your own values.

- Let's roll the clock forward and imagine that you are celebrating a milestone birthday – one of those that marks another decade of your life. A party has been arranged at one of your favourite local venues.

- Picture yourself arriving at that venue and walking through the doors to be greeted by the smiling faces of family members, friends and colleagues.
- Now let's imagine that the evening has progressed, and it's time to offer a toast for your birthday. A dear friend (someone whom you respect deeply) steps forward to provide a short speech about you. They talk about the type of person you are, the life you live, and the impact you have on the people around you.
- Take a moment to think about what you would want them to say. What qualities would you want them to notice about how you are living your life, how you are with yourself, how you are with others?
- Notice your mind's tendency to drift off to think about what that person would be likely to say if they were giving that speech today. Instead, the intention here is to focus on what you hope that person would say about you at a later point in time. Remember, there is time for you to commit to demonstrating those qualities, even if you do not feel like you've had the opportunity to do so recently.
- Now that you have given it some thought, write down the list of qualities on a notepad or in the Notes app on your phone. These qualities, which you have reason to cherish, are the personal values that you endorse.
- Looking at that list, think about how you might integrate those personal values into how you conduct yourself during the rest of today, and the days that will follow.

I recently used this approach with a client I'll call Sam. Sam, single and in his late twenties, was seeking support for difficulties with low self-esteem that were impacting his interactions with friends as well as colleagues in his job with a legal firm. Sam indicated that he had started to avoid social gatherings. The LAG (see p. 43) of psychological rigidity was setting in, and his wellbeing was being impacted. In our first meeting, he described experiencing a difficult childhood, characterized by frequent arguments between his parents – they eventually got divorced when he was a teenager. He indicated that he was bullied at school for several years. Sam's father would also be highly critical of him if he failed to perform well academically. In an early phase of the work, we established that fighting injustice and protecting the rights of others were key purposes for Sam. Through using the Birthday Speech exercise, Sam was able to identify the following personal values which he could incorporate into the broader work we were doing to empower him and shift his LAG to AWE:

- behaving kindly and helpfully towards others
- acting playfully and carrying oneself lightly
- living enthusiastically
- behaving wisely
- behaving adventurously
- treating oneself respectfully
- behaving assertively

Certain personal values we endorse may be more suitable for some situations than others. For example, while 'acting playfully and carrying oneself lightly' might be desirable for Sam in social situations, it might be less suitable for the formality of the courtrooms where his job requires him to work. Take a moment to review the list of your own personal values and consider whether these represent the breadth of the roles you assume in your life, e.g. colleague, friend, teammate, mother, leader. In doing so, you might notice that some personal values appear to be in opposition with one another. For example, in our work together, Sam queried whether his personal value of 'behaving assertively' might be at odds with 'acting playfully'. But rather than thinking that personal values are *in conflict*, it's helpful to understand that personal values occur *in context*. Sam was able to see that personal values like 'behaving assertively' *and* 'acting playfully' can coexist, and that these different personal values can come to the fore depending on the situation he is in. An important aspect of developing a flexible mind is to recognize that values can be deployed flexibly depending on the context.

Personal values are also dynamic – they can evolve and change over time. The personal values we endorse when we're single may differ from those we choose to prioritize when we are married. Similarly, the personal values that guide our actions early in the cultivation of a purpose can be distinct from those foregrounded later. For that reason, it is important to review our personal values on a regular basis. Life events, such as starting a new job, committing to a new project, starting or ending a relationship, or experiencing a bereavement can all provide important cues for this kind of review. Alternatively, we can proactively choose to schedule thirty minutes in our calendars every six months to revisit our personal values.

As with purpose, we should be vigilant to the risk of becoming too firmly attached to personal values. As helpful as values can be for guiding our behaviour, they shouldn't become rules. In the hustle and bustle of modern life, it often seems de rigueur to have 'non-negotiables' – credos that must always be displayed by yourself and others. My advice? Consider having 'Everything is negotiable!' at the top of the list. Otherwise, you risk being rigid and dogmatic rather than agile and responsive to the changing demands life brings.

Committing to pragmatic action

The final P is pragmatic action. It's pragmatic action that helps us to devise and implement plans for advancing our purpose that are tailored to the situations in which we find ourselves. The American educator Jessie Potter once remarked: 'If you always do what you've always done, you always get what you've always gotten.' Unless we are prepared to take pragmatic action, we will not have the opportunity to develop our purpose. For example, you could start a foreign-language course (to improve your ability to travel and meet new people), participate in discussions aimed at resolving conflict (promoting peace and reconciliation), reduce your carbon footprint by using alternatives to fossil fuels (combatting climate change), start writing a blog (sharing knowledge and insights with others), or raise funds for a mental health charity (supporting people's mental wellbeing). Pragmatic plans of action are the milestones that help us know we are connecting with our purpose.

New branches don't just suddenly appear on a tree. They emerge slowly but surely from growth buds. Similarly, actions in line with our purpose take time to build momentum. As Jeff Bezos, the founder of Amazon, once remarked: 'All overnight success takes about ten years.' It's no coincidence that we refer to people making their way in their chosen fields as 'budding' athletes, actors, musicians, film stars, entrepreneurs and so on, because they are growing their skills in an incremental way. Setbacks – whether they be failures, disappointments or rejections – will happen along the way. As I explained in the previous chapter, we can fall into the trap of trying to avoid the challenging emotions that accompany setbacks. We become passive rather than active – choosing not to 'branch out' in our own lives. I encourage my clients to be wary of pursuing what I call 'passive goals', which focus more on inaction and the avoidance of challenging emotions than action, e.g., *not* messing up, *not* drawing attention to themselves, *not* causing a fuss, *not* taking risks (we'll explore goals in more detail in the next chapter). As David Crosby, a founding member of The Byrds, sings in 'Everybody's Been Burned', 'You die inside if you choose to hide' – we wilt when we are not willing to grow towards what energizes us.

Earlier in the book, we learned how 'When . . . then' traps can prevent us from feeling more contented in the present moment (e.g. '*When* I have completed this project, *then* I will be able to relax'). But 'When . . . then' thinking has another pitfall: it can prevent us from taking decisive action in line with our purpose (e.g. '*When* I am feeling less anxious, *then* I will commit to seeking advice from experts'). We defer taking action to an unspecified point in the future. The key question here is: 'Will the time ever be right?' As the actor Hugh Laurie reportedly notes: 'It's a terrible thing, I think, in life to wait until you're ready. I have this feeling now that actually no one is ever ready to do anything. There's almost no such thing as ready. There's only now. And you may as well do it now.' Having doubts and being prepared to act are not mutually exclusive experiences – we can feel anxious *and* still do what matters. In his book *The Courage to Create*, the American existential psychotherapist

Rollo May pointed out that 'commitment is healthiest when it is not without doubt, but in spite of doubt'. We can do what matters, even if difficult emotions show up or the time doesn't feel right. Here's how that looked in my own experience.

Goin' Home

Having identified, that my soul was calling me home, in August 2018, I took a two-week break back in Northern Ireland. The relationship with my partner had ended, and I wanted to reconnect with the riches that my homeland has to offer. Along with my younger sister, I climbed Slieve Donard – Northern Ireland's highest mountain – and absorbed the fantastic views that its summit provides of the surrounding counties and the expanse of the Irish sea stretching out to the east. I took five days of surfing lessons on the north coast and felt revitalized by the seawater washing over me and the rush of catching my first waves. Finally, I finished my trip by meeting up with old friends in a pub in Moira, the town where I grew up. It was a special night – not least because I met the woman who would eventually become my wife. All roads were leading me back home!

A younger, less empowered version of me would have assumed that I couldn't relocate to Northern Ireland until I managed to secure a job. But the renewed commitment I had to acting authentically and purposefully meant that, on my return, I took the chance of discussing the situation with my managers at the University of Liverpool. To my delight, they were willing to support my request for flexible working arrangements that would allow me to work from home and to travel regularly to Liverpool for important meetings. In September 2019, I decided not to renew the rental agreement on my apartment in Liverpool. Despite the uncertainties about how the future would unfold, I took pragmatic action. I was goin' home.

Making choices

Trees have evolved to be decisive and deliberate in where they grow the branches of their crown. Willy-nilly won't cut it. Similarly, our time and effort are finite resources that need to be deployed in particular ways through the choices we make. Choices are central to our ability to act in line with our purpose and personal values. But how much freedom to choose do we really have? Our choices are constrained by the circumstances in which we find ourselves: the options available to us, our roles and responsibilities, gaping social inequalities, the limits of our capabilities, etc. 'Pragmatic' action is about recognizing that choices need to be optimized in light of the practical considerations we face in different contexts. The concept of 'reciprocal determinism', proposed by the late, great Canadian-American psychologist Albert Bandura, states that three factors influence our freedom to act – the environment, our individual characteristics (including how we think and feel), and the consequences of our behaviour. And it's not all one-way traffic – these three elements influence each other. Bandura himself stated that: 'Individuals are neither powerless objects controlled by environmental forces nor entirely free agents who can do whatever they choose.' Our choices are influenced by the context, and our choices also influence the context. For example, our choice of what series to watch on Netflix is prompted by what shows are available on the platform, what appeals to our sensibilities, and whether the first episode leaves us feeling interested enough to go back for more. In turn, the series that we watch to their conclusion on the platform will shape the decisions that Netflix make about what new shows get commissioned in the future. If I, along with millions of others, hadn't been enthralled by *Breaking Bad*, then *Better Call Saul* would never have been produced for me to enjoy.

In addition to 'external' contextual factors – such as when, where and in relation to what (e.g. family, career, recreation) a choice is being made – our choices are also influenced by 'inner context', including our unique personality traits, our ability to anticipate how others will respond and our decision-making style. In his book *Thinking, Fast and Slow*, Daniel Kahneman proposed that decision-making is influenced by two systems:

- **System 1 (Fast)** quickly triggers intuitive and automatic reactions based on assumptions formed from our previous experiences of the world. This system tends to be influenced by our emotional state and short-term drives.
- **System 2 (Slow)**, on the other hand, tends to be more considered and rational – guiding our decisions according to longer-term goals and aspirations.

Research has shown that we tend to use System 1 more when making choices relating to love and relationships – we intuit based on our feelings rather than hard rational facts. On the other hand, when the choice in question relates to our careers and employment, the more analytical reasoning associated with System 2 kicks in – a more considered weighing up of costs and benefits tends to be conducted.

The AWE of a flexible mind helps to transform our 'inner context' and the influence it has on the choices we make. For example, research has shown that practising mindfulness meditation, and the opportunities to be Anchored and Willing this provides, can impact our decision-making processes by Empowering us to reflect on our purpose and personal values, retain a focus on key objectives, and minimize the risk of acting in counterproductive ways. This is the work of System 2. In essence, developing a flexible mind helps us to identify the 'decision trees' that arise in our lives, and appreciate that we can branch *towards* our purpose and personal values rather than *away* from them, just because challenging emotions, thoughts and sensations have shown up. Don't wilt away, grow towards.

Choice overload

Having different options to choose from can be overwhelming. Harry S. Truman, the thirty-third president of the US, got so annoyed with economists initially recommending one option relating to fiscal policy, only to then contradict themselves by saying, 'On the other hand . . .' that he asked if there were any one-armed economists with whom he could consult instead! Truman was not the first to rue the dilemmas that different options bring. Aesop's fable of 'The Fox and the Cat' from around 600 BCE is a cautionary tale of the dire consequences of decision paralysis. While travelling on a journey together, a cat and a fox get into a discussion about who is the smartest. The fox boasts that he knows many clever tricks, but the cat confesses to knowing just one. At that very moment, a hunter's horn disturbs their discussion and a pack of ravenous dogs bound into view. In an instant, the cat scurries up the tree to hide in its abundant crown.

'This is my trick,' the cat calls down to the fox. 'Now you show me yours!' The fox, dithering over which of his many tricks to use, stays rooted to the spot. Alas, the story does not end well for our friend the fox . . .

In 1844, Søren Kierkegaard, the Danish philosopher, described the dread that can accompany our realization of the choices available to us as the 'dizziness of freedom'. Citing the example of someone standing on a cliff, he highlighted that it is not just the fear of falling that scares us, it's the knowledge that we could choose to throw ourselves off. The freedom to choose brings with it a sense of jeopardy. This sense of dread is, of course, not an entirely bad thing – it serves to sharpen our awareness of the importance of considering choices carefully.

More recently, the American psychologist Barry Schwartz, in his book *The Paradox of Choice: Why More Can be Less*, viewed the demands of having too many choices from a consumer's perspective. So-called 'choice overload' can sow concerns that we'll make the *wrong* choice, increasing the pressure on us to make the *right* one. Paralysis by analysis can set in. Rather than being Empowered to make a choice, we dwell on it too long – and when we overthink, we underperform.

A review of the research evidence concluded that the likelihood of choice overload on consumers depends on a range of contextual factors, including:

- **The perceived difficulty of the decision.** This can include factors such as how much time is available to make the choice, and the format in which the different choices are presented to us – seeing the different options seems to increase the likelihood of choice overload compared to being told what the options are.

- **The complexity of the choices**. This relates to factors such as how difficult it is to make comparisons between the different options, and whether a dominant option is present.
- **Uncertainty about preferences**. This relates to our ability to fully understand the costs and benefits that different options offer, and how easy it is to make comparisons between the costs and benefits offered by the respective options.
- **Decision goal**. If we are not clear on the particular purpose that the choice will serve or whether now is the best time to make the choice, it can increase the risk of choice overload.

But can research based on consumer behaviour really be applied to life choices? It's debatable, but it does highlight the possibility that choice overload can be avoided by identifying different options and considering the costs and benefits of each option relative to a set of clear criteria – from a flexible mind perspective, these criteria would be our purpose and personal values.

Paralysis by analysis can also occur *after* a choice has been made. It can be tempting, with the benefit of hindsight, to label choices as being 'good' or 'bad'. We can experience emotions such as regret, guilt, shame and self-blame if a choice we made leads to a less-than-desirable outcome. When we become entangled with these judgements and emotions, a state of inertia can develop; we can't move on from making ourselves wrong. This is where the AWE of a flexible mind can again be helpful: get Anchored into the here and now rather than being swept up in mental time-travel; be Willing to notice the stories your mind is generating about the choice and the emotions accompanying those stories; then, with kindness, give yourself credit for being Empowered to commit to making the choice when the situation required you to. Finally, recognize that moving forward, there will be opportunities to make new choices that align with your purpose and personal values. Each day brings fresh choices.

Lateral choices

Sometimes, rather than having too many options to choose from, it can seem like there are no viable options available to us at all. We can be convinced that the challenges we are facing seem insurmountable, and conceding defeat seems to be the only option. The crowns of trees face similar challenges when their access to the light energy is threatened by overcrowding from other trees. It can seem like there is nowhere left to go. But crowns are crafty; their branches grow out as well as up, and round as well as through. Being Empowered is the aspect of a flexible mind that allows us to demonstrate creativity and ingenuity when options seem limited. In 1967, the late Maltese psychologist Edward de Bono invented the phrase 'lateral thinking' when he published *The Use of Lateral Thinking*. In contrast to more conventional ways of trying to solve problems, which he referred to as 'vertical thinking', lateral thinking advocates for more creative, less obvious approaches, especially when our options seem limited.

It's easy for our minds to tell us that we are not very creative. But there are skills we can learn that can help. One such approach is the task unification technique, where an object that already serves a particular function is adapted to serve additional functions. The work of Rob Law, a British inventor, provides a great example of this. He had noticed how challenging it was for parents to manage both kids and luggage when travelling through airports. So, he took brightly coloured pieces of luggage, stuck four wheels on to the undercarriage, then attached a saddle-like seat for the child to sit on aloft the luggage, along with a set of handles at the front to hold on to, and a strap for the parent to pull both luggage and child along. Since the Trunki was first released in 2006, more than 5 million have been sold. It was Dr Martin Luther King Jr who said: 'The difference between a dreamer and a visionary is that a dreamer has his eyes closed and a visionary has his eyes open.' Rob Law had his eyes wide open.

Cereal entrepreneurs

In 2007, Brian Chesky and Joe Gebbia moved into an apartment together in San Francisco. If their names aren't so familiar, the company that they created will be. The two friends had recently graduated from the Rhode Island School of Design and had decided to head west. Chesky would later recall that his move to San Francisco was on a whim, and it put him out on a limb. His share of the rent was $1,150, and he didn't have enough money in his bank account to cover it. But as fate would have it, their move to San Francisco coincided with the Industrial Designers Society of America conference, which was being hosted in the city. Due to high demand caused by a large number of conference delegates, hotel accommodation was at a premium. Chesky and Gebbia came up with a solution by thinking *inside* the box – the box created by the four walls of their apartment. Gebbia had an air mattress, and they purchased another two. They set up a website to advertise to those attending the conference that they had space to accommodate three paying guests. For the princely sum of $80 per person per night, Chesky and Gebbia were offering delegates airbeds and breakfast. A thirty-five-year-old woman from

Massachusetts, a forty-five-year-old father of four from Utah, and a thirty-year-old man from India were happy to pay the money. The guests and the hosts enjoyed the experience; it was a win for all concerned. Not for the first time, nor the last, necessity was the mother of invention – and Airbnb was born.

Realizing they were on to something, Chesky and Gebbia invited Harvard graduate Nathan Blecharczyk to join the team to provide technical expertise. The three founders of the company ploughed their time, energy and money into the fledgling business. Frustratingly for the trio, others were slow to see the business's potential. Meetings with a multitude of angel investors failed to generate capital. It's rumoured that during a meeting with Chesky, Gebbia and Blecharczyk, one potential investor went to the toilet and never returned – kind of ironic, considering that the three partners didn't have a 'pot to piss in'! Chesky alone accrued debt of $30,000 on his credit card. It seemed that the fledgling company was on the brink of financial collapse.

In August 2008, the Democratic National Convention rolled into Denver. Airbnb used its technical know-how to help supporters of Barack Obama find accommodation in the city. Despite Chesky, Gebbia and Blecharczyk's hopes, the income generated was modest. They needed to make some lateral choices. Whereas previously they had focused on getting heads on beds, they decided to turn their attention to the breakfast instead. Making use of their contacts at the Rhode Island School of Design, they commissioned the design of cereal boxes that drew playfully on the political convention season. Breakfast cereals were purchased cheaply and repackaged into 500 (individually numbered) boxes emblazoned with a caricature of Barack Obama and the slogan 'Obama O's: The Breakfast of

Change'. The boxes sold like proverbial hot cakes – for $40 per box. They repeated the feat for the Republican party convention in Saint Paul, Minnesota, the following month. Of course, it was a caricature of John McCain against a red background, and the slogan 'Cap'n McCains: A Maverick in Every Bite' that adorned these boxes. The selling of these cereal boxes raised a staggering $30,000 for the company, keeping it afloat at a time when every dime counted.

At the last count, Airbnb now advertises properties in 100,000 cities and towns in more than 220 countries. At the time of writing, the company's market capitalization is valued at $107 billion. Airbnb's distinctive symbol is called the Belo, which it has named 'the symbol for belonging'. Airbnb's purpose, as outlined in their mission statement, is 'to create a world where anyone can belong anywhere'. In case you are wondering, the company has four core values: 1) Champion the mission, 2) Be a host, 3) Embrace adventure, and – last, but by no means least – 4) Be a *cereal* entrepreneur! As the company grows, it will doubtless experience challenges in its efforts to remain true to these values, but the story of its development helps illustrate what can happen when purpose, personal values and pragmatic action align.

Just as the crown of a tree traps energy from the sun to help the tree grow, the three Ps of purpose, personal values and pragmatic action constitute the Empowered aspect of a flexible mind. Purpose gives direction to our lives and honours our struggles. Personal values are the qualities that we wish to endorse in day-to-day life. And pragmatic action relates to what we choose to do in the situations we encounter. At times, pragmatic action may require us to demonstrate creativity and ingenuity in our efforts to further our purpose.

Over the course of this part of the book, we've explored how the roots, trunk and crown of a tree correspond to the three aspects of a flexible mind: Anchored, Willing and Empowered. But, like trees, we exist in environments that subject us to a range of stresses. In the final part of the book, we're going to turn our attention to how trees interact dynamically with their environment, and what this can teach us about how we can use flexibility in our own lives in order to thrive, whatever storms life may throw at us.

Empowered: Summary Points

- Being Empowered incorporates the Three Ps: purpose, personal values and pragmatic action.
- Purpose is not something we *find*, it's something we *form*.
- Personal values are the qualities that we bring to how we act in the world.
- A 'strong intention, light attachment' approach is important for sustaining our purpose and personal values.
- Our choices can provide us with opportunities to grow towards our purpose rather than wilt away from it.
- Thinking and acting creatively can help us to take pragmatic action in line with our purpose.

PART III

Interacting with the World Around Us

When a tree is firmly *anchored* in the ground, is *willing* to bend to and fro and allow nutrients to flow, and is *empowered* by the energy it captures, it possesses high levels of flexibility. But what does this flexibility afford the tree? Well, flexibility provides opportunities for the tree to respond to the various challenges and opportunities that it faces. For a tree to thrive, it must adapt to and synergize with changes in its surroundings. While spring and summer provide opportunities for growth, autumn and winter are times when the tree needs to become dormant. Across the changing seasons, one thing remains constant – the tree must defend itself from a range of different threats. Turbulent storms, winter frosts, dry summer spells, burrowing animals, competition from other trees, wood-devouring insects and/or invasive fungi can all pose problems for a tree.

Across the year, a tree needs to balance three competing demands – being productive when it can (*get*), defending itself against potential harm (*threat*), and consolidating during the fallow period of dormancy (*reset*). During the Get mode of the spring and summer, the tree uses water, nutrients and sunlight to photosynthesize so it can grow. In Threat mode, the tree utilizes inbuilt defences and diverts resources to deal with crises that threaten its existence. In Reset mode, the tree reduces its activity to conserve energy over the winter until the time is right to usher in a new period of growth.

A tree's ability to flexibly interact with its environment to manage competing demands so it can thrive provides an important parallel to how we can balance performing well with feeling well. If we are to thrive, we too must interact effectively with our environments by appropriately deploying our own Get, Threat and Reset motivational modes:

- **Get** mode facilitates our drive to achieve rewards and succeed.
- **Threat** mode equips us to detect and respond to danger – whether it is actually present or imagined.
- **Reset** mode provides opportunities to appreciate more fully ourselves and the world around us, and to reorientate to our purpose.

The existence of these three motivational modes and the distinctive ways that they direct attention, regulate emotions and guide our behaviour is supported by contemporary psychological theory, which draws on ideas from evolutionary science (see p. 305 in the Appendix for a summary of the three modes). High activation of one mode can lead to a downgrading of the others. And if these three modes of motivation are not sufficiently balanced over time, we – just like an unfortunate tree – will wither and wane.

In this section, you will learn more about these motivational modes and how the AWE aspects of a flexible mind equip us to either sustain or switch modes to optimize our ability to thrive. In the following three chapters, we'll focus on each of the modes in turn, starting with Get, then Threat, before finally looking at how we can Reset. By the end of this part of the book, you will understand the importance of asking yourself the following questions:

- Which motivational mode am I in right now: Get, Threat or Reset?
- What benefits is this mode serving in the situation I am in?
- What costs might this mode be incurring?
- Would I be best off sustaining this mode or switching to another mode, so that I can thrive in pursuit of my purpose?

While Part II focused on what we can do to develop the AWE of a flexible mind, Part III demonstrates how we can use it to make hay when the sun shines, prevail through the storms of life, and be renewed when the time is right.

CHAPTER 6

Get

The quaking aspen (*Populus tremuloides*) is an intriguing tree. It has small, rounded leaves with flattened stalks that flutter in the slightest breeze. This gives the impression that the tree is trembling – hence its name. But unlike humans, who tremble with fear, this aspen quakes with industry. It is what is known as a pioneer tree – these are trees that are the first to inhabit new spaces. To do so, it must grow quickly to avoid competition with other trees. This rapid growth requires large amounts of fuel, which can only be produced through photosynthesis. Unlike many other tree species, a quaking aspen can perform photosynthesis in its distinctive white bark as well as its leaves. The trembling of its leaves ensures that more light can penetrate its canopy to reach the bark below. But the quaking aspen pays a high cost for its productivity – its lifespan is very brief compared to other types of trees. It grows at a rate it cannot sustain. The story of the quaking aspen provides a cautionary tale for us all. 'Get mode' is the motivational system that helps us to be industrious and break new ground, but we must find ways of sustaining our efforts over the long haul.

In this chapter, we'll learn more about Get mode by addressing the following three questions:

1. What influences the types of rewards you are driven to seek?
2. What happens when your drive flips into *over*drive?
3. How can a flexible mind assist you with managing Get mode?

Spring into action

As we discovered in the previous chapter, clarifying our purpose brings clarity, coherence and orientation to what energizes us in life. Purpose helps us to map out our capacity for growth. But growth is an active process that requires momentum. Get mode is the motivational system that provides that momentum. The neurotransmitter dopamine has been identified as playing a prominent role in this mode. Broadly speaking, Get mode is fuelled by two main categories of rewards. Firstly, there are the forms of rewards that exist externally to us. These are also known as 'extrinsic rewards' and can include financial incentives (e.g. salaries or bonuses), indicators of status (e.g. work promotions), endorsements from others (e.g. 'Likes' on a Facebook post), sporting accolades (e.g. championship titles or the colour of a martial arts belt). Extrinsic rewards can also include lifestyle aspirations, such as a modish desire to own the newest smart phone, live in an exclusive neighbourhood or purchase expensive clothing brands. Consumerism is built on our willingness to pursue extrinsic rewards. As powerful as extrinsic rewards can be, they also have their limits. For example, an over-reliance on extrinsic forms of reward in corporate culture has been linked to employees demonstrating *less* proactive engagement in their work, higher staff turnover, and lower job satisfaction. Indeed, Dan Stone, a professor at the University of Kentucky, and his colleagues suggested that extrinsic rewards 'deliver short-term gain and create long-term problems'.

Secondly, there are less tangible, but more sustaining, forms of reward that exist *within* rather than *outside* us. Known as 'intrinsic rewards', these are akin to psychological yearnings (also referred to as psychological needs). Two American psychologists, Rich Ryan and Ed Deci, have pioneered scientific investigation into these yearnings through their development of Self-Determination Theory. Three psychological yearnings (which we'll represent using the acronym ARM) have consistently been identified across different cultural contexts:

Autonomy – the yearning to exercise agency in the choices that we make

Relatedness – the yearning to mutually share connection and care with others

Mastery – the yearning to develop our skills and capabilities

Ryan and Deci have likened these yearnings to 'innate psychological nutriments that are essential for ongoing psychological growth, integrity, and well-being'. Indeed, reviews of the research evidence have consistently shown that a failure to satisfy these intrinsic yearnings is associated with lower levels of wellbeing, lower levels of pleasant emotions, and increased levels of challenging emotions. This is backed up by my clinical experience – when clients come to me for support, my assessment of their difficulties often indicates that one or more of these yearnings is being frustrated.

I use a motoring metaphor with my clients to illustrate the different, yet potentially complementary, ways in which intrinsic factors operate. While the coherence and orientation of purpose act as a map for their journey, *autonomy* puts them in the driver's seat, *relatedness* guides them to think about who they would take along on the journey, and *mastery* helps them hone their ability to drive the car. Extrinsic factors, on the other hand, speak to whether they will receive a trophy or be paid handsomely for completing the journey.

Now, there's nothing inherently wrong with wanting to pursue extrinsic rewards – who wouldn't want to be well paid? – but it helps to be clear about the limitations of purely focusing on such rewards. For example, research has shown that focusing on money as a reward is linked with unhelpful and unethical behaviours, and can result in a reduced inclination to interact socially with others. When we are triggered to think about money, we are less able to savour the richness of simpler everyday pleasures, such as eating a piece of chocolate. By focusing on money, life seems less rich. Get mode can have an insatiable appetite when it comes to extrinsic rewards.

Do you recall Tal Ben-Shahar's concept of the arrival fallacy (see p. 87) – the sense of being underwhelmed when we do finally achieve a long-term objective? The risk of experiencing the arrival fallacy is increased when we focus too much on extrinsic rewards. Help can come from an unlikely source – nuts and sage. No, this isn't a recipe for making Christmas stuffing; these are acronyms that I use to draw attention to the dominance that extrinsic rewards can hold. We need to recognize that we have a squirrel-like tendency to scavenge for NUTs (the 'Next Unachieved Thing'), and that we can instead heed some SAGE advice ('Something's Always Gonna Entice') and savour the 'fruits' of our labour when they do arrive. This can also provide us with an opportunity to look beyond the trappings of success and take stock of how we are satisfying our yearnings for autonomy, relatedness and mastery. It's important to keep our eyes on the real prize.

Questioning our goals

To fully embrace the power of Get mode, it's important that we understand the different contributions that can be made by four distinct elements of our experience. These elements are:

- purpose
- goals
- tasks
- personal values

Thinking back to the motoring metaphor I use with clients, you'll recall that purpose acts as a map for our journey. To continue the metaphor, goals are sections of the journey we aim to complete that help us to chart the progress we are making, and tasks are the specific steps that we are required to take to reach particular mile-markers (e.g. stopping for fuel or consulting with others for directions). Tasks are the pragmatic actions that we complete as we progress towards goals. Finally, personal values, as we learned in the previous chapter, are the qualities that we choose to exemplify as we make our life journey – for example, these could include going about our lives considerately, inquisitively, thoughtfully, committedly, courageously, etc.

Having discussed purpose and personal values previously, let's turn our attention now to goals and tasks. Conventional wisdom advises us to be *smart* when we set goals. George T. Doran, a management consultant from the US, introduced the acronym SMART to high-light a need to set goals that are *Specific, Measurable, Assignable, Realistic* and *Time-related*. But goal-setting is merely the start of the process; Get mode requires us to get to grips with the details of *how* the goal can be achieved. That's when tasks come to the fore.

Let's imagine that some friends persuade you to join them in running a marathon. You haven't done a great deal of running in recent years, but you're up for the challenge. You and your friends identify a marathon that's scheduled for six months' time in a nearby city, and you've set your sights on completing the distance in under four hours. The SMART goal has been set. But now you need to mould the tasks linked to that goal to the context of your life. To do this, a process that I refer to as 'questioning our goals' can be indispensable. This involves addressing the following prompts:

- **Ask why** – What important life purpose and yearnings does this goal speak to? For example, pushing the boundaries of your physical fitness, raising money for a charitable cause, and/or enjoying the sense of comradery in achieving something special with your friends.
- **Ask for whom** – For whom are you working to complete this goal? For example, for yourself, for your friends, and/or for a needy charitable cause.
- **Ask whose** – Whose support and advice will you seek as you identify key tasks? For example, you might consult people who have completed a marathon, review online training plans to understand how best to build your fitness, seek advice from your family, and/or speak to the staff working in the sports store where you buy new running shoes.

- **Ask where** – In what places will you be able to do the tasks required to progress this goal? For example, on the road, in the gym, on the yoga mat, in an ice-bath, in the grocery store (nutrition), in your bed (getting good rest) and/or on the massage table.

- **Ask when** – When will you do the tasks, and how can they be timetabled into your calendar? For example, you may assign running to Tuesdays, Thursdays (incorporating some hill-sprints) and Sundays (incorporating incrementally longer runs week to week); yoga to Mondays; CrossFit to Fridays, and take rest days on Wednesdays and Saturdays.

- **Ask which** – Which personal values do you want to embody as you undertake these tasks and progress towards this goal, and how would you and other people notice those values in how you act? For example, you may want to be present, focused, dedicated and encouraging to others and yourself.

- **Ask what** – What practical, psychological and emotional barriers might you experience in completing the tasks linked to this goal? For example, you may need to juggle other commitments, manage inclement weather conditions, deal with injury setbacks, and handle self-critical thoughts and/or anxiety in the run-up to the event.

- **Ask how** – How can you overcome these barriers? For example, you could step back from some commitments or delegate certain tasks, engage the Empowered aspect of a flexible mind to come up with creative alternatives to out-door training when the weather is bad, and/or book regular sports-massage appointments to avoid injury.

Getting clear on these contextual details is the flexible way to ensure we achieve our goals. I have found this approach to be invaluable in my work with clients, whether I'm working with a schoolteacher who is planning a return to the classroom after a period of stress-related absence, an athlete returning to competition after injury, or a business executive who wants to set aside more time to spend with their family. Get mode prospers on this kind of data.

It's worth noting, however, that there will be times in life when we might lack clarity about the goal we want to work towards, even if our purpose is clear. While the absence of a specific goal can leave us feeling all at sea, using the Anchored and Willing aspects of a flexible mind can help us to notice the feelings of urgency, uncertainty and frustration that arise without being derailed by them. As we wait for our goals to crystallize, turning our attention towards our personal values can help. Values guide us through the fog. A question that is worth considering at these times is: **How do you want to be today as you navigate your way towards knowing what you will want to achieve tomorrow?** Even though our goals might remain unclear, we can still exude qualities such as being considerate, relaxed, engaged, diligent, enthusiastic or curious. The goals will be sure to follow.

Preparing for the future in the now

Mental imagery techniques can be an important tool when undertaking tasks to advance our goals. These techniques aren't just about imagining in advance what we will see in our 'mind's eye' as we complete those tasks (referred to as 'visualization'), it's also about more broadly anticipating what we will hear, smell, taste and feel as we do so. Mental imagery has been used extensively in the field of sports psychology to help athletes imagine completing tasks linked to their performance in the absence of overt physical movements. However, it has also been used to boost academic achievement, promote healthy lifestyles, and treat mental health difficulties.

In my work supporting clients in anticipating and preparing for tasks they will be undertaking, I use a seven-point evidence-based approach to mental imagery work that was pioneered by Paul Holmes and Dave Collins (two British psychologists based at Manchester Metropolitan University and the University of Edinburgh, respectively). Let me talk you through these points so you can use them to prepare for a particular task linked to one of your goals:

- Construct the imagery from your own point of view – experience it 'from the inside out' rather than from the viewpoint of someone watching you complete the task.
- If possible, assume the physical stance that you will take when undertaking the task (e.g. standing, sitting).
- Ideally, undertake the imagery work in the place where the task will be performed. If this is not possible, view photographs or videos of the location to help you picture it clearly in your mind's eye.
- Imagine completing the task in precise detail, just as it will be performed on the day.
- Imagine completing the task at the same speed that it will be performed – resist the temptation to speed it up or slow it down.

- If it's a task you will do routinely, develop the imagery to incorporate new skills you may learn along the way, or new insights you have gained.
- Anticipate the emotions that you will experience when completing the task (e.g. apprehension, excitement, fear), and incorporate the bodily sensations that accompany those emotions into the imagery.

When engaging in mental imagery work, it's not just about focusing on what you plan to do – it's about incorporating the personal values that you want to shine through as you undertake the tasks. This brings in the Empowered aspect of a flexible mind. Mental imagery is not just about preparing for *what* you will do, it's about preparing for *how* you will do it.

You can use your response to the seven-point mental imagery process to create an 'imagery script' – a detailed written account or audio recording that can be used to strengthen the imagery work. Jonny Wilkinson, the former England rugby fly-half, discussed using imagery scripts to prepare for the 2003 Rugby World Cup final in Sydney:

This visualization technique is a sort of clarified daydream with snippets of the atmosphere from past matches included to enhance the sense of reality. It lasts about twenty minutes, and by the end of it I feel I know what is coming. The game will throw up many different scenarios, but I am as prepared in my own head for them as I can be. If you have realistically imagined situations, you feel better prepared and less fearful of the unexpected.

What are the benefits of using mental imagery techniques? Well, a review of the research evidence found that athletes' use of mental imagery improved not just their level of performance but also their psychological experience of that performance. The review found that combining mental imagery with physically practising tasks was superior to physical practice on its own. Finally, the amount of imagery work that we do determines the impact it will have – the more imagery work we do, the greater the effects. However, it's worth noting that not all of us are equally able to use mental imagery. One in every fifty of us is affected by a condition known as aphantasia: an inability to form mental images. While mental imagery work may not be as helpful for those affected by aphantasia, there are many other tools in this book that will be useful.

You may wonder how using mental imagery to prepare for tasks you will be undertaking – whether it's a work presentation, a pitch for investment or asking someone out on a date – is compatible with a flexible mind's focus on being Anchored in the 'here and now'. Well, it's all a question of intentionality and awareness. There is an important distinction to be drawn between our minds drifting to the past or future in an absent-minded way compared to us deliberately allocating time for them to do so. Meta-awareness is key. By adopting a 'birds-eye' view of your attention, you can be fully aware that you are choosing to use the present to purposefully prepare for the future. 'Now' and 'then' can align.

The confidence trick

'Confidence' – or a lack of it – is often cited as a potential barrier to completing our goals. Whether it's a friend who isn't confident that they can learn conversational Italian for an upcoming work placement in Rome, or a colleague who isn't confident enough to interview for an upcoming promotion opportunity, a preoccupation with confidence can stop Get mode in its tracks. But it's not a lack of confidence that kills our goals, it's allowing *concerns* about a lack of confidence to prevent us from acting.

People working in high-performance environments often seem convinced about the importance of confidence for performance. Whether it's a football pundit, the boss of a Formula 1 team, the chief conductor of a philharmonic orchestra or the principal dancer of a ballet company, confidence is heralded as a cornerstone of success. As we've discussed, thriving has two key pillars – performance and wellbeing. How confident should we be about the supposed importance of confidence for performance? And how might confidence link with the second pillar – wellbeing?

When used in day-to-day conversation, the word 'confidence' (from the Latin *com fidere*, meaning 'with trust') tends to be used as an abbreviation of 'self-confidence'. Although definitions of self-confidence vary widely, it has been described as a person's 'perceived ability to accomplish a certain level of performance'. The eminent psychologist Albert Bandura wasn't a fan of 'confidence'. He described it as 'a nondescript term that refers to strength of belief but does not necessarily specify what the certainty is about'. Confidence, he said, 'is a catchword rather than a construct'. He preferred the concept of self-efficacy, which he defined as 'how well one can execute courses of action required to deal with prospective situations'. A teacher may or may not be confident about teaching a class, but being competent at developing lesson plans, organizing the learning environment and managing pupils' attention and discipline in the classroom – that's the stuff of self-efficacy. Whereas confidence is a belief *about* an ability, efficacy relates to how well we can actually *perform* that ability. Rather than getting too preoccupied with confidence, we might be better served by practising skills that help us build our levels of competence. This is a point that the great Jack Nicklaus, winner of eighteen professional major golf championships, highlighted when he said of confidence: 'There is only one way to obtain and sustain it: work.'

A major review of more than forty research papers that investigated the relationship between confidence and performance in twenty-four different sports concluded that the relationship is 'small in magnitude'. The authors of the review also emphasized that it is currently unclear whether confidence is a *cause* or *consequence* of better performances. While commentators and coaches might clamour to attribute an athlete's virtuoso performance to the abundance of confidence they bring to their game, it may well be that fantastic performances and rave reviews lead to increased confidence. So, despite the considerable airtime and column inches that confidence receives, there are still key questions that need to be answered. An important take-home message here is that we can over-egg the extent to which our Get mode relies upon confidence.

It is possible that, rather than being the presence of something, confidence may well be the absence of something else. Just like ignorance is a lack of knowledge, and a drought is a scarcity of water, confidence may well be the absence of counterproductive responses to anxiety and fear – us choosing not to respond to our emotions in ways that hinder our performance. While the world of high performance often stresses the importance of 'building confidence', I believe that we need to *excavate* confidence. We need to dig it out from beneath the layers of habits that we can develop in response to our doubtful thoughts and anxious feelings (such as quitting, dwelling on the prospect of failure, going 'into our shells' and criticizing ourselves). Practising the AWE of a flexible mind – getting Anchored in the here and now, being Willing to notice our thoughts and emotions without struggling against them, and being Empowered to take pragmatic actions in line with our personal values and purpose – can help us to break those habits, freeing us to do what we need to do in the moment it needs to be done. From a flexible mind perspective, the way to excavate confidence is not to get rid of worrying thoughts and anxious feelings, it's to respond to them in ways that allow us to continue to branch towards our purpose.

Next time you find yourself thinking, *I'm not confident enough to try it*, take a moment to identify specific thoughts and feelings that you might be experiencing. Perhaps you will realize that you are worried about messing up, and are dealing with associated feelings of anxiety. If that fits, recall the ARM (autonomy, relatedness and mastery) yearnings I highlighted previously, and see which of these may nestle at the heart of that anxiety. In this case, it could be the yearning for mastery – a desire to perform the task well. The anxiety is a messenger communicating how much this matters to you. You can then use your AWE flexibility skills of being Anchored, Willing and Empowered to shift your relationship with the anxiety. Rather than letting it impede your path forward, see if you can bring that

172

anxiety with you as you progress towards achieving your goal. As you commit to doing the task, you can use the strategic self-talk that we discussed in Chapter 4 (e.g. 'You can do this', 'Trust your processes', 'Let your values be your guide') to help bolster your sense of self-efficacy. If you don't give it a go, you'll never know how it'll go. Wayne Gretzky, widely regarded as the greatest ice-hockey player of all time, once said: 'You miss 100 per cent of the shots you don't take.' Take a shot at it.

Speaking to your future self

There are times in my work with clients when I could talk until I was blue in the face, and it would do no good. Less of me is what's required in those moments; the trick of being a good therapist is to know when to get out of the way. Allow me to explain. Jo, a client I was working with recently, had made great strides in clarifying her purpose, and we had identified a goal that she was working towards achieving. At the beginning of the session, we were reviewing her progress with a task that had been scheduled for the previous week. She hadn't completed it.

'I really wanted to be able to do it, but I'm worried that I'll look stupid,' she said. Her Get mode had ground to a halt. Consistent with the Willing aspect of a flexible mind, I invited her to swap the word 'but' for 'and' in what she had just said, and to notice what, if any, difference that might make. Saying, 'I really wanted to be able to do it, *and* I'm worried that I'll look stupid' highlights how our fears don't have to oppose our intentions – they can coexist with them. There could be a temptation here for me to encourage, persuade or cajole

Jo into action. But experience has taught me that, paradoxically, this can increase a client's ambivalence. It can trigger memories of times when their yearning for autonomy was thwarted by overbearing relatives or friends telling them what to do, and their resistance to the persuasion grows.

Instead, I do two things:

1. I help clients to compassionately acknowledge the thoughts and emotions that they are experiencing.
2. I encourage clients to listen not to me, but to themselves. Well, to a future version of themselves, to be precise. Trust me, it's a powerful conversation to have in those moments.

To approach this with Jo, I said the following:

Let's imagine that there is a version of you who exists two years in the future from now. That version of you is thriving; feeling fulfilled both professionally and personally, living in line with the purpose and personal values that matter to you. Now imagine that this contented and composed 'two-years-in-the-future Jo' was to walk into this room right now. What supportive advice would she give you about the choices that you can make in relation to the task we discussed? How might 'two-years-in-the-future Jo' justify the upset or inconvenience that could be experienced by making those choices? Picture the expression she has on her face as she says these things. Notice the glint of commitment and determination in her eyes.

By encouraging Jo to have a conversation with herself in this way, I reduced the potential for this to become a battle of wills between the two of us, and I helped her to connect again with the intrinsic drivers that are so powerful for helping us to commit to action. This is an approach that you can try for yourself. If you are struggling to make a decision, imagine what advice a fulfilled and contented 'two-years-in-the-future you' would offer. As you do that, imagine also how those words of support and encouragement would be communicated. Alternatively, you could consider harnessing the power of a flexible mind by asking yourself the following questions: 'What would an Anchored, Willing and Empowered version of me do in this situation? What advice would that flexible version of me give to me now?'

Facing up to challenges

Firing up Get mode is only the start of the journey. Effort needs to be sustained over time. Just as variations in the availability of sunlight and water impact the growth of a tree, our progress towards our goals will wax and wane according to the circumstances we encounter. But remember: **Progress isn't diminished by challenges; progress generates challenges**. When you commit to achieving a goal, you commit to experiencing challenges along the way. The Greek myth that tells of Jason and the Argonauts' quest for the Golden Fleece has endured through the centuries because of the challenges they faced. Where's the achievement in simply being handed the Golden Fleece? I'm pretty sure the version where Jason didn't have to yoke a plough to two fire-breathing bulls, sow dragon's teeth in the field those bulls ploughed, or battle an army of warriors that grew up from said teeth, would have skipped the big screen and gone straight to streaming. Challenges are part of the stories we share because challenges are inherent in the lives that we live. A life without challenges is a life unlived. You know this in your own life. Think of your proudest achievements. Now think about the difficulties you encountered on the road to those successes. And this will be the case moving forward, too. **It's going to be challenging to achieve your goals, but when you do, you'll look back and feel enormously satisfied both with what you've achieved and what you've overcome.**

Seeking out the 'maybe'

The momentum created by being in Get mode provides opportunities for us to leave the conforming zone – the rigid place where we get stuck when we pay too much attention to the stories our mind tells us – for the less familiar territory of the transforming zone. The transforming zone is an uncomfortable and uncertain place to be. David Bowie, the late, great musician, said in an interview in 1997:

> *If you feel safe in the area you're working in, you're not working in the right area. Always go a little further into the water than you feel you're capable of . . . Go a little bit out of your depth. And when you don't feel that your feet are quite touching the bottom, you're just about in the right place to do something exciting.*

The chatter in your mind will say that you can't do it, but you can show it you can. Bowie's observation is echoed by the experience of the cyclist Chris Boardman. In 1994, Boardman was crowned

UCI World Individual Time Trial Champion after completing the forty-two-kilometre course in forty-nine minutes and thirty-four seconds – that's an average speed of over fifty kilometres per hour. A time trial follows a particular format – riders set off at defined intervals and cover the same specified distance. The different start times mean you don't race directly against other competitors, and you don't know how quickly they are going. You just know that you need to complete the course as quickly as possible, but you have to balance your effort over the full distance of the event. So how do you know if you've got the balance right? Boardman's advice is to ask yourself: '[I]s my current pace sustainable?', and then to consider: 'If the answer is "yes", then you're not going hard enough, if the answer is "no", then it's already too late, so the answer you're looking for is "maybe".' The transforming zone is the realm of the 'maybe'. To sustain Get mode in times of challenge, we need to seek out the 'maybe'.

Here's a moment of 'maybe' from my own life.

Digging deep when the going gets steep

Kinnagoe Bay, an area along the Inishowen peninsula of north-west Ireland, is a place of breathtaking beauty, but there is no time to appreciate it. It's 21 August 2022, and I'm participating in the Inishowen 100, a one-day endurance cycling event that requires riders to complete 100 miles and 7,200 feet of ascent around the peninsula. I am seventy-four miles into the route, and I am just about to tackle the second major climb of the event – the road that rises from the beach at Kinnagoe Bay to Magilligan Point View, which sits 820 feet above.

THE TREE THAT BENDS

I had resisted the temptation to get involved in cycling for many years, preferring to focus on strength-training and running instead. But like many exercise enthusiasts in their thirties and forties, I had succumbed to the call of the Lycra. In the summer of 2021, I had completed my first endurance cycle around Lough Neagh, the largest lake in the British Isles, and I was hooked. In April 2022, I started training for the Inishowen 100, steadily building up the distances and climbs I tackled on my cycles in preparation. Bolstered by a solid routine – eat, cleat, sleep, repeat – I've managed to get plenty of miles in the bank.

Now that the time has come, a key objective for me is to complete the two legendary climbs of the Inishowen 100 without a foot touching the ground. I am riding in a group with Jackie, Stephen, Mark, Peter and Michael. We're all committed to getting each other to the finish line.

We have already had to contend with the first major climb at Mamore Gap; the steepest kilometre of road in Ireland, with an average gradient of 13 per cent that sharpens to 20 per cent in places. As I'd reached a particularly steep section about 150 metres from the top, my legs burned, my lungs gasped, and my heart raced. The voice in my head was pleading with me to stop. But I kept pedalling – one revolution after another. I was determined to conquer 'the Gap'. I was aware that I was not just doing this for me – a few weeks earlier, my brother-in-law and his wife had brought my eleven-year-old nephew and nine-year-old niece to this stretch of road to show them what I was taking on, so now I was doing it for them, too. A photographer perched at the brow of the hill captured my grimacing face as I arrived at the top. Rain had started to fall, but it was feelings of pride and relief that washed over me. There was no time to rest on our laurels, though; we descended the other side of the Gap, waves crashing rhythmically on to the shoreline stretched out below us.

Now, over fifty miles of undulating terrain later, it's time to take on the road up to *Magilligan Point View* – nearly three miles of continuous climbing.

'*This is where the fun begins!*' bellows a marshal with sardonic glee.

This is going to hurt.

Michael: 'Take this steady; it's a long drag. If you are feeling good, go for it, but leave something in the tank. Keep out of the red.'

The 'red' that Michael is referring to is the point at which our physical exertion exceeds our anaerobic threshold (AT). The AT is the point at which we are physically over-reaching, and there is a risk that cramping can become an issue. I am mindful that I need to leave enough energy in reserve to complete the remaining twenty-five miles of the cycle after this ascent. Although not as steep as Mamore Gap, the climb here is four times as long, and the impact on legs, lungs and heart is ratcheted up accordingly.

Michael: 'Dig in.'

Me: (silence)

The climb is relentless. It is said that the mind quits long before the body does. My mind is like a heckling spectator, ablaze with indignant protest, demanding that I stop and relieve the searing pain. But my feet continue to pedal, resisting the sirens' call of the road surface below. Although the top of the climb is tantalizingly close, it still seems a thousand miles away. I am in the realm of 'maybe'.

Flow

In recent decades, the concept of 'flow' has received growing attention in discussions about ways of optimizing our Get mode. It's not difficult to understand why. Flow, identified by Mihaly Csikszentmihalyi (pronounced 'chick-sent-me-high'), the late Hungarian-American psychologist, is an ethereal experience where our sense of self dissolves away, time distorts, and we seem to merge with our actions. Mike C, as he was affectionately known by his colleagues at University of Chicago, first identified 'flow' when he noticed that artists could get so swept up in their creative process that they would fail to register the need for food, drink and sleep. His interest piqued, he decided to conduct research to better understand what he had observed. Technical definitions of flow describe it as a state of total absorption in which our actions are experienced as effortless and enjoyable. Phrases such as being 'in the groove', 'in the zone', or 'dialled in' have also been used to describe it more informally. Research conducted with 500 families living in the US found that the top three activities for experiencing flow were: 1) arts and crafts, 2) sex, and 3) practising sports for competition. Of course, what induces flow will vary from person to person. For example, in my own life, I've most often experienced flow when I've been snowboarding or learning a tune on the guitar.

Three triggers have been identified as pre-requisites of flow:

1. The level of challenge associated with the activity must be slightly higher than our current level of skill – if our skill level is low and the degree of challenge is high, we will be

too anxious, and if our skill level is high and the degree
of challenge is low, we will be too relaxed. So, operating
in the realm of 'maybe' is conducive to experiencing flow.

2. The activity we're undertaking should have a clearly
   defined goal that links to our yearning for mastery, such
   as solving a Rubik's cube, mastering the double front flip
   on a trampoline, perfecting a dovetail joint in joinery, or
   nailing the drum line to Fleetwood Mac's song 'Go Your
   Own Way'.

3. You need to be receiving unambiguous feedback about
   your performance, either from others (e.g. a coach or
   mentor), or your own awareness (e.g. how balanced you
   feel as the snowboard glides across the snow, or the
   sound of the melody you can hear as you play the guitar).

There are at least six further dimensions that are key features of
the experience of flow:

1) We are concentrating intensely on the activity.

2) We retain a sense of being in control (i.e. our yearning for
autonomy is satisfied).

3) Our awareness merges with the actions we are undertaking.

4) There is a transformation in our experience of time.

5) We are devoid of self-consciousness.

6) The experience is autotelic – it is rewarding in its own right,
rather than relying on other types of reward, such as the approval
of others or the award of a prize. This is the intrinsic reward type
that we discussed on p. 161.

Understanding about flow continues to evolve. Questionnaires such as the Long Flow State Scale have been developed to measure it, and Steve Kotler, the American author and cofounder of the Flow Research Collective, has proposed a further nineteen triggers of flow in addition to the three prerequisites listed on the previous page. Increasingly, there is recognition that efforts to experience flow must be balanced with periods of rest and recovery.

What's so good about *flow*?

Research has indicated that flow helps us to glow; higher levels of flow are associated with higher levels of subjective wellbeing. A recent review of research also found that there is a small but consistent positive relationship between flow and superior performance in sports, as well as in computer-based games. But, as with confidence, it is unclear whether flow causes improved performance, or improved performance causes flow. It's also possible that any potential performance advantage that flow provides is indirect – for example, research has shown that anxiety, which adversely impacts on our ability to perform skills, tends to be conspicuously lacking when we experience flow.

Mike C wasn't that interested in whether flow increased the likelihood of successful outcomes. In fact, he warned that focusing on outcomes might detract from our ability to experience flow: 'When beating the opponent takes precedence in the mind over performing as well as possible, enjoyment tends to disappear. Competition is enjoyable only when it is a means to perfect one's skills; when it becomes an end in itself, it ceases to be fun'. It's worth noting that the title of Mike C's 1990 book was *Flow: The*

Psychology of Optimal Experience and not *Flow: The Psychology of Optimal Outcomes.*

I am circumspect about flow. As great as it is to experience, there's a risk that obsessing about it may be counterproductive for thriving. It shouldn't be the thing to fixate on. In fact, the harder we chase flow, the more elusive it can be. Like falling asleep, flow is more likely to happen when we let go of the conscious drive to achieve it. I see flow as a cherry on top of the thriving cake rather than the mix required to bake the cake. The Flow Research Collective have also acknowledged that flow can have a 'dark side', citing research that has linked flow with risk-taking and addictive behaviours, and Kotler himself has warned of the risk of people becoming 'Bliss junkies'. There will be times when we need to unhook from the pursuit of flow.

I believe that developing a flexible mind can help support our experience of flow whilst also guarding against the risk that we may become preoccupied with chasing it. In Part II. we learned how to enhance the Anchored and Willing aspects of a flexible mind by practising mindfulness. A review of seventeen different research studies found that an elevated capacity to be mindful is also associated with increased flow. In addition, harnessing the Empowered aspect of a flexible mind helps us to direct our skills and choices towards our purpose. So, it's not unreasonable to speculate that being Anchored, Willing and Empowered may provide opportunities to experience more flow. Research conducted with elite-level soccer players in Portugal revealed that their levels of psychological flexibility were associated with their levels of flow. However, further research is required to better understand this relationship. The strong intention, light attachment ethos of the Empowered aspect of a flexible mind will help us to stay true to our personal values and purpose rather than getting side-tracked by the pursuit of flow.

Let's go back to my cycle event:

Another revolution of my aching legs. The bike inches forward against the steep gradient of the hill. I feel myself slowing almost to the point of standstill. The heckling spectator inside my head is barking like mad`. . .

You're kidding yourself, it's too long a climb. You're not going to make it!

Another aching revolution`. . .

The heckling spectator: *Just a small break. You got up Mamore Gap; that's enough of a win for today.*

Another agonizing revolution`. . .

The heckling spectator: *Stop!!!*

I grip the handlebars, tilt my head down and keep going. I am now cycling past – over-riding, if you like – the heckling spectator in my mind. And then it happens. The road begins to flatten. The landscape opens in front of me. The tyres of the bike level out, and I realize I can change up through the gears once again. I have made it to the top! Reaching Magilligan Point View, I can see the curving, sandy shoreline of Benone Strand stretching out for miles along the north coast of County Londonderry hundreds of feet below. A sight for sore eyes (and legs!).

All that remains now is to cycle the relatively flat final section of the hundred-mile loop that takes us back to our starting point in the city of Derry/Londonderry. Gathering with the other cyclists in my group, we ride in close formation. The peloton has formed. The combination of needing to be highly attentive to the road surface, the position of the other riders, and high levels of physical exertion give rise to a sense that we are floating along the road surface with irresistible momentum. I can't differentiate the passing seconds from the scenery that speeds past. I don't know where the bike ends and where I begin. I am in flow.

While I am cycling on the flat, let's look at how I was able to negotiate the climbs. Getting in good physical shape, cycling in a group, and a desire to show my niece and nephew that challenging things can be done, had all certainly played their part. But something else was pivotal. Choosing to notice what I was experiencing made all the difference. As the voice of protest urged and cajoled me to stop, and feelings of doubt and uncertainty crept in, I realized that I didn't have to try to block them out; I could instead *move beyond* them. **A flexible mind allows thoughts and feelings to be present without being derailed by them.** This helps us to transcend thoughts and feelings rather than being constrained by them.

Perfectionism

It's late 1929, and Charlie Chaplin is a year into the production of his new film, *City Lights*. Not only is Chaplin the lead actor, director and producer, but he is also composing the film's score. Progress with filming has been slow. Chaplin is agonizing over a pivotal scene. In the movie, his Little Tramp character falls in love with a blind flower-seller (played by Virginia Cherrill). A key aspect of the story centres on the flower-seller initially mistaking the Little Tramp for a wealthy businessman. Chaplin, who had started filming without

finalizing the script, is struggling to come up with a plausible sce-
nario whereby this can happen ... Two previous attempts to shoot
the scene earlier in the year had failed. The shoot is running over,
and Chaplin's stress is impacting on the cast and crew.

Thankfully, a solution is eventually found. In the final version of the
scene, a large limousine – a rare sight and sound in 1920s Los Angeles
– draws up to the street corner to wait for its wealthy owner, where the
blind flower-seller is sitting with her carnations. At the same time, the
Little Tramp is seen trying to cross the road towards the street corner
through a queue of traffic that has ground to a halt beside the limousine. A police motorcyclist sits at the front of the queue. Always keen
to avoid officers of the law, the Little Tramp appears to have nowhere
left to go. But, enterprising as always, he finds a way through – quite
literally. He enters the rear left-hand door of the limousine, and then
exits through the rear right-hand door, emerging in precisely the spot
where the flower girl is located. It's the sound of the large limousine
door opening and shutting that alerts the blind flower-seller to the
supposed arrival of a wealthy potential customer.

There's no doubt that it's an entertaining watch. But astonishingly,
the scene, which runs for just over three minutes, required 342 takes
before Chaplin was satisfied with it – 342! Reflecting on it years later,
Chaplin said, 'I had worked myself into a neurotic state of wanting
perfection.'

Cherrill wasn't arguing. She said of Chaplin: 'He was a perfectionist, and, to us, it often seemed to be exactly the same ... When
he'd finally say: "It's a take," we'd breathe a sigh of relief, and then
he'd say: "Well perhaps just one more time."' Get mode can go rogue,
and perfectionistic striving is a key example of this.

Perfectionism is the obsessive preoccupation with attaining

perfection. It has several notable features, including feeling dissatis-
fied with the fruits of our labour, resisting support offered by other
people, indecisiveness about how best to proceed, and elevated levels
of self-criticism. While Chaplin's approach to directing *City Lights*
highlights how perfectionism can send our Get mode into overdrive,
perfectionism can also leave us reluctant to start in the first place.
Margaret Atwood, the Booker Prize-winning author of *The Hand-
maid's Tale*, warned about the dangers of this when she said in a
2013 interview with the *Telegraph*: 'If you're waiting for the perfect
moment, you'll never write a thing because it will never arrive.'

Three distinct forms of perfectionism have been identified:

- **Self-oriented perfectionism** arises when we place unreasonable expectations on ourselves to perform exceptionally.
  Although this can drive improvements in how we perform,
  fixating on the flawless can be destructive. It's a bit like
  swatting a fly with a baseball bat; it'll get the job done, but
  cracks will quickly appear. Self-oriented perfectionism can
  also lead to what is referred to as a 'fragile ego', when our
  sense of self is based on the results that we produce. If the
  outcomes we produce are substandard, then we conclude
  that *we're* substandard.
- **Other-oriented perfectionism** is when our perfectionistic
  expectations are directed at other people. We respond to
  those who fall short of the unreasonably high standards
  we set by being critical and hostile towards them. Unsur-
  prisingly, this form of perfectionism can have a particularly
  detrimental impact on our relationships – both personally
  and professionally.

- **Socially prescribed perfectionism** emerges when we feel obliged to adhere to unrealistic performance expectations that others have placed on us. Research has consistently shown that perfectionism of this kind is most strongly related to a range of mental health difficulties, including depression and anxiety.

The seeds of perfectionism can be sown early in our lives. Criticism and harsh judgements directed at us during our childhood and adolescence can lead us to believe that we are not good enough in the eyes of others. We strive to do better to compensate for our low sense of self-worth. Alarmingly, perfectionism is on the rise. A study led by two British psychologists, Thomas Curran and Andrew P. Hill, analysed data provided by more than 40,000 college students in the UK, the US and Canada. They found that all three forms of perfectionism detailed above had steadily increased over a twenty-seven-year period, and societal pressures were identified as a potential cause. Reflecting on the findings, Curran suggested that the increase may be linked to 'a strong need for young people to strive, perform and achieve in modern life,' explaining, 'Today's young people are competing with each other in order to meet societal pressures to succeed and they feel that perfectionism is necessary in order to feel safe, socially connected and of worth.'

For all its benefits, our use of social media provides ceaseless opportunities to compare ourselves with others. And the cards are stacked against us. Social media platforms draw revenue from advertisers who have a vested interest in preying on our insecurities. Apps such as Facetune and AirBrush allow people to transform their appearance in the photos they post online, and we end up comparing ourselves to manufactured versions of others. Moreover, the videos that go viral on platforms like Instagram and TikTok do so because they are extraordinary – the mere ordinary has viral immunity. All of this perpetuates a myth that we should be someone – or something – other than the flawed human beings that we are. But the travesty is that perceptions of perfection, like beauty, are in the eye of the beholder. While the audience watching the limousine scene in *City Lights* might think it's exquisite, the cast and crew involved in filming it were probably more equivocal when they saw it. Similarly, a person watching Charli D'Amelio, the social media influencer, perform the 'Renegade' dance on TikTok may well conclude that she had executed it perfectly, whereas D'Amelio might have uttered a 'Meh!' of indifference when the camera stopped recording. We can be our own harshest critics. Further research is required to determine if social media use is a cause of perfectionism, or if it merely acts as a canvas on to which we paint our own perfectionistic strivings. In all likelihood, it is both.

The path to imperfection

Flexible minds aspire to excellence rather than perfection. Excellencism – defined by the Canadian psychologist Patrick Gaudreau as the 'tendency to aim and strive toward very high yet attainable standards in an effortful, engaged, and determined yet flexible manner' – can be distinguished from perfectionism according to the reasonableness of the goals we set and the intensity of the effort we exert to achieve those goals. Organizational and workplace cultures may urge us to search exhaustively for those pearls of perfection based on the misguided assumption that perfectionism is 'good for business', but as we will see in the next chapter, this kind of thinking only serves to exacerbate the risk of burnout. Not only is building a culture of excellence rather than perfectionism more sustainable, it also seems to deliver better results. For example, research conducted by Gaudreau and his colleagues has demonstrated that excellencism is associated with better academic performance when compared to perfectionism.

The pernicious thing about perfectionism is that it drives our attention outward – the focus is on comparing ourselves and our actions with what is 'out there' in the world. Conveniently, this serves to divert our attention away from the challenging work of focusing inward – on the fears we have 'in here' about being *im*perfect, and the various implications we think this has for our existence. Redemption from perfectionism begins with realizing that the pursuit of perfection is born from an intolerance of our own imperfections. The being Willing aspect of a flexible mind can be particularly helpful in acknowledging and embracing our thoughts about imperfection and the fears that can accompany them. If we are willing to shift our relationship with imperfection in this way, we'll be less hindered by the corrosive effect that perfectionism can have on our ability to thrive.

Getting flexible with imperfection

Research has indicated that developing a flexible mind can help with managing perfectionism. Here's an approach that you can use to become more flexible when experiencing your imperfections:

- **Think about a domain of your life where perfectionism can show up.** Maybe you notice it in your work, home life, workouts or other activities you're passionate about. Take a moment to reflect on the costs that the perfectionism may be having on your lifestyle – your relationships with others, your energy levels, your mood, opportunities you may be missing out on, etc.

- **Identify a task that you will be required to do in relation to that perfectionism-prone life domain in the next couple of weeks.** For example, you may need to finalize a work report, perform at a music gig, bake a cake or prepare a video to share on social media.

- **Now imagine deliberately choosing to do that task imperfectly.** You might leave a typo in the work report, play a bum note in front of a crowd, leave the cocoa powder out of the mix for a red velvet cake, or go with the first take of the video for Instagram even though you fluffed the closing line.

- **Notice the fears that start to bubble up as you even contemplate doing this.** Maybe there are concerns about being criticized by others, or being judged a failure (by yourself or others). Perhaps you fear that something catastrophic will happen, or worry that you'll never be able to forgive yourself.

- **Take some time to locate where in your body you notice the sensations that accompany those fears.** In your mind's eye, imagine slowly tracing a line around the edge of those feelings of discomfort in your body.

- **Reflect on how you would respond to a friend or loved one if they shared with you that they were experiencing the same fears and discomfort.** How might you provide comfort to them? What words would you use to convey your support? What tone would you use to speak those words?

- **See if you can direct even some of that kindness and support towards your own fears**. Allow yourself to hear those same words, spoken in the same tone, to soothe your own discomfort.

Now that you've imagined how it would be to deliberately do something imperfectly, the choice is yours as to whether you'll go a step further and actually do it. After all, you can bake an imperfect cake *and* still eat it.

Putting on the brakes in Get mode

There is no denying that certain personal values oil the cogs of Get mode. Qualities such as tenacity, diligence and a commitment to excellence can play an important role in completing tasks and achieving goals. But, as we have already seen, personal values blindly applied irrespective of context can be a hindrance rather than a help. This is a point that Justine Musk, Elon's first wife, made in an essay she wrote for *Marie Claire* in 2010 – two years after their divorce. 'The will to compete and dominate that made him so successful in business did not magically shut off when he came home,' she wrote. As important as bringing personal values to the fore can be, we also need to be flexible in allowing them to recede when necessary. When we transition into new situations, we may need to turn over a new leaf.

As we discussed on p. 122 trees grow upwards, but they also grow *outwards*. It's a tree's multidirectional growth that enables it to position its leaves to best capture the sun's energy as it arcs across the sky throughout the day. This gives the crown of a tree its distinctive rounded appearance. We can be well-rounded, too – but to achieve this requires us to redirect the energies of Get mode to serve the breadth of the purposes that nourish us. Steve Barlett, entrepreneur, podcast host and author of the bestselling book *The Diary of a CEO*, captured the importance of getting to grips with Get mode when he said: 'Do I think hard work matters? Yes. Do I think hard work at the expense of your own health and wellbeing is a good idea? No. Do I think you should just endlessly hustle, hustle, hustle to become a successful entrepreneur? No.' Hustling matters, but so too does health. Like the quaking aspen that grows fast but dies young, many of us risk paying a high price for not recognizing when the brakes need to be applied.

How will we know when the time has come to reduce or redirect the activity of Get mode? Although meta-awareness can help, it's quite possible that we won't know. Remember that Get mode is greedy – it's a juggernaut hurtling down a freeway in the direction of 'more'. So, what can we do? Well, we can identify our exit points from the freeway well in advance, and enlist the support of fellow travellers to keep us on the right path. The following strategies can be helpful to consider when we are identifying a goal we wish to achieve.

Create a 'pre-commitment' pledge

This is a written agreement that we make with ourselves about what we'll do when certain outcomes occur. It can, for example, be used to block off options today that we're concerned we might be unable to resist in the future, like someone committing to buying only one tub of ice cream for fear that they might not be able to resist eating a second one. Or it can be used to clearly signal an endpoint to an activity once a goal has been achieved, like someone committing to stopping their guitar practice for the day when they've successfully learned a new song rather than starting to learn another one. A pre-commitment pledge for the purpose of limiting Get mode could include:

- a deadline date by which you will review progress on the goal
- the concrete indicators that will let you know whether the goal has been achieved
- what you will do to celebrate if you successfully achieve the goal, and how you will mark this with others (this can often be neglected in the moment, and we lose out on the opportunities to savour our 'wins')
- what you will do to commiserate if you are unsuccessful in achieving the goal (it's important for us to mark losses and be willing to experience the emotions that can show up)
- the wise and compassionate advice that you would give your future self about next steps if the goal were to be achieved, but also if it isn't
- what temptations you might experience, and why you might need to be wary of them
- a reminder of the breadth of purposes that matter to you and the need to take time to recoup your energy for future goals.

Invite people you trust to check in on you

This could involve sharing the pre-commitment pledge with them and asking if they would be willing to act as a guarantor to help you implement it. Alternatively, you can ask them to kindly challenge you if they are concerned about how much effort you seem to be investing in a particular goal. You can discuss with them what the telltale signs of you overinvesting might look like, what your likely response to their expressions of concern will be, and how they can compassionately respond to any resistance that your Get mode might generate. Finally, you can identify key phrases that they can say to you to help you 'come back to centre', such as 'Remember you're a human being, not a human doing', 'Strong intention, light attachment' or even 'Be more tree'.

During the spring and summer, trees get busy with water, nutrients and sunlight, powering their growth through photosynthesis. Similarly, in human terms, Get mode is vital for driving us to achieve our goals, whether they are linked to intrinsic or extrinsic rewards. Questioning our goals (see p. 163) helps us to see how context (both inner and outer) will impact our tasks. By employing mental imagery to rehearse the experience of completing those tasks, we can use the present to prepare for achieving our goals in the future. The AWE aspects of a flexible mind can help us adjust to the less comfortable aspects of Get mode, too – not only the uncertainty and anxiety that can come alongside growth and transformation, but also the risks that perfectionism might push us into perpetual overdrive, or the pursuit of flow might tip into an unhealthy obsession. Pre-commitment pledges and the 'strong intention, light attachment' ethos of a flexible mind can help us to both stay the course and cool the fervour of Get mode – even, as we'll see in the next chapter, when we are under Threat.

Get: Summary Points

- Get mode helps us to pursue rewards that are both externally and internally generated.
- Internal drivers include our yearnings for autonomy, relatedness and mastery.
- Setting goals is important, but Get mode prospers on data relating to *how* we can accomplish tasks relating to those goals.
- Using mental imagery helps us to prepare for the completion of tasks.
- Despite its popularity, confidence is a poorly understood concept; self-efficacy is something we can action more readily.
- Perfectionism can lead to Get mode going rogue. Excellencism is a more measured approach.
- Developing a flexible mind helps us to stay in Get mode when challenges occur, but also helps us to keep Get mode in check.

CHAPTER 7

Threat

To be a tree is to be exposed to the worst that nature has to offer. Storms pose a significant danger. Lightning strikes can damage branches, and strong winds can lash the base of trunks with a force equivalent to 220 tons. Forest fires can spread in seconds; on average, an area equivalent to sixteen football pitches is lost every minute due to forest fires across the globe. And then there is the damage that can be inflicted by other living organisms, such as fungi, bacteria and insects like the bark beetle. Being a tree is – pardon the pun – no walk in the park. And yet there are estimated to be more than 3 trillion trees on Earth. To prosper as they do, trees prevail over a whole host of threats. Many of the more than 73,000 species of trees on Earth have developed ways of protecting themselves based on the unique challenges they face in the environments in which they grow. Cedar, spruce, pine and conifer trees all produce substances called phytoncides, which have antibacterial and anti-fungal properties. The kapok tree, which grows in Central America, has large thorns embedded in its trunk that deter animals from getting too close. And then there are ponderosa pines, which have flame-retardant bark that can help the mature trees survive forest fires. However, these defensive measures come at a cost. The fuel a tree uses to protect itself from harm is fuel that it can't use to grow; a tree needs to carefully balance the needs of protection and growth. And there may well be times when a tree also needs to work collaboratively with its neighbours for support; a forest's green expanse of intermingling tree crowns can create a microclimate that limits the impact of extreme weather.

In this chapter, we will explore how we need to balance growth with responding to threats in our lives. By looking at Threat mode in more detail, we'll explore the benefits that it provides but also the drawbacks that can occur when our minds orientate to threat too much. Too much emphasis on merely surviving can get in the way of our ability to thrive. We will also see how a flexible mind can help us to deploy Threat mode in optimal ways. Over the course of the chapter, we will explore answers to the following three questions:

1. How is the impact of threats amplified by your own behaviour?
2. How can adjusting your 'sense of self' help you to manage Threat mode better?
3. How does a flexible mind help you learn from threat?

Perceiving threat

Among the more than 7,000 paintings in the Prado Museum in Madrid are several masterpieces by the fifteenth-century Dutch painter Hieronymus Bosch (also known by his Spanish moniker, El Bosco). The most well-known of Bosch's paintings displayed there is the triptych entitled *The Garden of Earthly Delights*. The three panels from left to right depict Eden, 'earthly delights' and Hell respectively. Which of the three panels do you think commands visitors' attention the most? Science has the answer. Researchers from Miguel Hernandez University invited visitors to the museum to wear eye-tracking glasses, and found that they spent on average sixteen seconds looking at Eden, twenty-six seconds looking at the 'earthly delights' centre panel (which is twice as big as the panels to its left and right), and a whopping thirty-three seconds viewing the depraved depiction of the inferno. People dwell on Hell more than twice as long as they do the Garden of Eden. Our attention is drawn irresistibly towards the dark and threatening stuff. We are motivated to take note of the perils that might befall us – this is the work of Threat mode.

If Get mode helps us strive, then Threat mode helps us survive. Whether the threat is clearly present (e.g. a flood in your home) or more symbolic (e.g. a flood of emails in your inbox), we are programmed to react to circumstances that can prove costly to us. Threats come in all shapes and sizes, including threats to our physical wellbeing (e.g. animals, disease, abuse or neglect by other people, unstable environments and extreme weather events), our social wellbeing (e.g. being shamed, rejected or ostracized by others) and our psychological wellbeing (e.g. experiences of trauma, stress and burnout). Threats don't just affect us as individuals; they affect the communities in which we live. Whether it's economic inequality, political turmoil or culture wars, societal schisms can emerge that threaten our sense of safety, stability and belonging. Clearly, there's a lot we can be concerned about.

When it comes to survival, prevention is better than a cure: if a vehicle is thundering down a road, stay on the sidewalk; if a dog looks angry, don't try to stroke it; if an angry mob is heading your way, walk in the other direction. When the situation merits it, avoiding threat is an incredibly valuable tactic. But there will be times when avoidance isn't possible, or we recognize that avoiding threat is going to incur too heavy a cost when it comes to our sense of purpose. Sometimes, we're going to have to take the hit. Suffice to say, our passage through life will bring its fair share of hits. Like a comet blazing a trail across the sky, we will lose parts of ourselves along the way. And what we will lose will not be insignificant. Our health, our relationships, people we care about, our income, our reputation, our hopes – not to mention sets of keys and the odd wallet or two. Everything can go. And it will hurt. But the scale of that hurt will be determined in part by how we respond to it.

Around 2,500 years ago, Buddha said to a student, 'During times of misfortune, two arrows are directed at us.'

The student listened attentively.

'If it hurts when an arrow hits us, is it not doubly sore if a second arrow hits us?' Buddha enquired of the student.

The student nodded without hesitation.

The Buddha then said, 'While we cannot do anything about the first arrow after it has hit, the second arrow is the way we react to the first. We can do something about the second arrow.'

The judgements we rapidly make about the struggles we face can amplify the impact that these struggles have on our lives. Our responses to threat can *become* the threat. Simone Weil, the twentieth-century French philosopher, made this point in a letter to her brother André: 'In struggling against anguish one never produces serenity; the struggle against anguish only produces new forms of anguish.' While a flexible mind won't stop the pain of that first arrow, it helps with the second.

An unfortunate quirk of humankind's capacity to mentally time-travel into the future is that we can *anticipate* being struck by an arrow that might never hit. The suffering these 'phantom arrows' can cause – worry as we wait for the outcome of health investigations, fear about falling flat on our faces when the big moment comes – is very real. So, our Threat mode doesn't need danger to be present – simply imagining danger can suffice.

The physiology of threat

Threat mode prepares us for the fight, flight or freeze response to fear through a set of involuntary physiological changes largely governed by the sympathetic nervous system. These changes include the redirection of blood to our muscles, a more rapid rate of breathing, increased blood-sugar levels, increased heart rate and enlarged pupils. The sympathetic nervous system is activated by the action of noradrenaline and adrenaline – hormones and neurotransmitters released by the adrenal glands that sit at the top of each of our kidneys. During times of stress, the adrenal glands also release the hormone cortisol. Cortisol helps to regulate the fuel available to our muscles by triggering the release of glucose from the liver into the blood. It also acts to stabilize our blood pressure and suppress inflammatory responses in the body. But in high concentrations, over prolonged periods of time, it can be harmful for us, contributing to problems such as high blood pressure and heart disease. Too much exposure to threat is not just bad for our physical health, it can also lead to profound impacts on our ability to thrive. If we constantly orientate to threat, we may miss out on opportunities to pursue our sense of purpose. As is the case with trees, a balance needs to be struck between surviving on one hand and thriving on the other. A failure to do so can lead to burnout.

Burnout

In the modern world, burnout is one of the most pervasive threats to our ability to thrive. Herbert Freudenberger and Christine Maslach, independently of each other, both coined the term 'burnout' in 1974. At that time, Freudenberger had been working as a psychoanalyst in private practice in New York City by day, and at St Mark's Free Clinic for young people by night. However, after a year of unrelenting double shifts, Freudenberger had a breakdown. Curious about his symptoms, and believing that they were linked to overworking, Freudenberger wrote an academic paper about the experience entitled 'Staff Burn-Out'. 'It is precisely because we are dedicated that we walk into a burn-out trap. We work too long and too intensely,' he wrote. Meanwhile, 3,000 miles away, a psychologist named Christine Maslach based at Stanford University used 'burnout' to describe the sense of detachment that can emerge in people working in the human services industry. She would go on to develop a questionnaire – the Maslach Burnout Inventory – to systematically measure burnout.

In 2019, burnout was included in the World Health Organization's (WHO) International Classification of Diseases, 11th Revision (a manual of diseases) as an 'employment-related factor' that influences our health. In the manual, three key dimensions of burnout are listed:

1. depleted energy levels (i.e. exhaustion)
2. higher levels of mental distance from our occupation, or feelings of cynicism related to that occupation (i.e. depersonalization)
3. a reduced sense of effectiveness (i.e. lack of personal accomplishment)

The inclusion of burnout in a 'manual of disease' attracted a lot of criticism, however, not least from Maslach herself. It was felt that calling it a 'disease' situated the source of the problem with the person and not the organization for whom they work. There was such a furore about this that the WHO had to urgently clarify that burnout was included as 'an occupational phenomenon', not as a medical condition.

A 2018 survey of 7,500 employees by the US management consultancy firm Gallup found that two-thirds of the respondents self-reported experiencing burnout at least some of the time in their jobs. The five factors most closely associated with an increased risk of burnout were threats relating to:

1. unfair treatment in the workplace
2. unmanageable workloads
3. lack of role clarity
4. poor communication and support from management
5. unreasonable time pressure

Research has shown that rates of burnout are on the rise. Burnout, it seems, is burning on. A series of surveys conducted with more than 10,000 office workers living in six high-income countries found that the proportion of people answering 'Yes' to the statement 'I feel burned out at work' rose from 38 per cent in May 2021 to 42 per cent in November 2022. The reasons for this rise are hotly contested: neoliberalism drawing towards its painful but inevitable conclusion, Millennials taking a generational stand, flaws in how burnout is measured inflating the figures – take your pick. However, what's beyond dispute is that the upheaval of the COVID-19 pandemic has caused us to look afresh at the work we do and whether it seems fair, reasonable and manageable. Meanwhile, the amount of work we do has actually increased since before the pandemic. A survey conducted in 2022 by ADP Research Institute found that, amongst the more than 32,000 employees from seventeen countries who responded, the average number of unpaid overtime hours worked every week increased from 7.3 hours prior to the pandemic to 8.5 hours after it. That's even more time dealing with the threat of work-related stresses, and less time for the restorative effects that leisure can bring. As Jim Harter, chief workplace scientist at Gallup at the time of writing, ironically pointed out: 'The intersection of work and life needs some work.' Even hamsters get off their wheels sometimes. It's important that we do, too.

What can we do to address burnout?

I would love to categorically state that developing a flexible mind will guarantee that you will not experience burnout. But I can't. The research evidence indicates that psychological interventions delivered to employees (such as counselling and cognitive behavioural therapies) have small, inconsistent or partial effects on burnout. Although noticing difficult thoughts without struggling against them, practising mindfulness, connecting with our purpose and clarifying our values can certainly help, tackling burnout requires a two-pronged approach – a point emphasized in Debbie Sorensen's excellent book *ACT for Burnout*. Change is necessary at both the level of the organization and the individual. Our acronym ARM applies here too. Organizations need to take steps to satisfy their employees' intrinsic yearnings for:

Autonomy – e.g. nurturing employees' sense of agency, ensuring adequate time and resources are available to undertake the work, and recognizing that employees need to balance their work with other commitments – including protected time away from work.

Relatedness – e.g. fostering psychologically safe workplaces, establishing trust, and demonstrating a genuine concern about the wellbeing of the person rather than the productivity of the employee.

Mastery – e.g. providing opportunities for continued professional development and giving constructive feedback to help the employee enhance their capabilities.

By consistently failing to satisfy one or more of these yearnings, employers fan the flames of burnout. And while organizations might feel that the offer of extrinsic rewards like salary hikes and promotions may be sufficient to extinguish those flames, they would be wrong.

A 'carrot and stick' approach helps. Countries such as Australia have introduced new laws that mandate managers to identify and address causes of workplace stress. But while we might feel powerless to change organizational cultures single-handedly, the AWE of a flexible mind can help us to work with others to bring about change. Just like a forest of trees, we can work collectively to change the harsh environments that we encounter.

Collective action

If modern life has taught us anything, it's that none of us make ourselves. While we might take personal responsibility for self-care, our wellbeing is affected by the social, political and economic circumstances that permeate our lives. Threats such as rising unemployment, experiences of discrimination, energy poverty, overstretched health services and financial crises take their toll. While the AWE aspects of a flexible mind can help us to respond more effectively to the *consequences* of these threats, they can also help us to address their *causes*. But this will require collective action by those who share a sense of purpose relating to tackling societal injustices – the #MeToo and Black Lives Matter movements are examples of this.

Sadly, the news is replete with reports of maltreatment and abuse occurring in prestigious institutions and organizations that ought to know better. High performers are certainly not immune to institutional harm. Those entrusted with the nurturing of talented people all too often end up posing threats to the wellbeing of those under their duty of care. For example, dancers attending the prestigious Royal Ballet School and Elmhurst Ballet School have gone on the record about the body-shaming and bullying that they were subjected to by teachers. Similarly, Jane Nickerson, the then-Chief Executive of Swim England, apologized for the body-shaming and bullying that swimming coaches had directed at elite swimmers. The Whyte Report, published in June 2022, provided shocking details of systemic emotional and physical abuse (including being forced to train with injuries and being denied food and water) against athletes under the auspices of British Gymnastics (BG). Ann Whyte KC, the author of the report, concluded that 'gymnast wellbeing and welfare has not been at the centre of BG's culture' – a culture which she described as 'unacceptable'.

If things are bad in the UK, they are no better in the USA. In 2017, Larry Nassar, the former doctor of USA Gymnastics, was sentenced to 175 years in prison for sexually abusing female gymnasts. Three years later, in 2020, Maggie Haney, an elite coach with USA Gymnastics, was suspended for eight years for the verbal abuse and mistreatment of athletes.

Of course, it's not just sport. It's politics, too. In April 2023, Dominic Raab resigned from his role as Deputy Prime Minister and Justice Secretary in the UK following the release of a report that ruled he had engaged in 'persistently aggressive conduct' towards colleagues. Raab appeared unrepentant. 'I strongly believe if the threshold for bullying is so lowered . . . then ultimately it will be the public that pay the price,' he said. Nit-picking over the 'threshold for bullying' is a slippery slope – four swear words in a rant is bad, while three swear words is fine? What Raab seems to be saying is that, provided the 'public' is being served, it's open season on his colleagues. It's not just that harm is being caused, it's that senior figures within organizations seem intent on justifying it.

Collective action won't occur if individuals are not prepared to act first. Todd B. Kashdan's book *The Art of Insubordination* showcases the role that nonconformist voices can play in challenging the status quo to bring about societal change. If that sounds like a recipe for anarchy, it isn't. Kashdan's focus here is on 'principled insubordination', which is defined as a form of defiance aimed at promoting societal change with minimal secondary harm. It's not a book about tearing things down, it's about building them anew – to effect change, dissenters need to be able to bring people along the road with them. Kashdan's book, which is broadly consistent with the flexible mind approach, provides a practical and evidence-based guide on how this can be achieved. Kashdan outlined four principles that we can use to bring other people with us:

1. **Work from the inside** – Invest time in building bonds with others and establishing a shared identity. The social capital that you accrue through committing to a group can be exchanged for support from group members for ideas that you propose.
2. **Spark curiosity, not fear** – Be diplomatic rather than dogmatic. Recognize that change is about winning hearts and minds.
3. **Project objectivity** – Use evidence to support your points, and clearly indicate when you are communicating facts and when you are expressing your opinion.
4. **Project courageous self-sacrifice** – Share with others the risks that you have taken and the sacrifices you have made in pursuit of the purpose you are promoting.

For me, an important aspect of harnessing the full potential of our *we*-ness is getting to grips with our *me*-ness. Working collaboratively with others is not just about self-sacrifice, it's also about sacrificing the restrictive perspectives we can take on the concept of 'self'. By better understanding the nature of the 'self', we can catch second arrows in flight and mitigate the threat that they pose. Let's turn our attention to that now.

Distinguishing the self from our identities

Clearly, our subjective experiences – including the perceptions, judgements and attributions that we make – are central to how we experience life. Everywhere we go, the self is there. It's been likened to a lens through which we see the world. But how well do you really know your 'self'? We are accustomed to defining ourselves in concrete terms of discrete personal and social identities: occupation, age, gender, race, sexuality, religion, ethnicity, political allegiance, sporting allegiances and, yes, even musical tastes (Ed Sheeran has his Sheerios and Taylor Swift has her Swifties). While these identities provide many benefits, such as building a sense of belonging and solidarity with others, there are also costs. The late Polish social psychologist Henri Tajfel's pioneering work on social identity theory highlighted that while we tend to align ourselves closely with others who share similar identities to us (forming what are referred to as the 'in-group'), we can fall into a trap of perceiving threat from others who don't share our identities (who are referred to as the 'out-group').

Our evolutionary history has sensitized us to the importance of aligning with a group and being cautious about perceived difference. This is particularly the case when opportunities and resources are in short supply, e.g. jobs, land, money, food and water. While the indications are that in-group favouritism has served some evolutionary advantages, it can also have dire consequences. Lack of familiarity and understanding about each other's motives and intentions can lead to distrust, fear and animosity mutually developing between 'in-group' and 'out-group'. Tajfel and his colleagues highlighted how 'in-group' membership can increase the risk of prejudice, discrimination and stereotyping towards 'out groups'. The processes of 'othering' between 'in-group' and 'out-group' can lead to a slew of 'isms': racism, sexism, sectarianism, ageism . . . And 'isms' cause schisms. Cruel and demeaning behaviour can quickly erupt when people stop seeing the person and start seeing a label. The Holocaust, the Ku Klux Klan, the genocide in Rwanda, the death of George Floyd, violence between football fans, the mob descending on the Capitol; all bear witness to the tragic effects that narrowly defining people by their social identities and allegiances can have. My experience of growing up in Northern Ireland taught me this well, but you will also know it in your own life. **While recognizing and celebrating difference is important, appreciating what is common to us all is potentially lifesaving.**

Not only can reductive notions of identity pose challenges for our relationships with others, they can also give rise to problems in our relationships with ourselves. This is particularly the case when we confuse who we are and what we do. While labels assigned to us by ourselves and others such as 'athlete', 'grafter', 'artist', 'nurse', 'adventurer', 'hard taskmaster', etc. can bring coherence, meaning and motivation to our lives, they can also be limiting. It can lead to a process called identity foreclosure. This is when we fix prematurely on particular identities and stop exploring and evolving our understanding of who we are. And when circumstances – whether it be retirement, illness, rejection or something else – conspire to prevent us from fulfilling those familiar roles, we cease to be our 'usual self'. A crisis of identity ensues.

Jimmy Greaves, who remains the all-time top goal-scorer in English top-flight football, retired in 1971 after a season with West Ham United when he had struggled to stay fit and sufficiently motivated. He was only thirty years old. It was a decision that he would come to deeply regret. He struggled to come to terms with life after football. By his own admission, he lost five years to alcohol dependency, which ended his marriage and brought chaos to his life. Reflecting on the difficulties that can arise when someone's sense of self becomes too entwined with their professional identity, Greaves drew a parallel between the fate of injured racehorses and retired sports people. 'They shoot horses, don't they, and I think that a lot of players would prefer to have been shot once their career was over, because they've found it very difficult to battle through life,' he said starkly. This story is sadly all too common – the highly structured nature of our professional lives can unravel all too quickly when the 'goal posts' either shift or disappear altogether. The memories of what we were for all those yesterdays obfuscates who we are today.

I have worked with sports people whose sense of self, just like Jimmy Greaves', has been left in tatters when their careers have been brought to an abrupt end by injury – they have been so entwined with their identity as an athlete that they don't know who they are now that their career has ended. Adopting a flexible mind can help us to appreciate that our sense of self is evolving rather than fixed. Rather than being bound ad nauseam to the same roles, we can make new choices in the situations in which we find ourselves that allow our sense of self to grow.

'I don't want to become my boss.' These words hung plaintively in the air long after they had left Gabriel's mouth. It was our first session together, and he was explaining why he had contacted me for support. Gabriel had been working for a large tech company for more than ten years. During that time, he had climbed the corporate ladder, and was now working as a senior executive. His commitment to the company had been rewarded, but it had come at a cost. His mood was low, he was cynical about the firm's vision, he felt irritable, his productivity had dropped off the edge of a cliff, his relationship with his CEO (whom he described as 'a bully') had soured, and he was burdened by guilt about not spending more time with his wife and young daughter. Burnout had hit. Gabriel was concerned that the Machiavellian world of big business was turning him into someone he didn't want to be. But being clear about who he *didn't* want to be had opened a door for us to think about who, and perhaps more importantly *how*, he *did* want to be. We'll come back to Gabriel and the progress he made later in the chapter.

Getting out of your own way

In his book *The Ego and the Id*, Sigmund Freud used the metaphor of a horse and chariot to distinguish between three distinct parts of the human psyche:

1. **The id**, the instinctual and unconscious part of the psyche, was likened to the horse.
2. **The ego**, the rational part of the psyche, was the metaphorical driver struggling to control the id.

3. **The super-ego,** the morally just and righteous part of the psyche, was represented by the driver's father, who stands in the back of the chariot offering advice to his son.

Since Freud originally introduced the concept of the ego, it has been commandeered by popular culture, and the word's meaning has morphed accordingly. These days, referring to someone's 'ego' or saying they have a 'big ego' is commonly used as a way of suggesting they have egotistical tendencies – that is, they are driven to maintain an excessively high self-image or are encumbered by an inflated opinion of themselves. Your ego likes to pit itself in competition with others. Not only does it want to be the best, it also wants to let other people know it is the best. The sense of self is dominated by a hunger for status and recognition.

Of course, a healthy dollop of self-regard and bold bravado can serve us well. Believing in ourselves and pursuing our interests are crucial ingredients for living a fulfilling life. But while it's important to give your ego its time in the driving seat, there will be times when it needs to shift into the backseat. Too much ego can leave us with a fragile sense of self. We end up being reduced to a list of achievements and accolades – becoming human *doings* rather than *beings*. When our sense of self is so heavily reliant on what we do, we ramp up the threat that experiences of failure and associated criticism can bring. It's not that we have failed, it's that we *are* failures.

Willem Dafoe, the four-time Oscar-nominated US actor, knows a thing or two about ego. In an interview with the *Guardian*, he pinpointed the pros – and the cons – that ego can bring. 'Of course, we need an ego to get out of bed,' he said. 'To want to do things, we have to have some sense of self. But we don't want to delude ourselves to think that we're one thing, to be *inflexible*, to think that we're special.' (My emphasis.)

As much as it would love to, the 'ego' need not be the 'be-all and end-all' of the self. Rather than fixating on preconceived notions of who we think we are (good, bad or indifferent), we can apply the 'strong attachment, light attachment' orientation to our sense of self. This so-called 'non-attachment to self' approach is gathering traction in high-performance environments and beyond. Drawing on Eastern philosophies, it advocates for a more flexible and expansive understanding of the nature of our experiences. Non-attachment to self is not about denying that the self exists. Nor is it about becoming indifferent to our interests – we can continue to care deeply about what matters to us. It's about recognizing that identifying one's 'self' with a desired outcome can lead to rigidity in how we think, feel and behave, and this can bring suffering into our lives. In contrast, non-attachment to self fosters a state of equanimous even-mindedness and poise whatever life might throw at us. This allows us to be less derailed by life's challenges and less carried away by our successes. Research has shown that non-attachment to self is associated with lower levels of distress and higher levels of wellbeing in both the general population and in high-performance populations. When we hold the 'self' more lightly, we can flex to situational demands with more vitality.

Paradoxically, it is through non-attachment to the self that we come to know ourselves better. By developing meta-awareness, we can become better skilled at appreciating that we are more than the quirky and fickle stories we tell ourselves about who we are. Despite what we might think, there is no fathomless void when we let go of the ego. Gaining this insight means our intentions can be directed more fully towards enabling the change we want to see in the world rather than appeasing the ego's sensitivities. Non-attachment helps us to connect more, not less, authentically with our purpose.

The Anchored, Willing and Empowered aspects of a flexible mind can help us to embrace a stance of non-attachment to self:

- Being **Anchored** helps us to be more fully present where we are, rather than being preoccupied with where the ego wants us to be.
- Being **Willing** helps us to notice the ego's stories about who we are, and not be swept away by the emotions that accompany these stories (including pride, envy, jealousy and anger).
- Being **Empowered** helps us to move beyond the ego's protestations about how things should be done in order to find creative ways of reconnecting with our purpose and personal values.

Losing your head (to gain greater insight)

How can we let go of our perceived sense of self? One response, proposed in the 1960s by the philosopher, spiritual teacher and author Douglas Harding, was to imagine that we have no head: no head full of busy thoughts, only a body and our sensory connections to the world around us. In his 1961 book *On Having No Head: Zen and the Rediscovery of the Obvious*, Harding presented the notion of 'headlessness' to help people more deeply connect with their experience rather than being constrained by restrictive understandings of the self. He proposed that by imagining we have no head, we can get a truer understanding of the nature of consciousness; by letting go of the idea that our 'I' is constituted by experiences, we get closer to the *essence* of our experiences. Harding's headlessness – or the 'the headless way' – is highly consistent with the non-attachment to self approach.

You may well be wondering how the concept of headlessness can be put to practical use. Sam Harris, the American philosopher and neuroscientist, provides some helpful tips and advice in his book *Waking Up: A Guide to Spirituality Without Religion* and on his podcast, also called *Waking Up*. But allow me to illustrate how I use it in my own life. When I practise mindfulness, my mind is often busy with thoughts – thoughts about things that need to be done, judgements about things that didn't go so well, worries about looming deadlines, etc. Observing these thoughts and broadening my awareness to notice my breath helps to anchor me to the present moment and stops me being swept away by those thoughts and urges to react to them. I rest my awareness on the felt experience of breathing in and out – the expanding of my chest or tummy as the air comes in, and the accompanying compression of those parts of my body when I breathe out. Occasionally, I will also take a moment to imagine that my head is not there. When I do that, my awareness doesn't disappear – it deepens. At the top of my body, where my head would normally be, there is instead only an expanding awareness of the place in which I am situated. I'm able to better appreciate how the physical form of the rest of my body is intimately connected to my surroundings. I blend into the chair in which I am sitting. I cease to be distinct from the sounds of the birds outside the window. I am more deeply connected with the world around me. I am freed from the restrictive grip that my ego can place on me. I am an integrated part of a myriad of unfolding events – one piece in the infinite jigsaw of existence. I have found this to be a very helpful approach in maintaining my own flexible mind.

In Chapter 2, I used the metaphor of a glass to capture how we are not our thoughts, emotions and sensations – we are the container into which these experiences are poured. Headlessness extends that idea further by recognizing that the glass is an integrated element of the wider universe – and the division between those integrated elements is not as distinct as we might think. As the German author and spiritual teacher Eckhart Tolle noted in his book *A New Earth*: 'You are not **in** the universe, you **are** the universe, an intrinsic part of it.'

Let's now turn our attention to how the flexible mind approach can be used to address some other specific threats that can arise in our efforts to thrive: imposterism (also known as imposter syndrome) and loss aversion.

Imposterism

When Ted met Ted

During his lifetime, the writer Theodor Geisel won a Pulitzer Prize, three Academy Awards and two Emmys, and was awarded no fewer than seven honorary doctorates. It's estimated that more than 700 million copies of his books have been sold worldwide. There's a fair chance that you have read at least one of them. Confused? Don't be. Theodor Geisel is better known by his penname: Dr Seuss. And yet, despite his incredible success, Geisel never forgot an embarrassing incident that happened during his formative years. In 1918, when he was fourteen years old, there was a competition run by the Boy

Scouts of America to see which scout could raise the most money for the organization. After raising the most money in his region, young Ted was invited to receive an award from none other than his namesake, the former President of the United States Theodore Roosevelt. Roosevelt was due to present awards to ten regional winners. Unfortunately, however, there was an administrative mix-up, and he was handed only nine awards to present. By the time the former president got to Geisel, who was the last boy in line, there were no awards left. 'What's this little boy doing here?' Roosevelt bellowed in a state of annoyed confusion. Geisel's misery was made complete when his scoutmaster unceremoniously pulled him from the stage to appease the irate former president. What had been set to be the proudest day of his young life had descended into a farce. In an interview conducted sixty-eight years later, Geisel recalled: 'All those eyes staring — staring right through me. I can still hear the people whispering, "Ted Geisel tried to get a medal and he didn't deserve it." I hear them saying, "What's he doing up there?" Even today, I sometimes find myself asking, "What am I doing here?"' Despite his later success, the sense of being an imposter never left him. We are left to wonder if Dr Seuss's famous book *Oh, the Places You'll Go!* was written as much for himself as it was for everyone else.

Understanding imposterism

The term 'imposter phenomenon' was first introduced in 1978 by Pauline Clance and Suzanne Imes, two American psychologists, to capture the experiences reported by more than 150 high-achieving women in the USA. It has subsequently been described as 'imposterism', 'imposter experience', 'imposter complex' and, most frequently, 'imposter syndrome' (this latter term has been criticized because it gives the impression that imposterism is a medical condition, which of course it isn't). Irrespective of what term is used, the sense of threat is the same – the person affected is convinced they're a fraud, deceiving themselves and others about the true nature of their abilities.

Hallmarks of imposterism include anxiety, perfectionism, self-doubt and fear of failure. The risk of experiencing imposterism is thought to increase with the novelty of the situations in which we find ourselves (i.e. if we are doing something unfamiliar), the visibility of our actions (i.e. if we know others can view and evaluate our performance), and the experience of being in a minority (i.e. if we are conscious of being different from most people around us).

A peculiarity in how we think – known as 'pluralistic ignorance' – can increase the likelihood of experiencing imposterism. Pluralistic ignorance is caused by a reluctance to share our self-doubts with each other – this distorts our worldviews by leading us to conclude that we are the only ones experiencing self-doubt. By opting not to talk about our own experiences of imposterism, we collude in perpetuating an illusion that imposterism is less common than it is. Far from being abnormal, imposterism may well be a normal reaction to adjusting to a new situation. Rather than *deceiving* other people, we are in a process of *conceiving* a new understanding of ourselves.

In my work with clients who describe experiencing imposterism, a consistent theme that emerges is how 'stingy' new work environments can be in satisfying our psychological yearnings for autonomy, relatedness and mastery. Being the 'newbie', we are left to wonder where our decision-making responsibilities might lie, how supportive and trustworthy colleagues are, and when – if ever – we might feel competent at completing the tasks we need to undertake. It takes time to adapt to new contexts. If imposterism was an actual medical syndrome, its most prominent symptom might well be 'psychological growing pains'! And the prescription? Recognition and validation of the experience, kindness towards oneself, sharing one's experiences with trusted people, and the accumulation of expertise over time.

The following process can help with counteracting the impact of imposterism. Over the next month, record on a notepad (or in the Notes application on your mobile phone) any feedback you receive from your friends, colleagues or family that relates to the following headings:

- **Qualities** – You possess qualities that they appreciate (while there may well be some overlap with your own personal values, be open to the possibility that others may value qualities you possess that you have not been aware of).
- **Skills** – You can perform skills and complete tasks that can make a difference in your personal and/or professional life.
- **Belonging** – You are a valued part of a group (e.g. a team, community or organization).

Setting a daily reminder on your phone will cue your memory to complete this task through the month. You might notice a reluctance to accept praise and recognition that may be directed your way. Søren Kierkegaard, the Danish philosopher we met in Chapter 5, once remarked: 'There is nothing with which every man is so afraid as getting to know how enormously much he is capable of doing and becoming.' So, see if you can feel that reluctance and still commit to collecting the information. That's the joy of a flexible mind – we can doubt and still do. At the end of the month, take time to review what you've recorded. Savour the feedback and be curious about the feelings that arise as you do so. Be curious also about which domains of life (work, recreation, family life, community, etc.) are providing this kind of feedback, and which are not. Don't confuse absence of evidence with evidence of absence – just because it isn't forthcoming from some quarters doesn't mean it doesn't exist. So, if you are staring at a blank page at the end of the month, don't despair; you may need to be more proactive in seeking feedback from others, even if you notice that your ego is deeply threatened by the prospect of it. That's flexibility in action.

It's important to emphasize that a defining feature of imposterism is that our perceived lack of belonging is attributed to flaws that are located squarely within us as individuals – we are contending with an inner dialogue that dictates: 'I'm not good enough and others are bound to catch me out.' But this shouldn't be confused with the lack of belonging that can emerge when those around us underestimate our ability and communicate to us, either explicitly or implicitly, 'You are not good enough and we will catch you out.' This latter example is not imposterism but a classic case of the in-group/out-group dynamic in action – it's not that your perception of your abilities has been falsely inflated, it's that they have been deliberately deflated by others. While the possibility exists that these two experiences can overlap, it's important to distinguish between them. Too often people from minoritized groups are left to feel like imposters when they encounter hegemonic and discriminatory cultures that are actively seeking to exclude them. Just because you feel like an outsider doesn't mean that other people don't want to put you outside.

Let's look at a situation when the AWE of a flexible mind helped me to manage my own feelings of imposterism.

Stand at ~~ease~~ freeze

I was trying to speak, but the words wouldn't leave my lips. I was standing in front of a company of more than 250 soldiers wearing combat fatigues. All eyes were on me, and the silence seemed to be stretching on for an inordinately long time. Beads of sweat were forming on my brow. The regiment was about to be deployed on peace-keeping duties to a hotspot in Africa, and I had been asked to provide a workshop on strategies that the soldiers could use to safeguard their mental wellbeing while overseas. When the senior sergeant initially contacted me out of the blue in the spring of 2022, he explained that he was putting together a coordinated package of training that would include input from medical doctors, physiotherapists and other health practitioners, so that the infantrymen and women could stay healthy while they were away. He wanted to know if I would come and speak to his troops as part of the package. I couldn't help but be impressed by the care and commitment he was taking to ensure that the group was as prepared as well as it could be. It was a 'yes' from me.

I had prepared for the session by talking with the senior sergeant in some detail about the trials and tribulations that soldiers face on tours of duty of this kind. I had also talked to psychologist colleagues who routinely work with military units in the USA about the work they do. Several stresses were highlighted. The climate would be wearing – particularly the heat and humidity – the variety and quality of the food produced in field kitchens would be limited, and the threat of physical illnesses, including malaria, would be ever-present. Then, of course, there was the uncertainty and concern about what contact with local warring parties might bring, and the pain of being away from friends and family who remained at home. Based on the information gathered, I had tailored the metaphors and techniques to be relatable to military life – for example, there was mention in the slides of 'being where your boots are' and 'making room in the kitbag for the worries'. I had also consulted relevant military policy documents to understand the organizational culture and values that the army espoused. I was ready. Or, at least, I thought I was.

The intention had been to begin the half-day workshop with a brief description of my experience and credentials before then setting out the aims for the session. While I had no military background to draw upon, I did have experience of working with conflict-affected populations in rural parts of sub-Saharan Africa – the kinds of settings the soldiers were about to be sent to. I had assumed that my experience of doing consultancy and training with those working in high-pressure environments – including athletes and coaches – would have prepared me well. But there was something about being in front of uniformed soldiers that I hadn't prepared for. Perhaps it was growing up in conflict-affected Northern Ireland, when soldiers of the British Army were on the streets, but the effect was unnerving. Suddenly, my mind was awash with thoughts that I didn't know enough about the lives that soldiers lead, and a fear the soldiers were going to be resentful that 'an outsider' was coming in to provide them with advice. The net effect was that my words were stuck in my throat. I glanced over at the senior sergeant, who frowned back at me. I was frozen to the spot on which I was standing. This was all going to go horribly wrong.

It was in that clutch moment that I came back to what I knew. I used the AWE aspects of a flexible mind to initiate a switch away from Threat mode and into Get mode. Specifically, I focused on being where my feet were, I curiously explored where the anxiety was manifesting in my body, and I breathed deeply into those butterflies in my stomach. I took a moment to acknowledge that the anxiety was an indication that I wanted to be true to the purpose that had brought me to the barracks in the first place – helping people to help themselves. I steeled myself, fixed my gaze on a young soldier at the back of the room and introduced myself to him – and, by default, everyone else in the room. The silence was broken, and the momentum built from there. I'm pleased to say that the workshop progressed well from that point on. A couple of soldiers came forward at the end, both asking if they could share the techniques and insights with their partners, who would have concerns of their own to deal with as they remained at home. I made sure that all the slides used during the workshop were shared with those who had attended, so that they could discuss them with those who mattered in their lives.

Loss aversion

We humans love to acquire new things. Whether it's the latest Apple gadget, Nike Air Jordans, more Instagram followers or the latest delivery from the wine club – gain is good. But as much as we love to acquire, we hate to lose what we already have. Streaming services like Paramount+ or Amazon Prime Video know it; that's why they offer you a free subscription for a month or two. Once you have it, you may be reluctant to relinquish it. Research suggests that for equivalent amounts, losses are twice as powerful as gains. If we are offered a chance to toss a coin to either lose £100 (tails) or win £100 (heads) most of us will not take up the offer. Loss is *very* bad. This asymmetry between being more driven to avoid losses than to achieve gains is called 'loss aversion' and it is one of the biases associated with our automatic instinctive decision-making processes (System 1, see p. 143) rather than our more rational ones (System 2). Loss aversion has been studied extensively in the field of behavioural economics, which focuses on the decisions that traders make in financial markets. The fear of experiencing a loss can lead traders to cash out when stock has gained marginally in value instead of holding off to see if it rises further.

Losses and gains are judged from reference points. These reference points can be based on the status quo (e.g. current income, levels of self-esteem or seniority within an organization), or on a target we've set for the future (e.g. a weekly training schedule and annual profit target), where not sticking to it would be a loss, while exceeding it would be a gain. Golfers are very familiar with reference points although they use the term 'par' to describe them. An eighteen-hole golf course will have a designated number of strokes in which golfers should complete the course – this is the course's 'par'. For example, the world-famous Old Course at St Andrews has a par of 72. In turn, each of its eighteen holes has its own par – fourteen of them are 'par 4', two holes are 'par 5', and a further two are 'par 3'. Let's use one of the 'par 4' holes as an example. If a golfer takes four strokes to get the ball into that hole, they are said to have 'made par'. If they get the ball in the hole in three strokes (i.e. one under par) they have achieved a 'birdie' – this is a gain. If they take five strokes (i.e. one over par), they score a 'bogey' – this is a loss. A research study that analysed 2.5 million putts made by 421 professional golfers found that when all other factors (including the distance and difficulty of the putt, etc.) were controlled, golfers putted more accurately for par than for birdie. Preventing a loss rather than achieving a gain resulted in better performance. **While potential gains might ask a question of us, potential losses demand a response**. Tiger Woods, who needs no introduction, backed up these findings when he said: 'You don't ever want to drop a shot. The psychological difference between dropping a shot and making a birdie, I just think it's bigger to make a par putt.'

Loss aversion is a threat response that can stop us in our tracks. But if we are to be true to our sense of purpose, then we need to take risks at times. A preoccupation with loss ends up depriving us of our ability to gain. **The thing we need to be most cautious about is being too cautious**. There are a several strategies consistent with the flexible mind approach that can be helpful for managing the sense of threat that loss aversion gives rise to:

- **Broad framing** – Rather than narrowly focusing on the merits/demerits of isolated decisions, we can instead recognize that we are managing a diverse 'portfolio' of commitments across various life domains (work, relationships, family life, recreation). Within that portfolio, there will be gains and losses across time – one bad investment will not break the bank.

- **Pre-commitment** – The pre-commitment pledge approach that was highlighted on p. 193 can be used to help us to identify a plan of action. This should include realistic consideration of the losses that may be incurred in the process.

- **Acknowledging gain fog** – We are prone to experiencing what I call 'gain fog' – a blind spot in our ability to foresee all the benefits that our choices can bring. Gain fog is a quirk of time. The devils we don't yet know might actually be better than those we do – it's just that we haven't had the opportunity to learn that yet. Recognizing the presence of gain fog can be a helpful step in mobilizing us towards taking appropriate risks. While being aware of what we stand to lose is important, acknowledging that we can't fully appreciate what we stand to gain is important too.

- **Appreciating experiences over outcome** – We can recognize that there is value to be derived from our experiences even if the outcome of our decisions is less than optimal. As Nelson Mandela once remarked: 'I never lose. I either win or I learn.'

Allow me to turn again to my work with Gabriel, whom we met on p. 212. He shared with me that his sense of dissatisfaction with his job had been growing steadily since the birth of his daughter four years earlier. But he felt trapped. As difficult as his work situation was, he was earning a good salary, which supported the lifestyle to which he and his family had become accustomed. At one stage, he had considered moving to a rival firm, but had dismissed the idea on the basis that the situation might be even worse there (better the CEO you know . . .). Gabriel acknowledged that loss aversion was serving to keep him where he was – stuck in the conforming zone. He was keen to explore how a flexible mind could help him get unstuck. In a session early on in the process of therapy, we spent time clarifying his personal values. He identified the following as his top five: being facilitative and supportive of the success of others, demonstrating integrity in what he was doing, nurturing relationships with friends and family, being 'progressively disruptive' (being prepared to do things differently to improve them), and being forgiving towards himself and others. Gabriel recognized that his current professional role was not conducive to endorsing these personal values, and that it was causing him to feel inauthentic. The concept of 'gain fog' resonated strongly with him. We focused on developing Gabriel's willingness to make choices in line with his personal values, even though he experienced doubt, uncertainty and fear as he did so. After discussing the situation with his wife, he took the decision to resign from his role. Rather than joining another firm and risking another misalignment between his personal values and their corporate values, he chose instead to set up his own consultancy firm. Gabriel was clear that he wanted to take a different approach that would afford him more autonomy in how he worked and allow him to be more present in his family life. Over the course of our work together, there was a reduction in the symptoms of depression and anxiety that he had been experiencing when we first met. Launching his own business and being more involved in looking after his daughter brought moments of stress as well as joy, but he was clear that he wouldn't want it any other way.

Lose without getting lost

Novak Djokovic, the Serbian tennis player, holds the world record for the most men's singles Grand Slam titles – twenty-four in total at the time of writing. It may come as a surprise to learn that across his career, Djokovic has won just over half (54 per cent) of the points that he has played. Along with all other top tennis players, Djokovic loses points nearly as often as he wins them. It's a similar picture for the most successful city traders and high-stakes poker players. The road to success is peppered with potholes of failure.

In an interview with the BBC, Djokovic alluded to the role that flexibility can play in offsetting experiences of loss if and when they do occur:

I used to be a bit more upset with myself if I didn't do something – it would be like, 'you're not good enough now,' or 'you are going to lose now' . . . One of the biggest lessons I have learned about mental strength in matches is that, if you lose your focus, if you are not in the present and things have started to go the wrong way for you, then it is fine. You just have to accept it, and then come back. I think that recovery, or how long you stay in that negative emotion, is what differentiates you from other players. The recovery is more important than working hard to stay in the present, because it is almost impossible to stay there all the time. It's about how quickly you can get back, and for me it is breathing, conscious breathing, that helps.

It's not whether we incur losses in our life, it's how we respond when we do – that's the second arrow that we can do something about. Even the minds of champions wander away from the present moment to premonitions of failure and catastrophe. Feelings of panic, fear and shame can start to take hold at times of defeat. No one is immune to experiencing difficult emotions. But if we are Willing to recognize and acknowledge the challenging emotions that can show up – rather than struggling against them – then we can 'recover' by using our breath to get Anchored once again in the here and now. It is like Jon Kabat-Zinn, the 'godfather of modern mindfulness', said of meditation, 'If your mind wanders away from the breath a thousand times, then your job is simply to bring it back to the breath every time.' We can then be Empowered to understand losses as being part and parcel of our journey towards purpose. Because when it comes to our purpose, no defeat is final.

Walking towards threat

There will be times when we will actively choose to walk towards threat – and the very real prospect of loss – to cultivate our sense of purpose. The story of basketball player Bill Russell and his Boston Celtics teammates illustrates this point well. In October 1961, the Celtics were invited to play an exhibition game against their fierce rivals the St Louis Hawks. The neutral venue of Lexington, Kentucky, had been selected for the encounter. In the lead-up to the game, two Celtics players – Sam Jones and Thomas 'Satch' Sanders – were refused service in the hotel coffee shop. The reason? They were Black. In a defiant act of collective action, their fellow Black teammates, Bill Russell (one of the greatest basketball players of all time, and the winner of no fewer than eleven NBA titles), K.C. Jones and Al Butler, joined the pair in deciding not to play in the game as a protest. Red Auerbach, the Celtics' legendary coach at the time, pleaded with the five players to stay and play, but when he understood the strength of their feelings, he drove them to the airport so they could catch a flight back to Boston.

When the Celtics players returned to Boston, they were pilloried for the decision that they had taken, receiving torrents of criticism from the team's own fanbase and the city's local press. Bill Russell stood firm. 'We've got to show our disapproval of this kind of treatment,' he said, 'or else the status quo will prevail. We have the same rights and privileges as anyone else and deserve to be treated accordingly. I hope we never have to go through this abuse again.'

Throughout his career, Russell used his platform to advocate for civil rights and fight discrimination, despite the fact that he and his family were subjected to racist threats and abuse. In 2010, Barack Obama awarded him the Presidential Medal of Freedom in recognition of his efforts to fight systemic racism. In recent years, other athletes such as former NFL player Colin Kaepernick and tennis superstars Venus and Serena Williams have taken courageous stances of their own in the fight against racism. The more a tree grows towards its source of energy, the bigger it becomes, and it can find itself a target for others. Sometimes remaining true to our purpose will mean encountering more threat than we otherwise would. If it matters enough to us, we might have to do it afraid.

Just as trees need to endure turbulent times, we too have to weather the storms of life that can jeopardize our ability to thrive. Threat mode plays a key role in helping us to respond to the dangers we encounter. While some dangers are clear and present in our environment, others lurk in the shadows of our minds, such as a distorted sense of 'self', imposterism and our aversion to loss. While threats – real and imagined – are a fact of life, adopting the AWE of a flexible mind can help ensure that our responses don't become 'second arrows' that compound the impact. Sometimes responding appropriately to threat requires more than just a focus on our individual situation. Tackling burnout, for example, might need coordinated action at both the level of the individual and the organization. Here, too, a flexible mind can help us mobilize collective action to help bring about systemic change. Threat might be unavoidable – and sometimes even necessary – as we cultivate purpose, but its impact can be mitigated, and there is always the chance for our final motivation mode – Reset.

Threat: Summary Points

- We have evolved to be attentive to potential danger that threatens our safety and wellbeing.
- Avoiding threats can be an incredibly helpful strategy, but it is not always possible – particularly when it comes to threats that we generate in our thoughts.
- The rising rates of burnout require collective action rather than just a focus on individual psychology.
- Sometimes, our response to potential threats can become the threat – our ways of coping diminish our ability to thrive.
- Better understanding the nature of the self and how this is distinct from our identities and roles provides opportunities for us to be less threatened by ego fragility.
- The feelings of threat associated with imposterism are less about *deceiving* others and more about the challenges of *conceiving* new identities and roles.
- The threat associated with contemplating change is heightened by loss aversion and gain fog – a blind spot in our ability to foresee the benefits that our choices can bring.

CHAPTER 8

Reset

To thrive, trees need to reset. Some resets, such as when a tree rebounds after a gust of wind, might take a fraction of a second. When trees bend in gales, they convert the kinetic energy from the wind into elastic potential energy in their trunks. Both the heartwood and the xylem (the layer of the trunk that transports water) play an important role in this process. These parts of the trunk use the elastic potential energy to reset the trees by swaying them back to centre after each gust.

Longer resets are necessitated by changing seasons. While the spring and summer are times for deciduous broadleaf trees – such as oak, birch and ash – to use Get mode to grow and develop, the autumn and winter are Reset seasons for consolidation and dormancy. In autumn, when the amount of daily sunlight begins to drop, the chlorophyll a tree uses to capture the sun's energy is drawn back from its leaves into the trunk. This causes the colour of the leaves to change to the distinctive brown, yellow and red hues so characteristic of autumn. Devoid of chlorophyll's lifeblood, the leaves fall to earth – giving autumn its other name, 'fall'. The loss of its leaves reduces the likelihood that a tree will catch the full force of winter gales that could damage it, and also prevents large volumes of snow from forming on branches that could cause them harm. The dormancy of autumn and winter is essential to the survival of deciduous trees. When trees such as oaks are grown indoors with an absence of the environmental cues that herald the arrival of autumn, they don't know when to shut off and they flounder. In this chapter, we will reflect on how for humans, too, the ability to reset (in ways both brief and bold) is an essential aspect of our ability to thrive.

Modern life provides no shortage of ammunition to ignite our Get and Threat systems. In a cartoon by Emily Flake in the *New Yorker*, people can be seen scattering from a rampaging Godzilla-like creature bringing carnage to a city. Amidst the chaos, one of the fleeing victims can be seen looking at her smart watch saying: 'Oh – I actually do want to log this as a workout.' In our rush to achieve our targets and remain safe, Reset mode can easily become the poor relation of our motivational modes.

If Get mode is about striving, and Threat mode is about surviving, Reset mode is about reviving. This revival comes from taking time to appreciate ourselves and the world around us, and reorientating to our purpose. Whereas Threat mode is linked to the sympathetic nervous system's 'fight, flight or freeze' response, Reset mode is linked to the parasympathetic nervous system, which helps our bodies to 'rest and digest' and is activated when we express compassion both towards ourselves and others – our ability to 'tend and befriend'. Just as activation of the sympathetic system stimulates stress responses, so activation of the parasympathetic nervous system results in an opposing range of changes within the body – the heart rate decreases, the pupils constrict, inflammation levels decrease, the production of saliva increases, and bile is released into the small intestine to aid digestion and nutrient absorption.

Resets come in different sizes and guises. In this chapter, I will draw a distinction between what I refer to as 'momentary moves' and 'bold moves'. As the name suggests, momentary moves are resets that can be undertaken in short periods of time, which can provide opportunities to Reset when the Threat or Get modes are highly activated. Bold moves, on the other hand, are more substantial, potentially counterintuitive undertakings that help us thrive over the longer term – just like trees shedding their leaves in the autumn and winter. One thing that both momentary moves and bold moves have in common is that neither happen by accident – we need to be deliberate in activating our Reset mode.

The idea of resetting will be anathema to many of us. So conditioned are we to respond to the persistent urges of Get mode and the incessant alerts of Threat mode that we feel disinclined to avail of Reset mode. But the costs of not doing so can be counted in the amount of fatigue, stress and disenchantment that we will experience – the antithesis of thriving. In this chapter, we will explore how adopting a flexible mind can help us to access Reset mode, both as part of our daily routines and in the situations when it might be particularly helpful.

We'll be addressing the following three questions:

1. What momentary moves can you take to reset?
2. What bold moves can you take to reset?
3. How will you know when it is time to reset?

Momentary moves

Let's start our exploration of resets with momentary moves, which are characterized by their ability to engender compassion, gratitude and/or wonderment. Collectively, these experiences are referred to as 'self-transcendent emotions'; they enable us to broaden our awareness to something or someone other than ourselves. Self-transcendent emotions of this type are inherently pro-social – they help with nurturing the bonds we have with other people.

- **Wonderment** helps us to recognize the interconnections between us, others and the world around us.
- **Gratitude** communicates to others that their actions are appreciated.
- **Compassion** allows us to express care towards others.

The self-transcendent emotions that can accompany momentary moves stand in sharp contrast to thoughts of self-doubt, self-criticism or self-recrimination, and self-conscious emotions such as feelings of shame, guilt or embarrassment that can flare up when Threat mode is activated. Momentary moves help us to adjust the emotional temperature – the cold chill of self-conscious emotions is offset by the warm flow of self-transcendent emotions.

As we will see, momentary moves are highly compatible with the AWE aspects of a flexible mind. Just as the Anchored and Willing aspects of a flexible mind help us to be more aware of the breadth of our current experiences and develop the ability to be open and curious about them, so momentary moves help us to broaden our focus and adjust how we relate to our experiences. The Empowered aspect of a flexible mind is consistent with the need to find the impetus and means to engage in momentary moves. When I introduce momentary moves to my clients, I explain that these can help build our flexibility to come 'back to centre' during turbulent times – like the tree trunk elastically swaying back to centre after a gust of wind. We'll take each of these three types of momentary moves in turn.

Wonderment

One of the most poignant examples of wonderment is that of astronauts looking back at the fragile beauty of Earth revolving slowly in the darkness of space – dubbed 'the overview effect' by author Frank White. Edgar Mitchell, an astronaut on NASA's Apollo 14 mission in 1971, said that viewing Earth from space provoked an 'overwhelming sense of oneness and connectedness . . . accompanied by an ecstasy . . . an epiphany'. But if a Virgin Galactic flight into Earth's mesosphere – a mere fifty-five miles above sea level – is beyond your price range, worry not. Moments of wonder can be found much closer to home.

In 1836, the great American author Ralph Waldo Emerson wrote: 'In the woods, we return to reason and faith. There I feel that nothing can befall me in life—no disgrace, no calamity (leaving me my eyes), which nature cannot repair. Standing on the bare ground—my head bathed by the blithe air and uplifted into infinite space—all mean egotism vanishes.' From Emerson's point of view, an escape into the forest is an escape from the ego and the tribulations of daily life. Policymakers agree. In 1982, Tomohide Akiyama, the then-Director

General of the Japanese Ministry of Agriculture, Forestry and Fisheries, initiated a programme of works relating to what is termed *shinrin-yoku* (Japanese for 'forest-bathing'), which aimed to get stressed-out city dwellers to visit areas of woodland and enjoy more restorative environs. Today, more than 90 per cent of the Japanese population live in urban areas, even though more than two-thirds of the country is covered in forest, so *shinrin-yoku* continues to be an important element of Japanese health policy.

To fully appreciate the wonders of the woods, it's important to leave two things behind – your devices and your desire to get somewhere. In his book *Shinrin-Yoku: The Art and Science of Forest Bathing*, Qing Li, the current President of the Society for Forest Medicine in Japan, writes:

Make sure you have left your phone and camera behind. You are going to be walking aimlessly and slowly. You don't need any devices. Let your body be your guide. Listen to where it wants to take you. Follow your nose. And take your time. It doesn't matter if you don't get anywhere. You are not going anywhere. You are savouring the sounds, smells and sights of nature and letting the forest in.

So, there you have it: simply immerse yourself in the rich sensory experience of the woods. You may or may not be relieved to know that there is no requirement to hug the trees.

Research studies have shown that forest-bathing is associated with a range of physical health benefits as well as a reduction in symptoms of mental health conditions. It seems, however, that the benefits of natural environments for our physical and mental health are not limited to just forests. Evidence collected in studies conducted in eighteen different countries indicated that by frequently visiting green spaces (parks, woodlands and open countryside), inland blue spaces (lakes and rivers) or coastal blue spaces (beaches, coastal pathways, etc.), we increase our levels of wellbeing and reduce the mental distress we experience. Several theories have been proposed to account for why this might be the case. One prominent example is Attention Restoration Theory. It was originally proposed in the late 1980s by Stephen and Rachel Kaplan – a husband-and-wife team who were both working as researchers at the University of Michigan at the time. The theory suggests that time in nature has a restorative effect on our attentional capacities – and not just because being in nature provides an opportunity to be away from familiar sources of stress, such as busy office environments. Nature is rich in what the Kaplans referred to as 'soft fascinations' – experiences that engender a sense of curious and effortless attention, such as dappled sunlight on the forest floor, or the sound of trees creaking and groaning in the breeze. These soft fascinations provide a break from the more demanding and effortful forms of attention demanded by our usual routines. Attention Restoration Theory emphasizes that the natural environment should be a place where you can feel at ease rather than on edge – forests where hungry grizzly bears are on the prowl should be avoided. Finally, the theory highlights the importance of the environment being a place of your choosing – one that feels intrinsically rewarding for you. It should be somewhere you're *pleased* to be rather than somewhere you feel you *ought* to be.

While moments of wonder arising in the natural world can provide important opportunities to access Reset mode, researchers have highlighted that collectively engaging in activities with other people can also do the trick. For example, taking part in religious or spiritual rituals, singing in unison, dancing in a group or being part of a crowd listening to music can all produce moments of wonder – which, in turn, are linked to a range of positive outcomes, including better quality of life, reductions in stress levels and improved wellbeing. Although there are different paths to moments of wonder, they all share the capacity to connect us with something more vast and less ordinary than our usual experiences.

Gratitude

Gratitude is an emotion that involves the recognition, acknowledgement and appreciation of those experiences in our lives for which we have reason to be thankful. Our gratitude can be directed towards any number of potential recipients – deities, mother nature, medical staff, window cleaners, aircraft pilots, the barista whose smile is as warm as the excellent coffee he serves you . . . But it seems that we often underplay the power of sharing our gratitude. Research conducted at the Booth School of Business, University of Chicago, found that we tend to underestimate the positive impact that our expressions of gratitude will have on others. This raises the risk of us being stingy with our gratitude. But being generous with our gratitude is not only good for others – it is good for us, too.

It was Tuesday, 1 January 2008, and John Kralik, attorney at law, was lost in the hills above Pasadena, California. If truth be told, he was lost before he even set out on his walk. The law firm that he had established was making zero profit, and he was going through his second divorce. Having initially blamed other people for divorce number one, with divorce number two, he was now recognizing that *he* was the recurring theme. Finding himself adrift and disorientated on the wooded hillside was an inauspicious start to what he had hoped would be a better year. His mood was as gloomy as the rapidly encroaching evening sky. Forest-bathing this was not. And then an inner voice spoke with a clarity that pierced the gloom: *Until you learn to be grateful for the things that you have, you will not get the things that you want.* If you're wondering where Kralik directed his gratitude first, he aimed it squarely at the dawning realization that the quickest way out of the hills was to ensure that each step took him downhill. He made it back to civilization.

By Thursday, Kralik's 'moment on the mountain' had already slid into the recesses of his mind. But then a reminder came from an unlikely source – his ex-girlfriend. Although they had ended their relationship just before Christmas, she had sent him a thank you card for the gift he had sent her. That little show of gratitude would go a long way. Spurred into action, Kralik decided to make good on his hillside epiphany. He began by sending a letter to his eldest son to thank him for the swish coffee machine he had given him for Christmas, and just kept going from there. Kralik made 2008 his 'year of gratitude' and would later write a book about it entitled: *365 Thank Yous: The Year a Simple Act of Daily Gratitude Changed My Life.*

Kralik observed an unexpected but nonetheless striking consequence of the gratitude he expressed. It spread. Gratitude can be infectious. The notes of gratitude that he wrote to his staff – apologizing that he had no money to give them as a Christmas bonus – prompted them to write notes of appreciation to each other. His son responded to his thank you note by taking him out for lunch and repaying $4,000 his father had gifted to him. Kralik observed other positive outcomes too. Letters of gratitude sent to clients who had settled their invoices promptly led them to paying even more promptly in future. Thank you notes to attorneys who referred cases to him prompted them to refer more cases. But Kralik wasn't doing it for secondary gain; he was doing it to get his focus beyond himself. 'The writing of thank you notes . . . gives you some way of focusing on that other person rather than on yourself, and the impact of what they did and the effort that they made to do something good for you. So, you take the focus off yourself,' Kralik said in a 2017 interview.

Kralik's experiences with expressing gratitude are backed up by research. Martin Seligman, the American psychologist dubbed 'the father of the positive psychology movement', was amongst the first to highlight the benefits of expressing gratitude to others. A study conducted by Seligman and his colleagues in 2005 found that participants who delivered a letter of gratitude to someone who had shown them kindness led to the largest increase in levels of happiness and the biggest drop in depression scores over the following month when compared with participants who received four other interventions and a control group. Since then, many other studies have examined the benefits that expressing gratitude have on a range of outcomes. A team of researchers from the University of New England in Australia combed through the findings of twenty-three studies that had investigated the impact that expressing gratitude had on levels of wellbeing. Their review concluded that expressing gratitude to others led to greater increases in wellbeing than completing normal daily activities or recalling memorable events, and was comparable to the effect of more active interventions such as using signature strengths, which involves selecting an aspect of our personality (such as optimism, zest or curiosity) that energizes us and integrating more of it into our daily routines.

If three-dimensional, in-person expressions of gratitude are not possible, don't despair. Expressing gratitude from afar can work just as well. The cornucopia of social media streams available to us today provide a dizzying array of opportunities to express our gratitude, whether we do it by text, FaceTime, Zoom, MS Teams, WhatsApp, the Telegram App, Facebook Messenger, etc. Whatever might be laying siege to your expressions of gratitude, not having the means to do it certainly isn't one of them. And, as the American author William Arthur Ward once noted, 'Feeling gratitude and not expressing it is like wrapping a present and not giving it.'

Interestingly, the review mentioned above concluded that keeping a gratitude list (i.e. noting down things for which we are grateful) was just as effective as expressing gratitude to others. Another review, this time conducted by a team of researchers based in Japan, pored over the findings of studies that had investigated the effectiveness of gratitude lists in occupational settings. Although a small number of these studies also gave the participants the opportunity to express gratitude towards others as a core element of the programme, the majority – eight out of the ten studies – did not. The review concluded that keeping gratitude lists leads to improvements in levels of stress and depression amongst employees. While gratitude interventions may not be vastly superior to other active interventions for helping us thrive, they can certainly play their part. There are also indications that the more often gratitude lists are completed, the greater the benefits on mental health. Gratitude needn't be a flash in the pan – it's something we can plan.

An approach I use with clients to help them with keeping a gratitude list uses the acronym THANKFUL as a prompt for eight aspects of our daily experiences for which we can potentially be grateful:

Today's opportunities – Was there something that happened today that gave your mood a lift?

Health – What aspect(s) of your wellbeing could you be appreciative of today?

Art and music – What piece of music or visual art might have made an impact on you today?

Nature – Was there an aspect of the natural world that you were grateful to experience today?

Kindness from others – Did someone go out of their way to be helpful or kind today?

Friends and family – Was there an interaction with a friend or family member that you're thankful for?

Unique/unusual – Was there something different that happened today that you're grateful for?

Lessons learned – What insights or wisdom might you be grateful for gaining today?

You might not be able to generate responses to each prompt every day, but hopefully they will provide some food for thought for notes that you can make in a journal, a Word document or in the Notes app on your smart phone.

It's important to recognize that the term 'gratitude' may not always have positive connotations. Research conducted in the UK, for example, has highlighted that talk of gratitude may conjure up undertones of indebtedness, a sense of guilt and/or feelings of awkwardness and embarrassment. Childhood memories of being 'encouraged' to say thank you can give rise to a mix of different emotions. Allow me to be clear: gratitude is not something you ought to do, nor is it something you owe other people. It's an experience of your own choosing.

Of course, things will happen that we will never be grateful for – travesties that severely test our mettle, tragedies that shake us to our core. While some setbacks can, with time, prove to be breakthroughs, many do not. And the pain we will experience will be profound. But, as I often point out to my clients, life is an 'and' rather than an 'or' thing. We can be confronted with huge challenges, *and* still find ways to be grateful for blessings both large and small that occur amidst all our trials and tribulations. Incorporating gratitude into our routines won't magic the pain away, but it will help us to get through the day. Importantly, practising gratitude also allows us to savour our successes and protects us from the pervasive discontentment of the arrival fallacy we discussed on p. 86. In this way, the momentary move of expressing gratitude can be an important part of downgrading Get mode when the situation requires it. The flexible mind skills of being Anchored, Willing and Empowered are all helpful for practising gratitude, allowing us to connect more deeply with the present moment, to notice and unhook from harsh judgements about the nature of our experiences, and to be creative in committing to pursuing goals in relation to practising gratitude.

Compassion

Compassion is defined as the capacity to understand the suffering of another living entity and the willingness to do something to alleviate that suffering. As such, compassion encompasses both empathy – the ability to understand and identify with the experiences of others – and a commitment to responding supportively. If we have not experienced a lot of compassion, we can be wary, sceptical and dismissive of it – it can seem indulgent, passive or weak. But what's indulgent about a nurse holding the hand of a gravely ill patient? What's passive about a vet tending to your injured pet? And what's weak about a four-ton elephant using its trunk to comfort a distressed member of its herd? (Yes, elephants express compassion too!) Compassion is a superpower. Expressing compassion has been central to the caregiving process that has allowed humans to prosper throughout our evolutionary history. But there's a potential target for our compassion that can be very challenging to reach. Allow me to illustrate this . . .

Let's imagine that a very close friend has been going through a difficult time, which has caused them considerable distress. It's the weekend and you have nothing planned. How much time and energy would you invest in taking care of your friend? You might, for example, come up with a plan to do something together, or just offer them a listening ear. Now, let's imagine it's the weekend and you have nothing planned, but the person going through a difficult time and experiencing considerable distress is *you*. Would you invest more, less or the same amount of time and energy in taking care of yourself than you were prepared to devote to your friend? It's a sad reality that many of us struggle to be as kind and compassionate to ourselves as we are to others. And the double whammy is that we regularly direct harsh criticism towards ourselves that we wouldn't say to another person. Imagine typing a self-critical judgement that recently popped into your mind (e.g. 'You are so stupid') as a WhatsApp message. Would you send that message to a close friend? You'd certainly think twice about it, yet all too frequently your inner critic trolls you with that kind of content.

Each of us has an inner critic that has been gestating for years, fed by an accumulation of criticism directed at us personally, or criticism we've witnessed being directed at others. While on one level the inner critic may help us to anticipate and reduce the risk of criticism from others, it can also cause considerable problems. For example, a review of the research findings from sixteen different studies found that students with a high level of self-criticism were more likely to be depressed over time. We might also find that our inner critic starts to play too prominent a role in influencing how we behave – for example, the perfectionist striving that we focused on on p. 185 can develop as an often-futile attempt to allay the inner critic's concerns. Momentary moves relating to self-compassion can help reduce the impact that the inner critic has on our behaviour.

According to Kristin Neff, a psychologist and pioneer in the art and science of compassion based at the University of Texas in Austin, self-compassion has three components:

1. **Mindfulness** – The ability to notice and be open to experiencing challenging thoughts about oneself without over-identifying with them (which, as noted previously, corresponds to the Anchored and Willing aspects of a flexible mind).

2. **Common humanity** – Being able to appreciate that experiencing challenges and failures is part of what it is to be human.
3. **Self-kindness** – The ability to direct compassion towards oneself, including at times of setback when self-critical thoughts might occur.

Research has consistently shown that low levels of self-compassion strongly predict the development and maintenance of a range of mental health difficulties. Psychological theories have proposed that the care we receive in early life can play an important role in influencing the extent to which we can be self-compassionate throughout our lives. If caregivers respond to our needs in a consistently compassionate way, then we are better placed to learn how to be compassionate towards ourselves. Unfortunately, not all of us will have been blessed with consistent compassionate care. The good news, however, is that self-compassion is a skill that we can learn throughout our lives, and increases in self-compassion are associated with better mental health. For example, a research study that followed 1,090 adults living in San Diego County, USA, for an average of five years found that increases in levels of self-compassion were associated with improvements in mental wellbeing across the adult lifespan. Interestingly, the same study found that greater increases across time in the compassion that participants felt *towards others* was also associated with improvements in mental wellbeing.

Psychological interventions aimed at boosting self-compassion – such as 'compassion-focused therapy' (CFT) and 'mindful self-compassion' – have also been shown to be effective for reducing the impact of experiences such as rumination, self-criticism, depression and anxiety. But learning to be more self-compassionate is not without its challenges. Experiencing shame (*I'm a bad person*), guilt (*I have done bad things*) and rejection (*I am not liked by others*) can leave us feeling unworthy of compassion from ourselves. We can also be fearful about the consequences that being self-compassionate might bring. For example, many of my clients express concerns such as: 'I'll be letting myself off the hook', 'My standards will slip', 'I'll lose my edge' . . . Threat mode rails against self-compassion. But self-compassion isn't weak, it's wise – it helps us flourish rather than flounder. If you notice that you are experiencing blocks and fears about practising self-compassion, using the principles outlined in Part II to develop a more flexible mind will be an important first step for ensuring that challenging thoughts and feelings about self-compassion don't impede your ability to benefit from it.

One tough mudder

Amelia Boone loves overcoming obstacles. She should; she's a world champion at it. The American excels in obstacle-course racing – a sport that requires competitors to jump through fire, crawl under barbed wire, scale walls, shimmy up ropes and traverse stretches of mud and water using only their own physical strength and stamina. It's a gruelling sport. Boone has won the Spartan World Championship and the World's Toughest Mudder on multiple occasions. She is also a qualified attorney and, at the time of writing this book, she works at Apple Inc.

Boone has had to deal with considerable obstacles away from the racecourse. In a post on her blog in 2019, she opened up about her experience of disordered eating and the treatment she was receiving for anorexia nervosa, which she had been battling for twenty years. A few months earlier, Boone had taken a leave of absence from her job in order to voluntarily attend an eating disorder treatment facility. 'I had a sense that there was more that could be had from life, and I needed to take a leap of faith to do it – one that required stepping out of my life for the short term in order to re-engage in it fully in the long term,' she wrote, before adding, 'Disorder and shame thrive in the darkness and silence, so I'm thrusting my disorder and shame into the light where [they have] no place left to hide.'

In a 2021 interview, Boone spoke in further detail about what she had found to be most helpful for dealing with feelings of shame. Reflecting on her experience of recent injury setbacks, she said:

> *You're angry, then you're angry at yourself for being angry, so you're ashamed of that, and then you get in this vicious shame spiral ... The only way out of it is to look at yourself with compassion. Instead of being angry at yourself, give love and self-compassion. One of the turning points for me was realizing how easy it is for me to forgive others for their faults, but I could never show that toward myself. It's been this active practice of learning to forgive myself.*

Putting self-compassion into practice

Research has shown that special forms of meditation collectively called 'loving-kindness and compassion meditation' (or LKCM), which anyone can practise, increase people's levels of self-compassion and compassion towards others. The origins of these kinds of meditation can be traced back to ancient times, and they have been a mainstay of Eastern philosophies such as Buddhism. LKCM are also referred to by the Pali word *mettā* (note the double 't' here, as opposed to the *meta* of meta-awareness), which translates as 'loving-kindness'. In recent years, their use has spread to a range of secular settings, including schools, prisons and mental health services, with the aim of alleviating distress and promoting wellbeing. Reviews of the research evidence have found that LKCM/*mettā* can be effective at reducing symptoms of anxiety and depression. Not only can these practices change how we feel, but they can also lead to structural changes in how our brains function.

When using *mettā* in my practice, I invite clients to sit comfortably with their eyes closed, or if they prefer, they can keep their eyes open and fix a soft gaze on the floor in front of them. I then guide them to think of a series of different people – one at a time. With each person in turn, the client is invited to direct the following kind and compassionate wishes to them: 'May you [i.e. the person I specify] be happy, may you be safe, may you be healthy, may you be free from suffering.' The series of people that I ask clients to think about starts with an initial focus on someone for whom they care deeply, before proceeding to themselves, then someone in their community whom they don't know particularly well, then someone towards whom they feel a level of acrimony, before finally focusing on all beings.

If any of that seems like it would be challenging to you, you are not alone. The Threat and Get modes can squeeze our capacity to be compassionate. Why would we practise compassion towards those who have wronged us? Well, it's not about forgetting their wrongs; it's about letting go of the resentment we feel towards them – resentment that can consume us from the inside out. As the fifth-century Indian sage Buddhaghosha once wrote: 'Holding on to anger is like grasping a hot coal with the intent of throwing it at someone else; you are the one who gets burned.' Compassion grows in the places where it is nurtured. It gets stronger the more it is practised, and practising it in relation to those who may have wronged us can do much to strengthen it.

A second example that I use with clients is the 'Compassionate Colour' exercise. Again, I invite the client to close their eyes if they are comfortable to do so. I then instruct them to draw their attention to a part of their body where they notice the air coming in and going out as they breathe. After they have noticed that felt experience of several breaths, I ask them to think of a colour they associate with the experience of compassion, which I describe to them as an experience of kind, resolute support. After allowing them time to reflect on this, I guide them to visualize the compassionate colour surrounding them. I ask them to imagine that the colour is entering through their heart area and slowly making its way through their bloodstream, infusing the experience of compassion throughout their body. I encourage the client to focus on the colour as having qualities of wisdom, warmth and kindness. The client is reminded that the sole purpose of this colour is to support them. I caution that blocks and barriers might arise in their thinking (for example, they may think that they don't deserve to benefit from the colour's support). I advise that if that happens, they should acknowledge these distractions and gently bring their focus back to their compassionate colour. After a minute or two of allowing the client to experience this, I draw the exercise to a close and ask them to open their eyes. We then reflect on their experience of the exercise and what they noticed. Finally, we discuss how the client can use their compassionate colour to create momentary moves in everyday life. Aisha, a forty-two-year-old schoolteacher, had been struggling with her inner critic for many years. When we completed this exercise together, she indicated that her compassionate colour was a warm orange shade. To help remind her of this exercise, she changed the lock screen on her smart phone to a warm orange.

Finally, there is also a very brief practice known as a 'self-compassion break' that can be used to help engender compassion towards oneself and others. This is a series of three statements that we can say inwardly to ourselves that capture the three components of self-compassion identified by Kristin Neff (mindfulness, common humanity and kindness). Examples of statements that capture these respective elements of self-compassion are as follows:

1. I'm going through a challenging time.
2. All people go through a challenging time.
3. May I respond with kindness.

Integrating self-compassion practices such as these into your daily routine can provide rich opportunities for momentary moves that will charge up your Reset mode. Building a more compassionate self will benefit both you and those around you.

Former ABC anchorman Dan Harris is, by his own admission, a reluctant convert to practising self-compassion. In a TED Talk enti-tled 'The Benefits of Not Being a Jerk to Yourself', Harris revealed how a review of his behaviour in the workplace had highlighted that he could be rude to junior members of staff, emotionally guarded, and authoritarian in his interactions. Making a commitment to get to grips with his anger and self-centredness led Harris to explore the role that self-compassion could play. He decided to sign up for an intensive nine-day programme in LKCM/*mettā*. The instructor of the programme explained to Harris that the quest to be nicer to other people needed to begin with him being nicer to himself. She instructed him and the other attendees on ways they could develop their abilities to express compassion to themselves. Harris wasn't convinced. He was too caught up in cycles of self-recrimination and frustration to engage with the instruction. But five days into the programme, he relented. In his TED Talk, he describes the fateful moment when he placed his hand on his heart and said to himself, in his own inimitable style: 'It's all good, dude. I know this sucks, but I've got you.' This extension of warmth towards himself was the first important step on a road that has helped him to improve his relationship with himself and others. 'Self-love, properly understood not as narcissism but as in having your own back, is not selfish; it makes you better at loving other people,' he says towards the end of his talk. Like Harris, we can use the words that work best for us. When it comes to self-compassion, it's not so much *what* is said but *how* it is said – a little bit of warmth, kindness and support go a long way.

Garbage in, garbage out

In business and computing, the phrase 'garbage in, garbage out' (GIGO) is used to capture how the quality of outputs is determined by the quality of the inputs – bad materials make for bad products. The same is true of our bodies and our minds. To thrive mentally, we need to provide our minds with the resources they need – and we need to do the same for our bodies. It's important that we do our best to establish routines in relation to sleep, exercise and nutrition that help us to safeguard our physical and mental health. This is an act of self-kindness, too. The Centre for Disease Control and Prevention in the USA recommends that adults have:

- a minimum of seven hours sleep per night
- a minimum of two and a half hours of moderate aerobic activity each week, along with strength exercises on two or more days a week working all the major muscles
- a healthy approach to eating (this means a diet that includes fruits, vegetables and wholegrains, a variety of sources of protein, and foods low in added sugar, sodium and saturated fat – and also that our calorie intake should be balanced against our energy expenditure)

Sleep (and opportunities to rest), exercise and good nutrition are of course topics that merit books of their own. I am a big admirer of Peter Attia's excellent book *Outlive: The Science and Art of Longevity*. Remember too that recommendations relating to sleep, exercise and diet are precisely that – recommendations, not rules. If we are too rigid in our fervour to adhere to recommendations, it can create more difficulties than it resolves. Again, the 'strong intention, light attachment' approach is apt here. Be flexible with those '*Oh crap, I'm not going to get my seven hours' sleep*' and the '*I'm a lost cause for missing the last two spin classes*' thoughts. We are all human and we will all err. It's important to forgive ourselves when we do. Momentary moves relating to self-compassion can help with that. Each new moment brings new choices that allow us to renew our commitment to following recommendations and advice that we have drifted away from.

Bold moves

In contrast to momentary moves, bold moves are a more significant – and potentially more radical – undertaking. These could be things like taking a career break, relinquishing a role or opting to change course to pursue a new long-term project. Bold moves take time to plan and implement, and they require us to commit to making courageous choices. When we have a clear purpose in mind, goals to achieve and yearnings to satisfy, we can be resistant to the idea of making bold moves. For many of us, continuing apace on the trajectory we are already on seems easier than choosing not to. The temptation is just to keep doing what we've been doing. But this inflexibility can breed exhaustion and disillusionment.

I use the phrase 'cups and candles' a lot with my clients. They operate in worlds where people frequently find themselves 'pouring from empty cups' and 'burning candles at both ends'. 'Cups and candles', then, is shorthand for the unrelenting pressure we can feel to do more, and the counterproductive impact this can have. It takes flexibility to relent. Bold moves are flexibility in action. When the situation requires it, bold moves help us to access Reset mode so that we can maintain our ability to thrive in the long run. They help us to step back, be inspired, realign with our purpose and replenish our energy levels. In recent years, there have been some high-profile examples of people being prepared to make bold moves.

The Danish chef René Redzepi is the co-owner of Noma, a three-Michelin-star restaurant in Copenhagen that won first prize in the World's 50 Best Restaurants Awards in 2021. Despite its phenomenal success, the restaurant will close at the end of 2024. Why? In an article in the *New York Times*, Redzepi described the pressures faced by those working in the fine-dining industry. 'It's unsustainable . . . Financially and emotionally, as an employer and as a human being, it just doesn't work,' he said. Instead of continuing to operate the restaurant, Redzepi will focus on developing a food-production company that he said would 'prove to the world that you can grow old and be creative and have fun in the industry . . . instead of [doing] hard, gruelling, low-paid work under poor management conditions that wears people out'.

In January 2023, Jacinda Ardern, who had been the Prime Minister of New Zealand for the previous five and a half years, made the shock announcement that she was resigning. In addition to coordinating her country's response to the COVID-19 pandemic, her premiership spanned several national tragedies, including a deadly attack on two Christchurch mosques and a volcanic eruption on Whakaari Island. During a news conference announcing her decision, Ardern said: 'I know what this job takes. And I know that I no longer have enough in the tank to do it justice. It's that simple . . . I am human, politicians are human. We give all that we can for as long as we can. And then it's time. And for me, it's time.' Eight months later, she was interviewed on ABC's *Good Morning America*. 'One of the things I wanted to do was be more present for my family, so I'm certainly trying to do that,' she explained to co-anchor Robin Roberts, before adding, 'But also, I still want to be useful.' And to that end, she had accepted a fellowship at Harvard University, which allowed her to pursue her passion for learning. Her work at the university focused on reducing the risks posed by online extremism. In the interview, she also revealed that she was furthering her commitment to environmental issues by becoming a trustee of the Prince of Wales's prestigious Earthshot Prize initiative. Adern's reset had been revitalizing.

Redzepi and Ardern provide high-profile examples of conscientious and determined people who have demonstrated a willingness to make bold moves and shift into *Reset* mode so that they can continue to move towards their purpose. But there are many less high-profile examples of people making bold moves.

The 'Great Resignation'

Since early 2021, when the COVID-19 pandemic was continuing to wreak its havoc, there has been a marked increase in the number of people voluntarily resigning from their jobs. The term 'the Great Resignation' has been coined to capture this trend. A 2023 report published by the PwC accounting firm, which surveyed more than 53,000 people working in the labour market across forty-six countries and territories, indicated that resignations were on the rise. This was the fourth such report published in successive years since 2019. More than a quarter of the employees surveyed in 2023 indicated that they were likely to change jobs in the coming year – up by nearly a fifth from 2022. Potential reasons for this highlighted in the report included employees feeling overworked, believing that they can't be themselves at work, and noticing a reduction in disposable income. In their reporting of the findings, PwC also highlight '(p)urpose, company culture and inclusion' as important considerations for those working in today's labour market. While the word 'resignation' makes for attention-grabbing headlines, quitting a job is only part of the story. What we may be looking at here is 'the Great Redirection'. The pandemic and associated disruption have provided us all with

THE TREE THAT BENDS

the opportunity to reflect, reprioritize and reorientate how we wish to live our lives – and many of us have made bold moves of our own.

Beautifully messy

As you formulate plans for a bold move, you can almost hear the howls of incredulity from others: 'You're going to do *what?!*' Even if you never hear it, you fear it – what will other people think? And then there are your own doubts and concerns ('I'm mad to even contemplate this'). In a documentary interview, the two-time Golden Globe-winning actor Jim Carrey is asked the following question by the American director and producer Judd Apatow: 'How hard is it to slow down, take breaks, to not feel the need to be the most successful person?' Carrey's response is brutally illuminating:

> *I wouldn't know what that feels like, Judd. I wouldn't know* [smiling broadly]. *Ah . . . it's fucking terrifying. It's fuck-ing terr-i-fy-ing. Because what if the train leaves, and you can never get back on? That's the key. What if it leaves, and I can never get back on, and they go, 'Too bad dude, you looked a gift horse in the mouth, [you] should never have done that.*

Contemplating bold moves can leave us feeling vulnerable, hollow and translucent: a ghost trapped in a spotlight's glare. All of which has the potential to tip us into Threat mode. However, Reset mode provides opportunities to address the vulnerability that arises when we contemplate bold moves.

The fear and reluctance we feel around making bold moves reveals itself in the obstinate language of our self-talk. For example, imperative phrases beginning 'I need to . . .' (e.g. 'I need to be per-fect'), 'I must . . .' (e.g. 'I must exude confidence at all times'), and 'I should . . .' (e.g. 'I should keep doing what I do best') popping up in our self-talk are indicators of the ego's desperate attempts to avoid the vulnerability that can arise at times of jeopardy. The underlying message is that we will be judged harshly by others and/or ourselves unless we act in a particular way. In addition, prohibitive phrases beginning 'I can't . . .' (e.g. 'I can't learn new skills'), 'I mustn't . . .' (e.g. 'I mustn't look inept'), 'I shouldn't . . .' (e.g. 'I shouldn't speak up in front of other people') that crop up in our self-talk are indi-cators that vulnerability is lurking close by. These forms of self-talk are intended to guard against the risk of messing up, looking silly or being on the receiving end of other people's disapproval. No one wants to feel the sting of self-conscious emotions such as embarrass-ment, guilt and shame. But complying with this self-talk means that we live life small. In avoiding the risk of being vulnerable, we lose out on opportunities to get into the transforming zone. In avoiding going out on the skinny branches, we lose out on the juiciest fruit. Adopting a flexible mind, and the Willingness aspect in particular, helps us to recognize that vulnerability is the gateway to transformation. In this way, vulnerability is *possibility*. In fact, transformation won't be possible if we aren't prepared to be vulnerable. Reset mode allows us to tend to feelings of vulnerability rather than being blocked by them, so that we can maintain our efforts to do what matters in the longer term.

'The beautiful mess effect' is a term that has been coined to capture the way we consistently appraise our own vulnerability more negatively than we do the vulnerability of others. Research evidence indicates that contrary to what we might think, other people tend to see our expressions of vulnerability as beautifully courageous rather than as a sign of us being an emotional mess. One potential explanation for this is provided by construal level theory. This theory proposes that our perception of threat is influenced by how psychologically distant we are from it. 'Psychological distance' is influenced by a range of factors, including whether a threat is expected imminently, whether it is physically close to us, whether it has affected people we know, and how likely it is to occur. Because our own sense of vulnerability is so immediate to us, the potential costs associated with it loom large on our psychological horizon. The threat is tangible. Because we are less intimate with other people's unique experience of vulnerability, we are better placed to appreciate the potential benefits, rather than the costs, of their sharing. What feels like vulnerability from the inside looks like bravery from the outside.

When we express rather than suppress vulnerability, it provides opportunities for us to receive support and care from others. Importantly, it also helps to build safety and trust for others to do the same. This is a point that Nick Cox, Director of Manchester United Football Club's Academy, alluded to when he said:

> *Part of your role as a leader is if you can show your own vulnerabilities and weaknesses and insecurities, then the people around you will do the same and there's a ripple effect . . . I think if I can do that to my immediate staff, they can then do that to the young people that they are then associated with . . . You have to model the behaviours that you expect everyone else in your organization to be able to demonstrate.*

Of course, consider carefully who you are prepared to be vulnerable with. Although people can respond supportively, it can't be guaranteed. So, if you are contemplating being vulnerable, do it on your own terms, and opt for people whom you can trust. By its very nature, however, being vulnerable will never feel completely safe. There will always be some risk to accompany the potential reward. Research has shown that people with higher levels of self-compassion view the prospect of expressing their own vulnerability no more negatively than they judge someone else doing the same. In this way, self-compassion can act as an enabler – it helps bolster our ability to show up to our own vulnerability. Every bold move requires its fair share of momentary moves.

A change is (nearly) as good as a rest

In addition to working directly with clients, a key part of my work involves offering supervision to other psychological practitioners who work with athletes, musicians and/or business executives. We discuss the work that the practitioner is doing with their clients so that I can support their ongoing professional development. Emma (not her real name) is one such practitioner with whom I meet monthly. Emma had sought supervision from me to develop her competency in using the flexible mind approach. Indeed, the three aspects of the flexible mind – being Anchored, Willing and Empowered – were also informing our approach to these supervision sessions.

Emma is a conscientious, committed and talented psychologist. She splits her employment between two roles. For half the week, she is employed as a performance psychologist for a professional rugby team. For the remainder of the week, she is employed as an academic member of staff at a university where she teaches and conducts research. She has held these roles jointly for the last ten years. Both roles are demanding, and she often works more hours than she is paid for in both jobs. The combined salary and benefits provide for a comfortable lifestyle, but Emma has been noticing she has limited time during the week to do the things that she enjoys. In the months leading up to the commencement of the supervision, Emma had been becoming increasingly disillusioned about the impact that she was having in each of her professional roles. She also reported feeling powerless to exercise changes in her life, and having thoughts that she was letting her husband down by not being more present with him. It was clear that Emma was experiencing conflicts in the goals that she was working towards in her salaried jobs, family life and her personal aspirations. Bottom line: if the situation persisted, Emma was on the road to burnout.

During an online supervision session one sunny spring afternoon, we discussed her current workload and explored options for reconfiguring her working week. The discussions provided an opportunity to revisit her sense of purpose. I asked Emma what she would ideally choose to be doing in her work if she wasn't having to contend with the feelings of disillusionment and stress. She paused for a moment's reflection. She had been an accomplished tennis player in her youth, and it was the sport that she was most passionate about. In an ideal world, she would want to do freelance work supporting a small number of professional tennis players with whom she could work intensively. When I enquired about what this role would provide her, Emma talked about the freedom to be creative and have greater autonomy in how she worked and who she worked with. It was notable how Emma's demeanour and facial expression changed during the conversation. Not only could I hear the enthusiasm in her voice, but I could also see it in her eyes.

The conversation shifted to thinking about next steps. We talked about what potential options she could explore. Emma suggested that she could try to reconfigure her work with the rugby team to assume more of a management role whereby she could delegate more responsibilities to the other psychology practitioners based at the team. She said she would also discuss the possibility of reducing her hours at the university. We talked about some of the barriers she might face in initiating those conversations. She was able to recognize that concerns about being perceived as 'entitled' or 'ungrateful' by her colleagues could stop the conversations with her employers before they even began, and that feelings of anxiety and trepidation were showing up. There were also worries about the impact the reduction in her guaranteed income and pension contributions would bring. At the end of the session, Emma and I identified two action points: 1) she would reflect on whether the reward of choosing to pursue her passion for freelance work with tennis players would be worth the doubts and anxiety that would inevitably show up; 2) she would identify the personal values she would like to demonstrate if she chose to discuss these options with her colleagues.

It was two months before we were able to meet again. In the meantime, there had been some important developments. Emma had talked with the management team at the rugby club, and they had agreed to reconfigure her post so that she would have more line-management responsibility for the other psychology practitioners and less involvement in the frontline delivery of interventions. She had also initiated a conversation with the university about workload and hours of employment. This discussion had prompted Emma's line manager to suggest that she should apply for a promotion in recognition of the important contribution she had been making in her role. Emma's response? She tendered her resignation. She was clear that more money and additional responsibilities weren't what she wanted. A fuse had been lit and it wasn't for being extinguished. She had decided to reset, and she was determined to follow through on it. A key motivation to act that Emma identified was the realization that she was being unkind – to herself. If she didn't make changes, she would be sacrificing her health and her purpose. The personal values of doing things authentically, courageously and committedly that she had identified as being important following the last session were shining through.

If, like Emma, you have noticed discontentment showing up in an area of your life (work, relationships, community life, etc.) the following questions, which contribute to a process I refer to as 'preparing for a bold move', will be helpful to consider:

- What would you ideally choose to be doing in that life domain if you weren't having to contend with the feelings of discontent?
- What impact would making that choice be likely to have on how you think, feel and act?
- What opportunities exist to implement those kinds of changes in that life domain?
- What barriers might you face in pursuing those opportunities?
- Do the potential benefits mean that those barriers are worth confronting?
- What options do you have for overcoming those barriers?
- What concrete steps will you now take?

Being deliberate in identifying and considering potential barriers when we are contemplating change is a crucial step. Gabriele Oettingen, a German psychologist based at New York University, and her colleagues refer to this process as 'mental contrasting' – we are contrasting the benefits with potential costs. Research has shown that engaging in mental contrasting increases the likelihood of achieving various goals, including adhering to nutritional plans, improving academic performance, engaging in physical activities, and improvements in other physical health outcomes.

Not long after that supervision session with Emma, I made a bold move of my own.

Writer's block

It was September 2023. I was in a hotel room on the twenty-eighth floor, and my eyes were tracing the route of a freeway that snakes westward towards Nevada's Spring Mountain Range. The sky had been a blanket of grey clouds all afternoon, but the sun was breaking through. And I was breaking through, too.

My wife Suzy and I were in Las Vegas to belatedly celebrate her fortieth birthday – the pandemic and associated travel chaos had put paid to the original plan. We were in town to see the Irish rock band U2 play at the brand-new $2.3 billion Sphere concert venue. The timing of the trip coincided with the rapidly approaching deadline for the completion of this book. In the months leading up to the trip, I had hoped that there might be cause for a double celebration – perhaps the manuscript might be finished, too? But as September drew close, it was clear that this wouldn't be the case. I was discovering that finishing a book project is harder than starting one. As you may well know, the creative process is not a linear one, and progress had slowed. I was experiencing a bout of 'writer's block', and the harder I pushed for inspiration, the more elusive it seemed to be. The trip to Las Vegas provided a welcome opportunity for a bold move towards a reset: spending quality time with the person I love, exploring new places and having different experiences.

On the first day of the trip, we visited the West Rim of the Grand Canyon. The journey took us through the arid, unforgiving landscape of southern Nevada and northern Arizona. Our first stop was the Eagle Point visitors' centre, which features a twenty-metre-long horseshoe-shaped glass skywalk that extends over the edge of the canyon. Looking down through the glass to the bottom of the canyon more than 4,000 feet below was an unforgettable experience. As I walked, I could see ravens flying hundreds of feet beneath my feet. After grabbing lunch, we proceeded to our second stop at Guano Point, which provided stunning views of the red and brown striations of rock that form the layers of the canyon walls. Wonder was in plentiful supply!

On the way back to Las Vegas, we stopped off at the Mike O'Callaghan–Pat Tillman Memorial Bridge, which affords excellent vistas of the Hoover Dam. Suzy and I walked out to the middle of the bridge. I took a moment to peer over the rail at the blue water of the Colorado river, 890 feet below. Like the view through the floor of the Grand Canyon Skywalk, the effect of looking down at the water was dizzying. For an instant, I was transported back to New Zealand in 2003, standing on the Ledge overlooking Queenstown, preparing for my bungee jump. The memory of the fear I'd felt before I jumped flashed through my mind, as did the awareness that facing my fear and jumping anyway had allowed me to experience something transformative on the other side of it. Walking back towards the coach, I reflected on how I was going to respond to the fears and concerns I was having about this book. The answer was clear – I would be kind to myself and true to the sense of purpose that had led me to start the book. I placed my hand on my chest and said silently to myself, 'Keep going – one word after another.'

On the Saturday afternoon of our trip, Suzy and I hopped into an Uber to make our way to one of the city's malls to buy gifts for family. As he drove us, our warm and friendly driver, a self-confessed burger connoisseur, gave us lots of great restaurant suggestions. Recognizing that his accent wasn't from the USA, I asked Lenny where he had lived prior to coming to Las Vegas.

'Guess,' he replied with a glint in his eye.

'Hmmm, Central Europe? Hungary, maybe?' I ventured.

'You're not the first person to guess Central Europe. I get Romania a lot.' He chuckled.

Intrigued and not knowing where to try next, I said, 'OK, tell us.'

'Iraq!' Lenny announced with glee. He went on to explain that he had worked for the US military as a translator, and had been granted a visa after being forced to flee the country.

'Some very bad things happened that meant I had to leave,' Lenny said.

He had managed to get a job working as a computer pro-grammer, but had recently been laid off, so he was working as an Uber driver for some steady income between jobs. I mentioned that, thanks to working on a project to develop and evaluate psy-chological and social supports for those forcibly displaced due to conflict, I knew a little about the types of challenges he may have faced. I asked him what had helped him get through. He responded by saying that while there is a lot that he could feel pessimistic about, that's not how he chooses to live his life. He has dreams and aspirations that he wants to pursue. He indicated that rather than struggling against the pain and misfortune of the past, he was willing to accept all those difficult yesterdays, so that he could focus on building a new life today. The hairs stood up on the back of my neck as I listened. Lenny was flexibility in action. Arriving at our destination, we thanked Lenny and wished him all the best for the future. As the car drove off, I stood on the tarmac outside the mall, slowly shaking my head, humbled by Lenny's grace, courage and humility.

We went to the gig on the Saturday night. It was breath-taking to see how U2 and their production team had utilized the Sphere's cutting-edge technology to combine their music with stunning visuals on the 160,000-square-foot LED display that lines the entire interior shell of the structure. There was a moment in the concert that moved me profoundly. As the band performed the song 'With or Without You', the visuals featured a huge orb floating on water behind them (a sphere within the Sphere). As the song progressed, the orb could be seen rotating on the water's surface, drawing ever closer. As it started to dwarf the audience, an aperture on the surface of the orb spun into view. The spinning of the orb stopped, and it became clear that aperture was expanding to encompass the entire audi-torium. As the song reached its crescendo, we were pulled into a dazzling kaleidoscope of white and gold light, which suddenly burst – genesis-like – into a patchwork of a thousand different animals that coated the entirety of the Sphere's inner lining. It was a stunning moment – a near-birth experience. A moment of wonder writ large. Bono later explained to the audience that the animals were all species native to the state of Nevada. The Skywalk, the dam, Lenny and U2. There was so much to marvel at during the trip. We felt blessed to have had the opportunity to be there.

On our last night, as we sped back to the hotel in a taxi, I smiled as I caught sight of the signage of a bookstore and coffee shop in the rear-view mirror. The name of the store? 'The Writer's Block'.

How will we know when to reset?

In Chapter 6, we discussed how strategies such as pre-commitment pledges, getting to know the early-warning signs of our own exhaustion, and inviting others to check in on us can be helpful for keeping Get mode in check. Well, they can be used to help us transition into Reset mode too. Just as a tree needs to be alert to the signs of the encroaching winter and use autumn to adjust accordingly, we can anticipate our own need to move into Reset mode and plan accordingly. Being proactive about building opportunities for momentary and bold moves when we are questioning our goals (see p. 163) will also reduce the risk that we neglect Reset mode.

Psychological periodization

The concept of periodization, which is used to help athletes physically prepare for competition, is relevant here too. Introduced in the

1960s by a Russian physiologist called Leo Matveyev, periodization involves an athlete preparing for an upcoming event by dividing their training into blocks (or 'periods') of training that vary in form, volume and intensity. This helps to build strength and fitness, reduce risk of injury and optimize performance when it matters most. Periodization allows athletes to focus on timescales of varying length: macrocycles, which typically involve planning for periods that last for years (e.g. the four-year cycles between competitions including the FIFA World Cup and the Olympic Games); mesocycles, which tend to relate to periods up to a month; and microcycles, which last up to a week. Irrespective of what timescale is used, rest and recuperation are key elements that will be specifically built into the programme. There are two main types of periodization: linear and undulating. Linear periodization involves cycles in which an athlete focuses on one goal, such as improving their strength, by progressively increasing the intensity of an exercise (e.g. the weight they are lifting) while simultaneously reducing the volume of that exercise (e.g. the number of times that the weight is lifted). Undulating cycles, on the other hand, allow an athlete to focus on developing two or more goals at the same time, such as increasing both strength and power (power being how much force can be exerted in a set time) by using either daily or weekly changes in both intensity and volume. Linear periodization is proposed to be better for beginners, whereas undulating periodization is suggested to be better for more experienced athletes.

A key aim of periodization is to improve athletic performance while preventing overtraining, and the risk of exhaustion and injury this can bring. In a similar vein, we can adopt what I refer to as a 'psychological periodization' approach to bring balance to our Get,

Threat and Reset modes. Both linear and undulating periodization draw attention to the need for us to be aware of the *number* of goals we might be aiming to achieve (e.g. applying for a work promotion might coincide with finding a new home), the *intensity* of the tasks we might be undertaking in relation to those goals (e.g. how much focused concentration might be required) and the *volume* of those tasks (e.g. the length of time that we allocate to undertaking them). In essence, with psychological periodization, we need to carefully consider how many goals we are simultaneously pursuing, adjust the time we allocate to tasks according to their intensity, and proactively build in opportunities for reset. Psychological periodization of this kind will require some planning, but my professional experience has shown that it can make a profound difference to our capacity to thrive.

It's important to emphasize that resets are intended to get us beyond our egocentric worldview rather than to furnish its ambitions. We can easily fall into the trap of 'using' Reset mode in an instrumental way, as a way of achieving some other end – for ourselves or others. Check your motivation. If you find yourself consistently using resets with the expressed aim of dreaming up the next big idea, that's a telltale sign that Get mode is still at the wheel. Or if you find yourself rushing to use resets only in a reactive way in the face of fear and anxiety – like engaging in LKCM/ *mettā* practices only when upset – that's a sign that Threat mode is reigning supreme. Do resets because you can. They are a key part of being and staying alive. Resets can be their own reward. That's what makes them counter-cultural – you won't know what will flow from them until you try them. Surrender to what they will bring. Relent more.

Like a tree dropping its leaves in the autumn, Reset mode offers us opportunities for revival, allowing the parasympathetic nervous system to both 'rest and digest' and 'tend and befriend'. Resets may not always require sustained periods of dormancy – a tree, for example, also resets by coming back to centre after a gust of wind. While resets might well be bold moves – major endeavours that help us to realign with our purpose – they can also be momentary moves – experiences of wonder, gratitude and compassion that reinvigorate our day-to-day lives. The concept of psychological periodization offers us a way of adjusting the intensity and volume of the tasks we undertake. So pervasive is the 'go, go, go' attitude of modern life that the very idea of accessing Reset mode can feel problematic, yet the AWE of a flexible mind encourages us to question the path that others (and indeed we ourselves) expect us to take and instead make the choices – and resets – that are uniquely right for us.

Reset: Summary Points

- Reset mode helps us to better appreciate ourselves and the world around us, and reorientate to our purpose.
- Momentary moves help us to access Reset mode through the experience of compassion, gratitude and/or wonderment.
- Self-compassion is a skill that we can learn to help with the experience of self-criticism and feelings of shame.
- Bold moves are larger commitments that help us to step back, get inspired, realign with our purpose, and feel renewed.
- Avoiding the experience of vulnerability limits our opportunities for transformation.
- Care should be taken to ensure that Reset mode doesn't simply become a means to an end. Reset is its own reward.
- We should be proactive in planning opportunities to reset.

CONCLUSION
Thrive

All too often, popular culture tells us that we will only achieve our goals through relentless sacrifice. But increasingly, the 'success is sacrifice' mantra is being exposed as a kind of Orwellian 'double-think' – ideas packaged together that are inherently contradictory. We are waking up to the reality that some of the approaches we can take to performing well in our chosen field can come at the cost of maintaining good levels of wellbeing. To my mind, that's not success, that's distress. Rising rates of burnout have signalled the need for a rethink. The concept of thriving has helped to highlight that we can do what matters without reducing ourselves to tatters.

All our lives are an unfolding game of give and take. Thriving is no different. While it is tempting to understand thriving as a balance between wellbeing and performance, this can be misleading. It could create a sense that there is some magical 'sweet spot' where harmony between wellbeing and performance can be maintained ad infinitum. But this belies the fact that the cultivation of purpose and doing what matters will be inconsistent in the demands it places on us. Sometimes, the emphasis will fall more on performing, and at other times the focus will shift to placing more attention on our wellbeing.

In this way, **thriving is a process of *blending*, in complementary ways, our efforts to both excel and feel well by flexibly striving, surviving and reviving according to what the situation requires.**

In essence, this book can be boiled down to 'Three threes and a tree'. The 'three threes' are:

1. the three aspects of a flexible mind (Anchored, Willing and Empowered)
2. the three psychological yearnings that provide intrinsic rewards (Autonomy, Relatedness and Mastery)
3. the three motivational modes (Get, Threat and Reset)

The tree has been our central metaphor throughout this book, used to illustrate how the three aspects of a flexible mind can help us to switch – or, indeed, maintain – motivational modes depending on what the situation demands. Just like us, trees thrive by flexibly responding to the challenges and changes that arise in their environments. The roots, trunk and crown of the tree are all integral to that process, just as being Anchored, Willing and Empowered are integral to our own thriving.

Striving, surviving and reviving

Over the course of the book, we learned that our evolutionary history has hardwired us to experience three motivational modes that govern our behaviour – Get, Threat, and Reset (see the diagram overleaf). These motivational modes exert a strong influence on how our attention is deployed and the choices that we make:

- **Get** mode steers our attention towards potential reward and motivates choices that direct us *to strive* for rewards.
- **Threat** mode directs attention to sources of danger – both real and imagined – and spurs choices that help us to *survive*.
- **Reset** mode invites us to bring our attention to the world around us and facilitates choices that provide opportunities for us to *revive*.

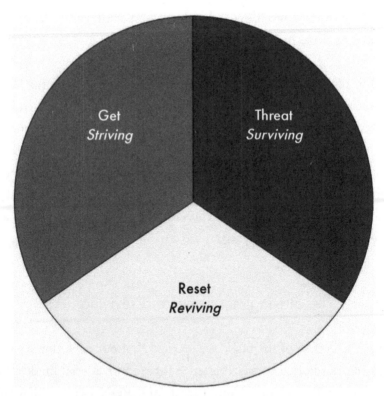

The three modes of motivation

There will be times when behaviours consistent with Get mode's striving (e.g. pursuing, persevering, competing) will be most appropriate for the contexts in which we find ourselves. But equally, there will be times when behaviours that are characteristic of Threat mode's surviving (e.g. asserting, defending, protecting) or indeed Reset mode's reviving (e.g., appreciating, nurturing, reorientating) will be more appropriate. Yet, we can become overly reliant on our perceived 'strong suits' – our tried and trusted ways of behaving. When this happens, we can get stuck in a motivational mode; we lose sight of the context and become rigid in how we react. This can create problems. Too much Get mode, and we risk experiencing burnout; too much Threat mode, and life feels devoid of joy and vitality; too much Reset mode, and we struggle to build momentum in cultivating purpose. Instead, we must dynamically adjust our motivational modes to the situations in which we find ourselves.

The necessity of aligning motivation with context is evident in nature – and it's not just trees. Octopuses, squid and cuttlefish (collectively referred to as cephalopods) are species of sea life that can change the colour of their bodies. Thousands of cells called chromatophores that sit below the surface of their skin allow this transformation of colour. This process can be used to flash distinctive zebra-like designs across their bodies when they strive to attract a mate, or red when they're warning other cephalopods not to approach. At other times, they must survive the presence of predators by changing colour to blend in with their surroundings. All of this happens within a blink of the octopus's eye. It's crucial that these colour changes are precisely matched to what the context requires. At best, a failure to do so would prevent the cephalopod from finding a mate; at worst, it would make it top billing on the lunch menu of a host of aquatic predators. As Leon C. Megginson, then a Professor in the Business School at Louisiana State University, once wrote: 'It is not the strongest species that survive, nor the most intelligent, but the ones most adaptable to change.' The price of not adjusting to changes in our context can be catastrophic. For us humans, it is the flexibility formula – *Flexibility = Anchored × Willing × Empowered* – that allows us, like trees and cephalopods, to align our motivational mode to our context.

Bringing it all together

Over the course of the book, I have shared a range of practical tips intended to help you develop a flexible mind and navigate both within and between the Get, Threat and Reset modes, whatever your circumstances. But just reading the insights and techniques that I have shared throughout this book is not a magic formula for thriving, any more than reading a recipe book written by Gordon Ramsay guarantees a tasty meal. *You* are the most vital ingredient. You need to put the guidance into practice. Understanding flexibility is one thing, but enacting it will be crucial to helping you thrive.

To help consolidate your efforts to thrive moving forward, you might find it helpful to use a two-stage process that incorporates the various components of *The Tree That Bends*.

First, check in on your motivational mode. This can be done by asking the following questions:

- Am I in Get, Threat or Reset mode right now?
- How is this mode serving the situation I find myself in?

- What costs might it be incurring? (Where do I stand on the 'Is my current pace sustainable?' question mentioned in Chapter 6?)
- Would I be best off staying in this mode or switching to another mode to maintain my ability to thrive in cultivating my purpose?

Now use your flexibility skills.

- Be Anchored in the here and now, and recognize that you have thoughts and feelings – those thoughts and feelings don't have you.
- Be Willing to notice the stories your mind might be generating about the situation, and the feelings that are showing up with those stories with an attitude of detached curiosity.
- Be Empowered in either changing your behaviour or sticking with it to honour your purpose.

We also need to be flexible, and self-compassionate, about flexibility itself; it's important to recognize that we won't be flexible *all* the time. The key thing is to notice when we've become rigid in our responding – that's the moment of 'awakening' that can allow us to bring to bear the AWE of a flexible mind. Developing our meta-awareness (for example, by practising mindfulness) will help us with those noticing skills.

It's also worth noting that other people may not universally welcome the progress that you make when you apply these steps. It's possible that others will be frightened by your flexibility and the freedom that it affords you. It may throw into sharp relief the lack of freedom that they have owing to their own persisting inflexibility. Don't be deterred. We all have to assume responsibility for our own thriving.

The wish to thrive is as old as humankind itself. While critics of neoliberalism might question the desire to thrive, seeing it as part of some cynical, advanced-capitalist grand plan to enslave you so that corporations can carry on getting richer, the processes of striving, surviving and reviving have been integral to what it is to be human throughout our entire history. Hopefully you've read enough in this book to know that thriving is about staying true to your own purpose, not someone else's.

Allow me to emphasize the following points about thriving:

- There's absolutely nothing wrong with wanting to do things well. The yearning for mastery is one of our three basic psychological needs. And there's nothing wrong with wanting to feel well. **But there *is* something deeply concerning about ignoring indications that we are *not* thriving**, such as: being overworked and feeling burned out; feeling distant from what matters to us; living our lives too much in the past or in the future; and lagging in rigid, restricted patterns of behaviour that are diminishing our ability to pursue what we are passionate about in life.

- Some might question whether the concept of thriving puts too much responsibility on you to be the agent of change and lets societal institutions 'off the hook'. Well, **for societies to change, individuals have to act**. And when we join forces and engage in collective action to address injustices that are limiting our ability to excel and feel well, this can bring about considerable change. The Arab Spring, Black Lives Matter, the #MeToo movement and campaigns against press intrusion have all prompted societal reckonings demonstrating what can be done when people coordinate their actions.

- Thriving is not an overly individualistic concern. It is in part; you matter, after all. Being able to have autonomy and exercise personal agency in the choices you make is a yearning that we all share. But a flexible mind's capacity to help us engage with our purpose means that others can rally to the flag we fly – or we can rally to the flags that others fly. In my work with clients, I have been struck by the ways in which people want to make a difference to those around them, whether it's through contributing to charitable causes, fighting injustice or protecting the planet. It's all too easy to assume that people's base motives are selfish. To me, that's a lazy and cynical assumption. Sure, people want to be comfortable and to make sure that those they care about are too. But there is a difference between being *selfful* – ensuring that our own needs are adequately met – and being *selfish*. Striving for achievements and enhancing our wellbeing need not be at the cost of everyone else – indeed, many of my clients derive a sense of wellbeing from supporting and feeling connected with others. This speaks to the final psychological yearning of relatedness. **Our ability to connect with others is important, not just for our psychological wellbeing but also for our physical health.**

- Thriving is not a subversive ploy contrived by big business. Far from it. Unscrupulous business leaders have reason to fear thriving as a focus of our attention, because it shines a revealing light on the more superficial 'well-washing' approaches that they might be tempted to use. Well-washing has been defined as practices, intentional or otherwise, that seemingly promote wellbeing cultures within an organization, but in fact offer only a tokenistic concern while failing to tackle the root causes of stress. Examples include organizations making a big deal about employees' mental health every 10 October to mark World Mental Health Day, but not addressing workplace bullying – or the folly of companies offering 'wellness days' that staff don't take up because they feel so anxious about the workload that will be waiting when they return to their desk. Even approaches that can be effective can be cynically co-opted to keep staff on site and be productive for longer – behold, the work email that reads: 'No need to seek mindfulness classes anywhere else; we're making them available in the building at the time you were meant to be eating lunch.' **The desire to thrive invites us to notice the extent to which our time, energy and effort are being co-opted without our informed consent**. That's the stuff that erodes another key psychological yearning – the need for autonomy. Emphasis on thriving helps to ensure we don't become complicit in our own exploitation.

Toxic Positivity

It's become vogue in recent years to label experiences as 'toxic' – so much so that the *Oxford English Dictionary* named 'toxic' as its word of the year for 2018, beating stiff competition from other contenders including 'gaslighting' and 'overtourism'. It seems that nothing is immune from being tainted with the pervasive, corrosive harm that toxicity brings – people, environments, workplaces, cultures, relationships, political agendas and masculinity can all become toxic. Even positivity can be toxic. Yes, too much positivity can be greeted with scepticism, suspicion and, um . . . negativity. The term 'toxic positivity' was coined to capture a collective delusion that we should be able to negate, erase, suppress or avoid the challenging thoughts and feelings that can accompany our experiences by reframing them as something positive. Toxic positivity dictates that life only has its upside. **But restricting the emotions we are willing to experience obstructs rather than enhances our opportunities to thrive.** We lose out on opportunities to understand the important functions that more challenging emotions can serve. While the positivity of maintaining a cheery disposition can bolster us in the face of setbacks, problems emerge when this approach is blindly applied, irrespective of the situation. Negativity has its role as well as its limits – in some contexts, it can help us anticipate and plan for undesirable outcomes or engender the support and encouragement of others, but if overused it becomes restrictive. Context matters, and as contexts change, we must retain the capacity to shift our outlook. We would never set out on a car journey having decided in advance to respond to each set of traffic lights in a particular way (e.g. to proceed with joyful abandon) irrespective of the colour they show. Instead, we stop at the red lights when they appear, we proceed when we see green lights, and we exercise some caution with amber lights. We don't deny the reality of the situation and the implications that it might have for us. This is what flexibility affords us: an ability to respond appropriately to the situations in which we find ourselves.

So, flexibility is not toxic positivity. Flexibility is about feeling it all. Whatever you're feeling isn't wrong. It doesn't need to be fixed, swapped out, suppressed or avoided. Your emotions, whatever they are, need to be acknowledged and understood: understood as an experience that *you have* (rather than an experience that *has you*), an experience that helps to highlight what you care about, and an experience that you can respond to in line with your purpose and personal values. Indeed, it's about resisting the urge to reductively judge emotions as being either positive or negative. There can be learning, cause for pause and possibilities in all the emotions we experience.

An unexpected beneficiary

I had started writing this book for you, but it turns out that I have also been writing it for myself. A friend of mine is fond of evoking the biblical verse 'Physician, heal thyself' (Luke 4:23). The inference of the proverb is that we need to guard against advising others to behave in certain ways when we are not prepared to do so ourselves. To support my own ability to thrive, I have decided to make a bold move of my own. The university at which I work allows employees to take a career break of up to twelve months of unpaid leave. After twenty-eight years of being in and around universities in Glasgow, Liverpool and Belfast, I realize that it is time for me to reorientate to my sense of purpose. A few things have happened over the course of writing this book that have culminated in me choosing this opportunity to reset. There have been incredible highs – I got married and became a stepdad to an amazing teenager. And there have been lows – for example, earlier this year I experienced a herniated disc in my neck, which, it turns out, is not just a pain in the neck, but also a pain in the back, shoulder and arm. Sadly, I also lost a friend to suicide: a talented, kind and conscientious person who was deeply appreciated by others. As I read through the messages of tribute posted on social media, my heart was heavy, weighed down by the cruel irony that the person who would have benefited most from reading them couldn't. This gave me much pause for thought. Both the highs and the lows have served to highlight what matters in my life. As important to me as research and teaching are, I also value opportunities to communicate important messages beyond the confines of academic settings, as well as the opportunities to learn new skills that help me to help others. I want to do deep work to support clients, train others and write for the public. I've had to contend with the vulnerability that has shown up as I've considered stepping away from a regular salary, the support of colleagues and the familiarity of well-established routines. As stultifying as loss aversion and 'gain fog' can be, the voice within that's articulating the need for a reset to help me thrive is too clear and insistent to ignore.

My Get and Threat systems have dictated the tempo and focus of my efforts too much in recent times. The needle on my 'thrivometer' has sometimes wavered – and yours will, too. I've used the Anchored, Willing and Empowered aspects of a flexible mind to modulate my focus on striving to initiate momentary moves, before finally making a bold move to access the opportunities to revive that Reset mode provides. And it takes effort. It would be disingenuous of me to pretend otherwise. We can't become complacent with our efforts to thrive.

Life throws heavy and unexpected punches, but developing a flexible mind will help us to roll with the blows and come back to centre so that, despite it all, we can prevail. Our capacity to face challenges is far more flexible than our minds give us credit for. I wish you well with your own next steps, as you harness the power of the tree within.

Appendices

The Tree That Bends

The Crown – *Empowered*
Acting in line with our personal values and purpose.

The Trunk – *Willing*
Accepting that our minds generate stories, and being willing to turn towards rather than away from the emotions that accompany those stories.

The Roots – *Anchored*
Situated in time and place, and able to recognize that thoughts and emotions come and go.

APPENDIX 2

The Primary Emotions

(See Chapter 2)

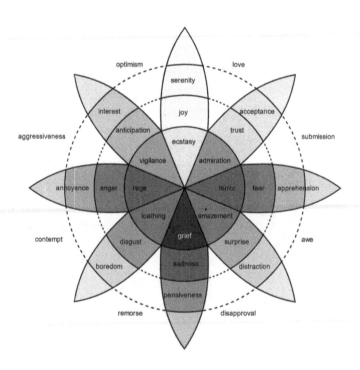

Anger arises when we feel that we are being undermined, perceive that an injustice has occurred, or experience a deep sense of frustration. It can incorporate elements of hostility and tension. When we are angry, we may express our displeasure and annoyance by shouting or swearing, and/or we may even engage in physical aggression against the source of our ire; all of which are behaviours that run the risk of planting the seeds for further problems. The experience of anger may serve to obscure other challenging emotions, such as fear or embarrassment – at least in the short term. The challenges of managing anger appropriately have been recognized for eons. It was Aristotle who warned that: 'Anyone can become angry – that is easy, but to be angry with the right person and to the right degree, at the right time, for the right purpose, and in the right way – that is not within everybody's power and is not easy.' According to Plutchik, **rage** is an intense form of anger. Other words that we may use to capture the experience of anger could include 'grumpy', 'irritated', 'cross' or 'livid'.

Fear is the emotion that is most intimately linked to an imminent sense of threat. Indeed, fear (and the related experience of **anxiety**) ratchets up our bodies' vital systems (e.g. increased heart rate, increased breathing, reduced blood flow to extremities, increased muscle tension) to enable us to be aggressive (fight), escape the situation (flight) or buy time (freeze) in response to threats. Plutchik proposed that **terror** is an intense version of fear. Despite the key role that fear can play in keeping us safe, research has shown that when fear starts to dominate our emotional experience, the effects on our psychological and physical health can be profound. Other words that we may use to capture the experience of fear could include 'petrified', 'terrified', 'quaking' or 'alarmed'.

Sadness is an emotional state that occurs when something or someone who is important to us is lost (e.g. the death of a loved one, the end of a relationship, a wish that did not come true). In addition to feelings of unhappiness, sadness can also involve a sense of despondency or defeat. Our expressions of sadness can act as a stimulus to encourage others to either provide support or cease aggression. There are risks that sadness may be confused with clinical depression. Sadness is a normal emotional reaction experienced at sombre moments, and it usually passes with time. Clinical depression, on the other hand, is a disorder that includes a combination of psychological symptoms (e.g. feeling worthless or inappropriately guilty), physical symptoms (e.g. changes in appetite, fatigue and/or sleep problems) and social symptoms (e.g. loss of interest in activities previously enjoyed). Care needs to be taken not to treat sadness as a disorder and to assume that experiences of sadness need to be treated clinically. If you are concerned about whether you may have clinical depression as opposed to sadness, then speaking with your physician or general practitioner is the best course of action. Unfortunately, the overlap with aspects of clinical depression, along with fears and concerns about how mental health can be portrayed in popular culture, means that some might be reluctant to speak about their sadness. This is a shame, as it limits the opportunities people have to seek out and receive support when experiencing sadness. Other words that we may use to capture the experience of sadness could include 'disappointed', 'disillusioned', 'pessimistic' or 'tearful'.

Joy is an emotion that is characterized by feelings of delight or extreme gladness. The word 'joy' comes from the French word *joie* (meaning 'jewel'). It can arise following experiences of deep connection with others, the relief of suffering, pleasurable sensory experiences, or experiences of achievement either by yourself or someone close to you. Joy is a coveted experience, but it can be both fleeting and elusive. As the poet Mary Oliver once wrote: 'If you suddenly and unexpectedly feel joy, don't hesitate. Give in to it . . . don't be afraid of its plenty. Joy is not made to be a crumb.' According to Plutchik, **ecstasy** is an intense form of joy. Other words that we may use to capture the experience of joy could include 'glee', 'contentment', 'delight' or 'elation'.

Disgust is a strong aversion to sensing (seeing, hearing, smelling, tasting or feeling) something that is revolting, whether it is an inanimate object, a living thing, or a type of experience. Disgust can serve important survival roles by keeping us away from potential contamination and moral transgressions. There is a strong cultural influence on what can trigger disgust – for example, sights and smells that are commonplace in market stalls in one part of the world can provoke visceral reactions of disgusts in others. Disgust can also be experienced when moral rules are broken, or societal taboos arise. The Greek tragedian Sophocles said: 'All is disgust when a man leaves his own nature and does what is unfit.' Other words that we may use to capture the experience of disgust could include 'repulsion', 'aversion' or 'distaste'.

Surprise is an emotional response that occurs when the unexpected happens. The artist and naturalist John Muir Laws suggests: '[S] urprise is a gift. It is your mind's way of telling you that something in your environment is not the way you thought it was.' Surprise is closely associated with the physical 'startle' response, a reflex that we are born with. Surprise can only be experienced briefly. I challenge you to try to remain surprised for any real length of time – you might be briefly surprised by how difficult this is. Across the world, surprise tends to be associated with the same characteristic facial expression – eyebrows and upper eyelids are raised, and the lower jaw drops down (often accompanied by a gasp). It has been suggested that surprise helps to quickly mobilize our attention to what is new and/or hard to predict in our environment so that we can respond appropriately. Other words that we may use to capture the experience of surprise could include 'shocked', 'amazed', 'astounded' or 'flabbergasted'.

Anticipation is an emotion that arises when we ponder upcoming experiences. It comes in different flavours: blushed with pleasure or bespeckled with nervous energy. There is an exquisite vividness to the sensations that accompany anticipation. Other words that we may use to capture the experience of anticipation could include 'excitement', 'apprehension', 'contemplation' or 'expectation'.

Trust is an emotion that centres on how dependable we perceive the world to be. When we experience trust, we have a high level of confidence in how reliable processes, objects and other people are. Trust is a crucial component in establishing a sense of safety and security in our relationships with others. Stephen R. Covey, the American educator, said: 'Trust is the glue of life. It's the most essential ingredient in effective communication. It's the foundational principle that holds all relationships – marriages, families, and organizations of every kind – together.' Plutchik proposed that **admiration** is an intense form of trust. Other words that we may use to capture the experience of trust could include 'faith', 'reliance', 'belonging' or 'assuredness'.

APPENDIX 3

LAG versus AWE

(See Chapter 2)

Aspect of AWE	What is it?	How can it be enacted?	What do low levels look like? (i.e. the LAG counterpart)
ANCHORED	Fully present in time and place, and able to recognize that thoughts and emotions are momentary experiences that come and go.	• Bringing an attitude of curiosity and interest to both familiar and unfamiliar experiences. • Recognizing that we are the *context* in which our thoughts and emotions occur.	**Lost** inside your head, detached from what is happening around you, ruminating about the past, or worrying about the future.

WILLING	Prepared to recognize the mind's story-generating tendencies, and ready to turn towards rather than away from the emotions associated with those stories.	• Being vigilant to our urges to control, suppress or avoid thoughts and emotions. • Practising being open and receptive to thoughts and emotions.	**Avoidant** of situations that evoke strong emotions, and buying into stories that you wouldn't be able to cope.
EMPOWERED	Engaging in a range of behaviours across a range of life domains that speak to your sense of purpose and personal values.	• Connecting with purpose, clarifying personal values and taking pragmatic actions in line with your purpose. • Appreciating that different types (or forms) of behaviour can serve your purpose. • Choosing to persevere or change tack depending on whether behaviours are moving you towards or away your purpose.	**Grinding** out familiar routines according to the same old rules, even when these cease to move us towards what matters to us.

AWE Exercises

(See Chapters 3, 4 and 5)

Anchored (roots)

Bird's-eye view on attention

- **Separate** – Get out of your head and be where your feet are instead. Feel the solidity of the ground on which you stand.
- **Elevate** – Recognize that your attention is being stretched by your mind's tendency to time-travel to the past or the future.
- **Navigate** Reorientate by pulling your focus towards what needs to be done now. You've noticed, now get refocused.

The u-Phone

- Imagine that there is a device called a 'u-Phone' on which your current experiences can be viewed as a feed.
- Your attention is like this u-Phone. You can engage with some of the feed or choose to scroll on.
- Just as the u-Phone allows you to switch to different apps,

you can use your meta-awareness to purposefully switch your attention.

- Just as you can notice the u-Phone and the apps running on it, so too can you notice what you are paying attention to, and how.

Be curious

- **Notice what you can see** – Pick three objects and describe their shape and colour to yourself.
- **Notice three things that are in contact with your body** – What sensations of temperature, pressure or texture are there in the contact between your body and these objects?
- **Listen to the different sounds you can hear** – Where are those sounds originating from? How loud are they? If it's quiet, be curious about whether there are any variations in the sound of that silence.

Savour moments of achievement

Focus your attention on your experiences – Toggle your awareness between the events happening around you, and the thoughts, feelings and sensations that accompany those events. Notice urges to multi-task or become distracted, and instead see if you can maintain your focus for just a few seconds longer.

Catch 'killjoy thoughts' in flight – If you notice thoughts that seek to dampen down your joy, undermine achievements or move you on to the 'next thing', know that you don't have to comply with them. Imagine instead embracing those thoughts in a warm, celebratory hug.

Don't keep it all inside – Many of us were raised to be alert to the risk of appearing arrogant or complacent, but try to move past this and embrace your successes. Communicate your good feelings with others, and share moments of joy with those who matter in your life.

Practise mindfulness

Use apps and other forms of mindfulness guidance to develop meta-awareness.

Willing (trunk)

POPLAR

When you experience challenging or difficult feelings, work through the following steps, represented by the acronym POPLAR:

Pick up on the fact that the situation has provoked a strong emotional reaction in you.

Observe the most prominent emotion – is it anger, fear, shame, guilt, panic or something else?

Pinpoint your immediate urges to react. For example, depending on the circumstances, you might be tempted to quit, remove yourself from the situation, send a strongly worded email, placate the other people present, etc. See if you can allow the urges to be there without reacting to them.

Locate where in your body you are *feeling* the prominent emotion – is it in your chest, abdomen, head or somewhere else?

Assign physical properties to the felt experience of the emotion.

If it had a colour, what colour would it be? If it had a weight, would it be? If it had a texture, what would it have?

Recognize that you can hold the emotion in that moment, the next moment, and even the moment after that . . . and that you can choose to respond in a way that is consistent with how you want to be in the world.

A roving reporter

To help you get unstuck from your thoughts, imagine that you are a reporter broadcasting live from the scene of your thoughts, speaking to camera and relaying a concise summary of events into a microphone.

Author your own life

Use motivational self-talk and instructional self-talk.

Empowered (crown)

These exercises are focused on the 'three Ps': purpose, personal values and pragmatic action.

Purpose: What energizes you?

Personal values: How can you transform that energy into how you act?

Pragmatic action: How can you maximize the likelihood of your actions delivering desirable outcomes?

A day on purpose

Imagine a day free of doing the stuff you don't want to do. A day without humdrum chores, spent doing only things you feel passionate about.

- How would you choose to spend that day?
- What matters enough for you to spend it *that* way?
- What difference, if any, would you hope that doing that might make?
- How would you know that it had been a day well spent?
- How would you feel at the end of that day?
- If you could have more of those kinds of feelings in your life, would you want them?
- Now take a moment to think about how you might do more of that stuff – even 1 per cent more – in your average week. What one concrete action could you take next week to help you to do that?

Personal values clarification

- Think about what you admire about how your friends, family members and colleagues conduct themselves.
- Now think about the qualities you admire in people whom you have never met.

Birthday Speech

Imagine you are celebrating a milestone birthday. A party has been arranged, a room full of family members, friends and colleagues. As the evening progresses a dear friend (someone whom you respect deeply) steps forward to give a short speech about you. They talk about the type of person you are, the life you live, and the impact you have on the people around you. Take a moment to think about what you would want them to say.

- What qualities would you want them to notice about how you are living your life, how you are with yourself, how you are with others?
- Focus not on what that person would say about you today, but on what you would like them to be able to say about you at a later point in time. (Remember, there is still time for you to commit to demonstrating those qualities.)
- Write down the list of qualities on a notepad or in the Notes app on your phone. These are the personal values that you endorse.
- How could you integrate those personal values into how you conduct yourself during the rest of today, and the days that will follow?

Pragmatic action: Setting goals

- Watch out for passive goals – these are defined by the absence rather than presence of particular outcomes e.g., Don't mess up. Don't fail. Instead, focus on setting active goals that clearly detail the outcomes that you are trying to achieve.
- Don't wait for the 'right time' – the only time you truly have is now.
- You may have to act whilst still feeling anxious. Action and experiencing difficult emotions can co-exist.

The Three Modes of Motivation

(See Part III)

Motivational mode	Focus	Function	How it manifests	Biochemical agents
Get	Achievement-focused (e.g., status, money, sustenance, sexual gratification)	Striving	Behaviours: Achieving, striving, pursuing and consuming Feelings: wanting, desiring and longing	Dopamine (neuro-transmitter)

Threat	Threat-focused • Actual (e.g., aggression from others) • Imagined (e.g., worrying that we will fail)	Surviving	Behaviours: Fight-flight-freeze Feelings: Anxiety, fear, criticism, hostility defensiveness and suspiciousness	Cortisol, noradrenaline and adrenaline (hormones)
Reset	Self-transcendent and nurture-focused	Reviving	Behaviours: Appreciating the world around us, reorientating to our purpose, expressing warmth and/or kindness towards oneself or others Feelings: Peace, contentment, warmth, a sense of being cared for	Endorphins and oxytocin (hormone)

APPENDIX 6

Get, Threat, Reset Exercises

(See Chapters 6, 7 and 8)

Get

Questioning your goals

- **Ask why** – What important life purpose and yearnings does this goal speak to?
- **Ask for whom** – For whom are you working to complete this goal?
- **Ask whose** – Whose support and advice will you seek as you identify key tasks?
- **Ask where** – In what places will you be able to do the tasks required to progress this goal?
- **Ask when** – When will you do the tasks, and how can they be timetabled into your calendar?
- **Ask which** – Which personal values do you want to embody as you undertake these tasks and progress towards this goal, and how would you and other people notice those values in how you act?

307

- **Ask what** – What practical, psychological and emotional barriers might you experience in completing the tasks linked to this goal?
- **Ask how** – How can you overcome these barriers?

Preparing for the future in the now

- Construct the imagery from your own point of view – experience it 'from the inside out' rather than from the viewpoint of someone watching you complete the task.
- If possible, assume the physical stance that you will take when undertaking the task (e.g. standing, sitting).
- Ideally, undertake the imagery work in the place where the task will be performed. If this is not possible, view photographs or videos of the location to help you picture it clearly in your mind's eye.
- Imagine completing the task in precise detail, just as it will be performed on the day.
- Imagine completing the task at the same speed that it will be performed – resist the temptation to speed it up or slow it down.
- If it's a task you will do routinely, develop the imagery to incorporate new skills you may learn along the way, or new insights you have gained.
- Anticipate the emotions that you will experience when completing the task (e.g. apprehension, excitement, fear), and incorporate the bodily sensations that accompany those emotions into the imagery.
- When engaging in mental imagery work, it's not just about

focusing on what you plan to do; it's also important to incorporate the personal values that you want to shine through as you undertake these tasks.

Speaking to your future self

Let's imagine that there is a version of you who exists two years in the future from now. That version of you is thriving: feeling fulfilled both professionally and personally, living in line with the purpose and personal values that matter to you. Now imagine that this contented and composed 'two-years-in-the-future you' was to walk into this room right now. What supportive advice would they give you? How might 'two-years-in-the-future you' justify any upset or inconvenience caused by making those choices? Picture the expression they have on their face as they say these things. Notice the glint of commitment and determination in their eyes.

Seeking out the 'maybe'

When you are striving to achieve a goal, ask the following question: 'Is my current pace/ effort sustainable?' The sweet-spot answer to this question is, 'Maybe.' The transforming zone is the realm of the 'maybe'.

Getting flexible with imperfection

- **Think about an area of your life where perfectionism can show up.** Maybe you notice it in your work, home life, workouts or other activities you're passionate about. Take a moment to reflect on the costs that the perfectionism may be having on your lifestyle – your relationships with others, your energy levels, your mood, opportunities you may be missing out on, etc.

- **Identify a task that you will be required to do in relation to that perfectionism-prone life domain in the next couple of weeks.** For example, you may need to finalize a work report, perform at a music gig, bake a cake or prepare a video to share on social media.

- **Now imagine deliberately choosing to do that task *imperfectly*.** You might leave a typo in the work report, play a bum note in front of a crowd, leave the cocoa powder out of the mix for a red velvet cake, or go with the first take of the video for Instagram even though you fluffed the closing line.

- **Notice the fears that start to bubble up as you even contemplate doing this.** Maybe there are concerns about being criticized by others, or being judged a failure (by yourself or others). Perhaps you fear that something catastrophic will happen, or worry that you'll never be able to forgive yourself.

- **Take some time to locate where in your body you notice the sensations that accompany those fears.** In your mind's eye, imagine slowly tracing a line around the edge of those feelings of discomfort in your body.

- **Reflect on how you would respond to a friend or loved one if they shared with you that they were experiencing the same fears and discomfort.** How might you provide comfort to them? What words would you use to convey your support? What tone would you use to speak those words?

- **See if you can direct even some of that kindness and**

support towards your own fears. Allow yourself to hear those same words, spoken in the same tone, to soothe your own discomfort.

Threat

Bringing other people with us

- **Work from the inside** – Invest time in building bonds with others and establishing a shared identity. The social capital that you accrue through committing to a group can be exchanged for support from group members for ideas that you propose.
- **Spark curiosity, not fear** – Be diplomatic rather than dogmatic. Recognize that change is about winning hearts and minds.
- **Project objectivity** – Use evidence to support your points, and clearly indicate when you are communicating facts and when you are expressing your opinion.
- **Project courageous self-sacrifice** – Share with others the risks that you have taken and the sacrifices you have made in pursuit of the purpose you are promoting.

Tackling imposterism

Over the next month, record on a notepad (or in the Notes application on your mobile phone) any feedback you receive from your friends, colleagues or family that relates to the following headings:

- **Qualities** you possess that they appreciate (remember, others may value qualities you possess that you have not been aware of).
- **Skills** you perform or tasks you complete that make a difference to you or to someone else in your personal and/or professional life
- **Belonging** or signs that you are a valued part of a group (e.g. a family, team, community or organization).

Setting a daily reminder on your phone will cue your memory to complete this task through the month.

Reset

THANKFUL approach to gratitude

Being attentive to the following eight aspects of our daily experiences may be helpful for eliciting gratitude:

Today's opportunities – Was there something that happened today that gave your mood a lift?

Health – What aspect(s) of your wellbeing could you be appreciative of today?

Art and music – What piece of music or visual art might have made an impact on you today?

Nature – Was there an aspect of the natural world that you were grateful to experience today?

Kindness from others – Did someone go out of their way to be helpful or kind today?

Friends and family – Was there an interaction with a friend or family member that you're thankful for?

Unique/unusual – Was there something different that happened today that you're grateful for?

Lessons learned – What insights or wisdom might you be grateful for gaining today?

Compassionate colour exercise

- Close your eyes if you feel comfortable doing so. Alternatively, fix your gaze on a point on the floor in front of you.
- Draw your attention to a part of your body where you notice the air coming in and going out as you breathe.
- After you have noticed that felt experience of several breaths, think of a colour that you associate with the experience of compassion – the experience of kind, resolute support.
- Visualize that compassionate colour surrounding you.
- Imagine that the colour is entering through your heart area and slowly making its way through your bloodstream, infusing the experience of compassion throughout your body and the qualities of wisdom, warmth and kindness that it brings.
- Remember that the sole purpose of this colour is to support you.
- If blocks and barriers arise in your thinking (for example, if you find yourself thinking that you don't deserve the colour's support) acknowledge these 'distractions' and gently bring your focus back to the compassionate colour.
- Focus on the colour and its compassionate qualities for

another minute before opening your eyes and progressing with the rest of your day.

Self-compassion break

Repeat the following three phrases to yourself:

- I'm going through a challenging time.
- All people go through a challenging time.
- May I respond with kindness.

Preparing for a bold move

Think of a life domain (work, relationships, community life, etc.) where discontentment might be showing up. Now consider the following questions:

- What would you ideally choose to be doing in that life domain if you weren't having to contend with the feelings of discontent?
- What impact would making that choice likely bring to how you think, feel and act?
- What opportunities exist to implement these kinds of changes in that life domain?
- What barriers might you face in pursuing those opportunities?
- Do the potential benefits mean that those barriers are worth confronting?
- What options do you have for overcoming those barriers?
- What concrete steps will you now take?

Glossary of Acronyms

ACT – Acceptance and Commitment Therapy

ARM – Autonomy, Relatedness and Mastery (three psychological yearnings)

AWE – Anchored, Willing and Empowered (three aspects of a flexible mind)

CBT – Cognitive Behavioural Therapy

CFT – Compassion-Focused Therapy

LAG – Lost, Avoidant and Grinding (three aspects of experiential avoidance)

NUT – Next Unachieved Thing

PDF – Persistently Denied Feelings

SAGE – Something's Always Gonna Entice

Support for Mental Health and Wellbeing

If you are experiencing difficulties with your mental health and wellbeing, contact your general practitioner. If you or someone else is experiencing a mental health emergency, call 999 or go to your local accident and emergency department.

If you need help urgently for your mental health, but it's not an emergency, call 111.

Information and advice are also available from the following UK organizations:

Alcoholics Anonymous
Alcoholics Anonymous provide advice and support for those experiencing difficulties with alcohol use.

https://www.alcoholics-anonymous.org.uk/

0800 9177 650

Mind

Mind is a charity that offers information and advice to people with mental health problems and lobbies government and local authorities on their behalf.

https://www.mind.org.uk/information-support/
0300 123 3393

Rethink Mental Illness

Rethink is a charity working to improve the lives of people severely affected by mental illness.

https://rethink.org/
0808 801 0525

Samaritans

A charity that offers support to distressed people through a network of listening volunteers.

Find your local branch at:
https://www.samaritans.org/branches/
116 123 (support available 24 hours a day, 365 days a year)
Email: jo@samaritans.org

Acknowledgements

I want to begin by thanking my wife Suzy for the time, space and support that she afforded me during the writing of this book. I know that time at the computer was time away from you, and that came at a cost. Thank you for your patience, wisdom and listening ear. I love you. Big shout-out to Nicole, the best stepdaughter I could ever wish to have. It's been fantastic to watch you blossom into the very talented person that you are. Bobby the dog, thanks for taking me on walks and providing me with opportunities to see the woods for the trees when my mind felt full.

My parents, George (a retired horticulturalist) and Claire (a retired midwife), helped me and my two sisters to understand the rich rewards that nurturance can bring – whether that be garden plants, family pets, fellow human beings or big ideas worth pursuing. I love you both. This book is dedicated to the memory of my uncle Tom White, who was a huge presence in my life. Sadly, the completion of the first draft of the manuscript coincided with his passing. I'm sorry that Tom – a talented poet – never got to read it. I miss our conversations.

I am blessed to be part of a fantastic community of ACT trainers.

ACKNOWLEDGEMENTS

Deep gratitude in particular to the following people from whom I have learned much over the years: Steven C. Hayes, Kelly Wilson, Kirk Strosahl, Robyn Walser, D. J. Moran, Hank Robb, David Gillanders, Russ Harris, Ray Owen, Louise McHugh, Louise Hayes, Joe Oliver, Eric Morris, Rob Archer, Jim Lucas, Nic Hooper, Dennis Tirch, Beate Ebert, Hannah Bockarie and Chris McConnell. Their work, and the discussions I have had with them, have inspired and informed the content of this book.

In my own work, I have the privilege of sharing conversations with very talented applied psychology practitioners working in high-performance environments. These conversations helped me to refine some of the ideas that have been included in the book. Special mentions to Steve Ward, Karl Steptoe, Aidan Kearney, Miia Chambers, Laura Swettenham and Trevor Jones.

When times have been tough, I have benefited greatly from the sage advice and compassionate support of Rosco Kasujja, Jennifer Nardozzi, Laura Golding and Mary Loudon. Thank you from the bottom of my heart.

Special thanks to Lydia Thompson for granting me the opportunity to interview her about her experiences during the Rugby World Cup final and the months that followed. I am also deeply indebted to the clients with whom I have worked over the years, and will be eternally grateful for the trust that they placed in me.

Where would I be without my friends? Chris Logan, Roisin Logan, Stephen Smyth, Jim Hoskinson, Paddy Steele, David Carlisle, Pete Torney, Craig Turkington, Ben Stewart, Mark Sloan, Andrew Jordan, Michael Gourley, David Croot, Graeme Eddie, Anthony Allison, Dave Eustace, Ally McInroy and Keith Crawford: thanks for the good times and stories that we have shared.

ACKNOWLEDGEMENTS

Tom Henry has provided fantastic mentorship in helping me develop as a writer – thank you for supporting me to find my authorial voice. My literary agent, Jaime Marshall, has been a calm and considered presence throughout this process. Jaime, thanks for believing in me – and believing in the book.

Many thanks to the team at Quercus Books. How apt that the publisher of *The Tree That Bends* has a name that means 'oak' in Latin. I will be eternally indebted to Victoria Millar and Tara O'Sullivan for their careful reading of draft manuscripts and their contribution to making the book what it is. Thanks also to Jane Sturrock for her support throughout the project.

Thanks to Steve Doogan at Steve Doogan Illustrations (https://www.doogan.ie/) for the wonderful tree illustrations that have been used inside the book.

As I was writing this book, a client mentioned that he was reading a book by forest scientist and author Peter Wohlleben entitled *The Hidden Life of Trees*. I was delighted to learn that I wasn't the only one drawing parallels between trees and humans. While Peter's book explores the human-like aspects of how trees thrive, I have sought to return the favour by highlighting the tree-like aspects of how we can thrive. So, thank you to our trees, the lungs of our planet; as we take care of nature, nature will help take care of us.

Notes

Introduction

p. 6 **'I miss my daughter'**: Vallely, P (2006, March 7). 'Vicar struggles to forgive the terrorists who killed her daughter'. *The Independent.* https://www.independent.co.uk/news/uk/this-britain/vicar-struggles-to-forgive-the-terrorists-who-killed-her-daughter-6107339.html.

p. 6 **'Psy-Flex, CompACT-10, MPFI, and AAQ-II'**: Psy-Flex: see Gloster, A. T., Block, V. J., Klotsche, J., Villanueva, J., Rinner, M. T., Benoy, C., . . . and Bader, K. (2021). 'Psy-Flex: A contextually sensitive measure of psychological flexibility'. *Journal of Contextual Behavioral Science*, 22, 13–23;

   CompACT-10: Golijani-Moghaddam, N., Morris, J. L., Bayliss, K., and Dawson, D. L. (2023). 'The CompACT-10: Development and validation of a comprehensive assessment of acceptance and commitment therapy processes short-form in representative UK samples.' *Journal of Contextual Behavioral Science*, 29, 59–66;

   MPFI: Rolffs, J. L., Rogge, R. D., and Wilson, K. G. (2018). 'Disentangling components of flexibility via the hexaflex model: Development and validation of the Multidimensional Psychological Flexibility Inventory (MPFI)'. *Assessment*, 25(4), 458–482.

   AAQ-II: Bond, F. W., Hayes, S. C., Baer, R. A., Carpenter, K. M., Guenole, N., Orcutt, H. K., . . . and Zettle, R. D. (2011). 'Preliminary psychometric properties of the Acceptance and Action Questionnaire-II: A revised measure of psychological inflexibility and experiential avoidance'. *Behavior Therapy*, 42(4), 676–688.

p. 6 **'pathways in the medial prefrontal cortex area of the brain that are implicated in flexibility':** Cho, K. K., Shi, J., Phensy, A. J., Turner, M. L., and Sohal, V. S. (2023). 'Long-range inhibition synchronizes and updates prefrontal task activity'. *Nature*, 617(7961), 548–554.

p. 6 **'low levels of psychological flexibility are consistently associated with worse levels of wellbeing':** Ong, C. W., Barthel, A. L., and Hofmann, S. G. (2023). 'The Relationship Between Psychological Inflexibility and Well-Being in Adults: A Meta-Analysis of the Acceptance and Action Questionnaire (AAQ)'. *Behavior Therapy*, 55, 26–41.

p. 7 **'research studies conducted with athletes':** Mooney, J. (2022). 'Psychological flexibility and well-being in sport'. Doctorate in Clinical Psychology Dissertation. The University of Liverpool (United Kingdom).

p. 7 **'effectiveness of ACT for improving wellbeing and addressing a range of physical and mental health difficulties':** ACT has most commonly been evaluated as an intervention for those experiencing depression, anxiety, substance use disorders, and chronic pain. The results of a recent review that investigated the effectiveness of ACT across these different outcomes highlighted that ACT was generally better when compared with 'control' conditions (i.e. inert experiences, such as staying on a waiting list) and the majority of other forms of intervention – its effectiveness was shown to be comparable with that of Cognitive Behavioural Therapy (CBT), which is regarded as a 'gold standard' psychological intervention for many types of difficulties. See: Gloster, A. T., Walder, N., Levin, M. E., Twohig, M. P., and Karekla, M. (2020). 'The empirical status of acceptance and commitment therapy: A review of meta-analyses'. *Journal of Contextual Behavioral Science*, 18, 181-192.

ACT has also been evaluated as an approach for boosting subjective wellbeing, which is a measure of how we experience the quality of our own lives. See: Stenhoff, A., Steadman, L., Nevitt, S., Benson, L., and White, R. G. (2020). 'Acceptance and commitment therapy and subjective wellbeing: A systematic review and meta-analyses of randomised controlled trials in adults'. *Journal of Contextual Behavioral Science*, 18, 256–272.

p. 7 **'improving day-to-day functioning, quality of life, pain intensity and mood of people experiencing chronic pain':** Ma, T. W., Yuen, A. S. K., and

Yang, Z. (2023). 'The efficacy of acceptance and commitment therapy for chronic pain: A systematic review and meta-analysis'. *The Clinical Journal of Pain*, 39(3), 147–157.

p. 8 **'ACT interventions can improve self-reported levels of flexibility'**: Brandon, S., Pallotti, C., and Jog, M. (2021). 'Exploratory study of common changes in client behaviors following routine psychotherapy: Does psychological flexibility typically change and predict outcomes?'. *Journal of Contemporary Psychotherapy*, 51(1), 49–56; Ciarrochi, J., Bilich, L., and Godsell, C. (2010). 'Psychological flexibility as a mechanism of change in acceptance and commitment therapy'. In R. A. Baer (Ed.), *Assessing Mindfulness and Acceptance Processes in Clients: Illuminating the Theory and Practice of Change* (pp. 51–75). Context Press/New Harbinger Publications; Lakin, D. P., Cooper, S. E., Anderson, L., Augustinavicius, J., Brown, F., Carswell, K., . . . and Tol, W. A. (2023). 'Psychological Flexibility in South Sudanese Female Trauma Survivors in Uganda as a Mechanism for Change Within a Guided Self-Help Intervention'. *Journal of Clinical and Consulting Psychology*, 91(1), 6–13.

p. 8 **'people who are not mental health experts can be trained'**: Arnold, T., Haubrick, K. K., Klasko-Foster, L. B., Rogers, B. G., Barnett, A., Ramirez-Sanchez, N. A., . . . and Gaudiano, B. A. (2022). 'Acceptance and Commitment Therapy informed behavioral health interventions delivered by non-mental health professionals: A systematic review'. *Journal of Contextual Behavioral Science*. 24, 85–196.

p. 8 **'*Doing What Matters in Times of Stress*'**: World Health Organization. (2020). *Doing What Matters in Times of Stress: An Illustrated Guide*. WHO.

p. 8 **'adapted to specifically support wellbeing and performance in sport, music and workplace settings'**:
ACT in Sport: White, R. G., Bethell, A., Charnock, L., Leckey, S., and Penpraze, V. (2021). *Acceptance and Commitment Approaches for Athletes' Wellbeing and Performance: The Flexible Mind*. Palgrave Macmillan; Lundgren, T., Reinebo, G., Näslund, M., and Parling, T. (2020). 'Acceptance and commitment training to promote psychological flexibility in ice hockey performance: A controlled group feasibility study'. *Journal of Clinical Sport Psychology*, 14(2), 170–181; Juncos, D. G., and e Pona, E. D. P. (2022).
ACT in music: *ACT for Musicians: A Guide for Using Acceptance and*

Commitment Training to Enhance Performance, Overcome Performance Anxiety, and Improve Well-Being. Universal Publishers.

ACT in workplace settings: Bond, F. W., Lloyd, J., Flaxman, P. E., and Archer, R. (2016). 'Psychological flexibility and ACT at work'. *The Wiley Handbook of Contextual Behavioral Science*, Wiley Blackwell, 459–482; Flaxman, P. E., Bond, F. W., and Livheim, F. (2013). *The Mindful and Effective Employee: An Acceptance and Commitment Therapy Training Manual for Improving Well-Being and Performance.* New Harbinger Publications.

Chapter 1: High performance, high price?

p. 15 **'"It's all retch and no vomit"'**: Laxton, M. (2014, 31 August). 'Alan Watts – Motivational speech – What do you desire?' [Video file]. YouTube. https://www.youtube.com/watch?v=6j-nYa6ex7U

p. 16 **'When I win, I don't feel happy'**: Tignor, S. (2021, 4 September). 'Naomi Osaka isn't enjoying herself even when she wins—so you can understand her need for a break from the game'. *Tennis.* https://www.tennis.com/news/articles/naomi-osaka-isn-t-enjoying-herself-even-when-she-wins-so-you-can-understand-her-

p. 16 **'Dave Alred's *The Pressure Principle*'**: Alred, D. (2016). *The Pressure Principle: Handle Stress, Harness Energy, and Perform When It Counts.* Penguin.

p. 16 **'*No Limits: How to Build an Unstoppable Mindset*'**: Lynch, A. (2021). *No Limits: How to Build an Unstoppable Mindset.* Independently published.

p. 17 **'I underestimated or judged it wrong'**: Hunter, A. (2024, 26 January). 'Jürgen Klopp blames fatigue for decision to leave Liverpool at end of season'. *Guardian.* https://www.theguardian.com/football/2024/jan/26/jurgen-klopp-to-step-down-as-liverpool-manager-at-end-of-season#:~:text=I%20judged%20it%20wrong.,to%20England%20in%20the%20future.

p. 17 **'I gave everything, physically and mentally'**: Brookes S. (2023, 4 February). '"I'm suffocating ... the player is gobbling up the man": Man United's Raphaël Varane opens up on his struggles and WHY he's quitting France duty at 29, despite being next in line to be his country's captain'. *Daily Mail.* https://www.dailymail.co.uk/sport/football/article-11712679/Man-Uniteds-Raphael-Varane-opens-struggles-hes-quitting-France-duty-29.html

p. 18 '"resilience" can variously describe': Fletcher, D., and Sarkar, M. (2016). 'Mental fortitude training: An evidence-based approach to developing psychological resilience for sustained success'. *Journal of Sport Psychology in Action*, 7(3), 135–157.

p. 18 'a 2015 article in the *New York Times*': Seghal, P. (2015, 1 December). 'The Profound Emptiness of "Resilience"'. *New York Times*. https://www.nytimes.com/2015/12/06/magazine/the-profound-emptiness-of-resilience.html

p. 19 'Everything can be taken from a man': Frankl, V.E. (1963). *Man's search for meaning: an introduction to logotherapy*. Washington Square Press.

p. 20 'It can be incredible and unsustainable': Scarborough, A. and Tattershall, C. (Directors) (2022, 29 August). *End to End*. [Film]. Hurley and the Directors Paint Studios.

p. 21 'The so-called availability bias': Tversky, A., and Kahneman, D. (1973). 'Availability: A heuristic for judging frequency and probability'. *Cognitive Psychology*, 5(2), 207–232.

p. 22 '*The Mental Toughness Handbook*': Zahariades, D. (2020). *The Mental Toughness Handbook: A Step-By-Step Guide to Facing Life's Challenges, Managing Negative Emotions, and Overcoming Adversity with Courage and Poise*. Art Of Productivity.

p. 22 'the four Cs': P. Clough, K. Earle, D. Sewell. (2002). 'Mental toughness: the concept and its measurement'. In Cockerill (Ed.), *Solutions in Sport Psychology*, Thomson, 32–43.

p. 22 'conceptualization of mental toughness has been criticized and concerns have been raised': Crust, L., and Swann, C. (2011). 'Comparing two measures of mental toughness'. *Personality and Individual Differences*, 50(2), 217–221; Gucciardi, D. F., Hanton, S., and Mallett, C. J. (2012). 'Progressing measurement in mental toughness: a case example of the Mental Toughness Questionnaire 48'. *Sport, Exercise and Performance Psychology*, 1, 194–214; Sheard, M., Golby, J., and Van Wersch, A. (2009). 'Progress towards construct validation of the Sports Mental Toughness Questionnaire (SMTQ)'. *European Journal of Psychological Assessment*, 25, 186–193.

p. 23 'A review of the research evidence by Andreas Stamatis': Stamatis, A., Grandjean, P., Morgan, G., Padgett, R. N., Cowden, R., and Koutakis, P. (2020). 'Developing and training mental toughness in sport: a systematic review and meta-analysis of observational studies and pre-test and post-test experiments'. *BMJ Open Sport and Exercise Medicine*, 6(1), e000747.

p. 23 'an editorial in the *British Journal of Sports Medicine*': Bauman, N. J. (2016). 'The stigma of mental health in athletes: are mental toughness and mental health seen as contradictory in elite sport?' *British Journal of Sports Medicine*, 50(3), 135–136.

p. 23 'US Olympian figure skater Sasha Cohen': Rapkin, B. (Director) (2020, 29 July). *The Weight of Gold.* [Film]. Podium Pictures.

p. 24 'Daniel Gucciardi, a leading researcher in mental toughness': Gucciardi, D.F. (2017) 'Mental toughness: progress and prospects'. *Current Opinion in Psychology*, 16, 17–23.

p. 24 'In Damon Zahariades' *Mental Toughness Handbook*': Zahariades, D. (2020). *The Mental Toughness Handbook: A Step-By-Step Guide to Facing Life's Challenges, Managing Negative Emotions, and Overcoming Adversity with Courage and Poise.* Art Of Productivity. (pp. 17–18, 31).

p. 25 '*Extreme Ownership: How U.S. Navy Seals Lead and Win*': Willink, J., and Babin, L. (2017). *Extreme Ownership: How US Navy SEALs Lead and Win.* St. Martin's Press.

p. 25 'In a 2019 podcast, in which he fielded questions from listeners': Ferriss, T. (2019, 25 November). 'Jocko Willink Takeover – On Quitting, Relationships, Financial Discipline, Contrast Baths, and More (#395)' [Podcast Transcript]. *The Tim Ferriss Show.* https://tim.blog/2019/11/25/jocko-willink-takeover-transcript/

p. 25 'Martin Luther King Jr addressed in the 1963 book *Strength to Love*': King, M. L. Jnr. (1963). *Strength to Love.* Harper Row.

p. 26 'a firmness of mind and/or a plucky spirit': Online Etymology Dictionary (n.d.). 'Grit'. https://www.etymonline.com/word/grit

p. 26 '*Grit: Why Passion and Resilience are the Secrets to Success*': Duckworth, A. (2017). *Grit: Why Passion and Resilience are the Secrets to Success.* Vermilion.

p. 27 'pushback from sections of the scientific community about the concept's credibility': Datu, J. A. D. (2021). 'Beyond passion and perseverance: Review and future research initiatives on the science of grit'. *Frontiers in Psychology*, 11, 545526.

p. 27 'programmes aimed at enhancing grit may have little effect on performance and success': Credé, M., Tynan, M. C., and Harms, P. D. (2017).

'Much ado about grit: A meta-analytic synthesis of the grit literature'. *Journal of Personality and Social Psychology*, 113(3), 492.

p. 27 **'core claims about grit have either been unexamined':** Credé, M. (2018). 'What shall we do about grit? A critical review of what we know and what we don't know'. *Educational Researcher*, 47(9), 606–611.

p. 27 **'very strong statistical relationship between grit and conscientiousness':** Credé, M., Tynan, M. C., and Harms, P. D. (2017). 'Much ado about grit: A meta-analytic synthesis of the grit literature'. *Journal of Personality and Social Psychology*, 113(3), 492.

p. 27 **'Duckworth and her colleagues have conceded that there is overlap between the two':** Duckworth, A. L., Peterson, C., Matthews, M. D., and Kelly, D. R. (2007). 'Grit: perseverance and passion for long-term goals'. *Journal of Personality and Social Psychology*, 92(6), 1087–1101. (p. 1089).

p. 27 **'guilty of the "jangle-fallacy"':** Ponnock, A., Muenks, K., Morell, M., Yang, J. S., Gladstone, J. R., and Wigfield, A. (2020). 'Grit and conscientiousness: Another jangle fallacy'. *Journal of Research in Personality*, 89, 104021.
The jangle-fallacy can be contrasted with the jingle-fallacy, which occurs when a single term is used to describe phenomena that are actually different. The jingle and jangle fallacies are described in a 2012 paper by Robert Roeser and colleagues, and are based on work conducted in 1904 by Edward Thorndike and in 1927 by Truman Lee Kelley. See: Roeser, R. W., Peck, S. C. and Nasir, N. S. (2012). 'Self and Identity Processes in School Motivation, Learning, and Achievement'. In P. Alexander and P. Winne (Eds.), *Handbook of Educational Psychology*. Psychology Press (pp. 391–424).

p. 27 **'grit has been criticized for prioritizing "consistency" over "adaptability"':** Datu, J. A. D. (2021). 'Beyond passion and perseverance: Review and future research initiatives on the science of grit'. *Frontiers in Psychology*, 11, 545526.

p. 29 **'A Method of Estimating Plane Vulnerability':** Wald, A. (1980). *A Method of Estimating Plane Vulnerability Based on Damage of Survivors.* CRC 432, July 1980. (Copies can be obtained from the Document Center, Center for Naval Analyses, 2000 N. Beauregard St., Alexandria, VA 22311.)

p. 29 **'160,000 farms spread across Northern Ireland and the Republic of Ireland':** Forde, A. (2021, 9 December). 'Farm census: number of farms fall and 33% of farmers over 65'. *Irish Farmers Journal.* https://www.farmersjournal. ie/farm-census-number-of-farms-fall-and-33-of-farmers-over-65-667311;

Cullen, L. (2021, 16 December). 'More land being farmed in Northern Ireland, census shows'. BBC News. https://www.bbc.co.uk/news/uk-northern-ireland-59682757#:~:text=There%20are%20approximately%20 25%2C000%20farms%20in%20Northern%20Ireland.

p. 30 'Simon Sinek has used the concentric rings of his "Golden Circle analogy"': Sinek, S. (2011). *Start with Why*. Penguin Books.

p. 32 'The Swedish psychologist Anders Ericsson and his colleagues found that': Ericsson, K. A., Krampe, R. T., Tesch-Römer, C. (1993). 'The role of deliberate practice in the acquisition of expert performance'. *Psychological Review*, 100, 363–406.

p. 32 'in his bestselling 2008 book *Outliers*': Gladwell, M. (2008). *Outliers: The Story of Success*. Little, Brown.

p. 33 'a ratio of around 3:1 for productive work time vs time to relax': Gifford, J. (2020, 19 June). 'The Rule of 52 and 17: It's Random, But it Ups Your Productivity'. *The Muse*. https://www.themuse.com/advice/the-rule-of-52-and-17-its-random-but-it-ups-your-productivity

p. 33 'They define thriving as simultaneously': Brown, D. J., Arnold, R., Reid, T., and Roberts, G. (2018). 'A qualitative exploration of thriving in elite sport'. *Journal of Applied Sport Psychology*, 30(2), 129–149.

p. 33 '[T]o thrive in life is not only marked by a feeling of happiness': Su, R., Tay, L., and Diener, E. (2014). 'The development and validation of the Comprehensive Inventory of Thriving (CIT) and the Brief Inventory of Thriving (BIT)'. *Applied Psychology: Health and Well-Being*, 6(3), 251–279. (p. 272).

p. 33 'Su and her team developed self-report questionnaires': Wiese, C. W., Tay, L., Su, R., and Diener, E. (2018). 'Measuring thriving across nations: Examining the measurement equivalence of the Comprehensive Inventory of Thriving (CIT) and the Brief Inventory of Thriving (BIT)'. *Applied Psychology: Health and Well-Being*, 10(1), 127–148.

p. 33 'explored the concept of thriving in sport': Brown, D. J., Arnold, R., Fletcher, D., and Standage, M. (2017). 'Human thriving'. *European Psychologist*, 22(3), 167–179; Brown, D. J., Arnold, R., Standage, M., Turner, J. E., and Fletcher, D. (2021). 'The prediction of thriving in elite sport: A prospective examination of the role of psychological need satisfaction, challenge appraisal, and salivary biomarkers'. *Journal of Science and Medicine in Sport*, 24(4), 373–379; Brown, D. J., Arnold, R., Reid, T., and Roberts,

G. (2018). 'A qualitative exploration of thriving in elite sport'. *Journal of Applied Sport Psychology*, 30(2), 129–149.

p. 34 **'There is growing recognition that high levels of wellbeing'**: White, R.G., Bethell, A., Charnock, L., Leckey, S., Penpraze, V. (2021). *Acceptance and Commitment Approaches for Athletes' Wellbeing and Performance: The Flexible Mind*. Springer International Publishing, Palgrave Macmillan.

p. 34 **'being in a good mental state is really important'**: Brown, D. J., Arnold, R., Reid, T., and Roberts, G. (2018). 'A qualitative exploration of thriving in elite sport'. *Journal of Applied Sport Psychology*, 30(2), 129–149.

p. 34 **'our ability to thrive is determined by an interaction'**: Brown, D.J., Arnold, R., Fletcher, D. and Standage, M. (2017). 'Human Thriving'. *European Psychologist*, 22:3, 167–179

p. 35 **'The aim of the project'**: UK Sports Institute (2018). 'EIS performance psychology: Project Thrive'. English Institute of Sport. https://uksportsin-stitute.co.uk/resource/eis-performance-psychology-projectthrive/

p. 35 **'the tough and gritty "No compromise", which proved divisive'**: 'Wagstaff, C. R., and Quartiroli, A. (2023). 'A Systems-Led Approach to Developing Psychologically Informed Environments'. *Journal of Sport Psychology in Action*, 14(4), 227–242.

p. 35 **'"Win well" and "Grow a thriving sporting system"'**: UK Sport (n.d.). 'Powering success, inspiring impact'. *UK Sport's Strategic Plan 2021–31* https://www.uksport.gov.uk/-/media/uks-strategic-landing-images/uk-sport-strategic-plan-2021-31.ashx

p. 35 **'an online platform called Groov'**: Groov (n.d.) Workplace science platform. https://www.groovnow.com/product/overview

p. 35 **'on the *How's the Head?* podcast, Kirwan said'**: Malone, T. (n.d.). 'Rugby – "I'm dead, I'm walking around, but I'm dead": John Kirwan tells Quinny about his mental health'. *Off The Ball*. https://www.offtheball.com/best-of-otb/john-kirwan-mental-health-1035329

Chapter 2: Flexibility: from LAG to AWE

p. 37 **'Charles Darwin, in his book *The Expression of the Emotions in Man and Animals*'**: Darwin, C. (1872). *The Expression of the Emotions in Man and Animals* (P. Ekman, Ed.).

p. 38 **'A technical definition of emotions suggests'**: Paul, E. S., and Mendl,

M. T. (2018). 'Animal emotion: Descriptive and prescriptive definitions and their implications for a comparative perspective'. *Applied Animal Behaviour Science*, 205, 202–209.

p. 38 '***Show Your Anxiety Who's Boss***': Minden, J. (2020). *Show Your Anxiety Who's Boss: A Three-Step CBT Program to Help You Reduce Anxious Thoughts and Worry*. New Harbinger Press.

p. 38 '**Research has found that emotions can also be infectious**': Herrando, C., and Constantinides, E. (2021). 'Emotional contagion: A brief overview and future directions'. *Frontiers in Psychology*, 12, 712606.

p. 39 '**Daniel Goleman popularized in his bestselling book**': Goleman, D. (1995). *Emotional Intelligence: Why It Can Matter More Than IQ*. Bantam Books.

p. 39 '**Goleman defines emotional intelligence (EI) as**': Goleman D. (1998). *Working with Emotional Intelligence*. Bantam Books (317).

In recent years, EI has become increasingly influential in the business world, and has also been applied in other high-performance contexts. See: Laborde, S., Dosseville, F., and Allen, M. S. (2016). 'Emotional intelligence in sport and exercise: A systematic review'. *Scandinavian Journal of Medicine and Science in Sports*, 26(8), 862–874.

p. 39 '**higher levels of EI were consistently linked to higher levels of well-being**': Sánchez-Álvarez, N., Extremera, N., and Fernández-Berrocal, P. (2016). 'The relation between emotional intelligence and subjective well-being: A meta-analytic investigation'. *The Journal of Positive Psychology*, 11(3), 276–285.

p. 39 '**Robert Plutchik introduced his "Wheel of Emotions"**': Plutchik, R. (1980). 'A general psychoevolutionary theory of emotion'. In R. Plutchik and H. Kellerman (Eds.), *Emotion: Theory, Research and Experience – Theories of Emotion Vol. 1*. Academic Press. (pp. 3–33).

p. 41 '**celebrated Lebanese-American poet Kahlil Gibran explains why**': Gibran, K. (1923). 'On Joy and Sorrow'. *The Prophet*. Knopf.

p. 44 '**"experiential avoidance" – is a major contributor to mental health difficulties**': Ong, C. W., Barthel, A. L., and Hofmann, S. G. (2024). 'The Relationship Between Psychological Inflexibility and Well-Being in Adults: A Meta-Analysis of the Acceptance and Action Questionnaire (AAQ)'. *Behavior Therapy*, 55(1):26–41; Hayes, S. C., Luoma, J. B., Bond, F. W., Masuda, A., and Lillis, J. (2006). 'Acceptance and commitment therapy:

Model, processes and outcomes'. *Behaviour Research and Therapy*, 44(1), 1–25; Kashdan, T. B., Morina, N. and Priebe, S. (2009). 'Post-traumatic stress disorder, social anxiety disorder, and depression in survivors of the Kosovo War: Avoidance as a contributor to distress and quality of life'. *Journal of Anxiety Disorders*, 23(2), 185–196; Karekla, M., Karademas, E., and Gloster, A. (2019). 'The common sense model of self-regulation and acceptance and commitment therapy: Integrating strategies to guide interventions for chronic illness'. *Health Psychology Review*, 13, 490–503.

p. 44 **'Evidence is also emerging that suggests that bodily markers':** Karekla, M., Demosthenous, G., Georgiou, C., Konstantinou, P., Trigiorgi, A., Koushiou, M., . . . and Gloster, A. T. (2022). 'Machine learning advances the classification and prediction of responding from psychophysiological reactions'. *Journal of Contextual Behavioral Science*, 26, 36–43.

p. 48 **'the "sunk-cost fallacy", which was originally proposed by psychologist Richard Thaler':** Thaler, R. (1980). 'Toward a positive theory of consumer choice'. *Journal of Economic Behavior and Organization*, 1(1), 39–60.

p. 50 **'Choice . . . is what defines and validates a life':** Hollis, J. (1993). *The Middle Passage: From Misery to Meaning in Midlife*. Inner City Books. (p. 106).

Part II

p. 63 **'a tree, which requires to grow and develop':** Mill, J. S. (2002). *On Liberty*. Dover Publications.

Chapter 3: Attuned

p. 65 **'The roots of a tree form':** 'Tree Roots,' The Daily Garden (2018, 15 November). https://www.thedailygarden.us/garden-word-of-the-day/tree-roots

p. 66 **'looks without seeing, listens without hearing':** Gelb, M. (2000). *How to think like Leonardo Da Vinci: seven steps to genius every day*. New York, N.Y., Dell Pub. (p. 97).

p. 67 **'Pete Carroll, the Super Bowl-winning former head coach':** Gervais, M. (host). (2016, 27 April). 'Competing to be your best (No. 27)' [Audio podcast episode]. *Finding Mastery*. https://findingmastery.net/pete-carroll/

p. 67 **'But how much time are we spending actually thinking'**: Tseng, J., and Poppenk, J. (2020). 'Brain meta-state transitions demarcate thoughts across task contexts exposing the mental noise of trait neuroticism'. *Nature Communications*, 11(1), 1–12.

p. 67 **'Research . . . which tracked the moment-by-moment contents of people's thoughts**: Killingsworth, M. A., and Gilbert, D. T. (2010). 'A wandering mind is an unhappy mind'. *Science*, 330(6006), 932–932.

p. 67 **'Mind-wandering may well serve important functions'**: Smallwood, J., and Andrews-Hanna, J. (2013). 'Not all minds that wander are lost: the importance of a balanced perspective on the mind-wandering state'. *Frontiers in Psychology*, 4, 441; Baird, B., Smallwood, J., Mrazek, M. D., Kam, J. W., Franklin, M. S., and Schooler, J. W. (2012). 'Inspired by distraction: Mind wandering facilitates creative incubation'. *Psychological Science*, 23(10), 1117–1122.

p. 67 **'It is associated with poor performance in various educational activities'**: Szpunar, K. K., Moulton, S. T., and Schacter, D. L. (2013). 'Mind wandering and education: From the classroom to online learning'. *Frontiers in Psychology*, 4, 58178; Unsworth, N., McMillan, B. D., Brewer, G. A., and Spillers, G. J. (2012). 'Everyday attention failures: an individual differences investigation'. *Journal of Experimental Psychology: Learning, Memory, and Cognition*, 38(6), 1765.

p. 67 **'reduced vigilance to what is happening'**: McVay, J. C., and Kane, M. J. (2009). 'Conducting the train of thought: working memory capacity, goal neglect, and mind wandering in an executive-control task'. *Journal of Experimental Psychology: Learning, Memory, and Cognition*, 35, 196–204; McVay, J. C., and Kane, M. J. (2012a). 'Drifting from slow to "d'oh!": Working memory capacity and mind wandering predict extreme reaction times and executive control errors'. *Journal of Experimental Psychology: Learning, Memory, and Cognition*, 38, 525–549; McVay, J. C., and Kane, M. J. (2012b). 'Why does working memory capacity predict variation in reading comprehension? On the influence of mind wandering and executive attention'. *Journal of Experimental Psychology: Learning, Memory, and Cognition*. 141, 302–320.

p. 68 **'Attention allows us to maintain alertness'**: Mark, G. (2023). *Attention Span: Finding Focus for a Fulfilling Life*. William Collins. (p. 36).

p. 68 **'Both endogenous and exogenous attention'**: Ester, E. F., and Nouri,

A. (2023). 'Internal selective attention is delayed by competition between endogenous and exogenous factors'. *Iscience*, 26(7).

p. 69 **'It's claimed that, on average, we shift our attention'**: Mark, G. (2023). *Attention Span: Finding Focus for a Fulfilling Life*. William Collins.

p. 69 **'The "switch-cost effect" emerged from observations'**: The switch-cost effect was first identified in 1927 by American psychologist Arthur T. Jersild. For more, see: Vandierendonck, A., Liefooghe, B., and Verbruggen, F. (2010). 'Task switching: interplay of reconfiguration and interference control'. *Psychological Bulletin*, 136(4), 60.

p. 70 **'a phenomenon called "vigilance decrement"'**: Pattyn N., Neyt X., Henderickx D., Soetens E. (2008). 'Psychophysiological investigation of vigilance decrement: Boredom or cognitive fatigue?' *Physiology and Behaviour*, 93:369–378.

p. 70 **'our attention is drawn to what is recognizable'**: Jha, A. (2021). *Peak Mind: Find Your Focus, Own Your Attention, Invest 12 Minutes a Day*. Piatkus Books.

p. 70 **'Records from the fourth century CE reveal that monks'**: Kreiner, J. (2023). *The Wandering Mind: What Medieval Monks Tell Us About Distraction*. Liveright Publishing.

p. 71 **'nearly half of us (49 per cent) felt that our attention span was shorter'**: 'How people focus and live in the modern information environment'. (February 2022). Kings College London – The Policy Institute https://www.kcl.ac.uk/policy-institute/assets/how-people-focus-and-live-in-the-modern-information-environment.pdf

p. 71 **'Research has linked increased smart phone and social media use'**: Abi-Jaoude, E., Naylor, K. T., and Pignatiello, A. (2020). 'Smartphones, social media use and youth mental health'. *Canadian Medical Association Journal*, 192(6), E136–E141.

p. 71 **'A study that recruited nearly 30,000 young adults'**: Sapien Labs (2023). 'Age of First Smartphone/Tablet and Mental Wellbeing Outcomes'. Results from the Global Mind Project, https://sapienlabs.org/wp-content/uploads/2023/05/Sapien-Labs-Age-of-First-Smartphone-and-Mental-Wellbeing-Outcomes.pdf

p. 72 **'A range of AI-powered apps such as'**: Kuki, https://www.kuki.ai/about; Replika, https://replika.com/.

p. 72 **'Whether these chatbots are safe'**: Cox, D. (2024, 4 February). '"They thought they were doing good but it made people worse": Why mental health apps are under scrutiny'. *Guardian.* https://amp-theguardian-com. cdn.ampproject.org/c/s/amp.theguardian.com/society/2024/feb/04/ they-thought-they-were-doing-good-but-it-made-people-worse-why-mental-health-apps-are-under-scrutiny

p. 72 **'computer programmes such as Freedom':** Freedom, https://freedom.to/

p. 74 **'Gloria Mark's excellent book *Attention Span*':** Mark, G. (2023). *Attention Span: Finding Focus for a Fulfilling Life.* William Collins.

p. 77 **'Research studies have demonstrated that mindfulness meditation':** Hargus, E., Crane, C., Barnhofer, T., and Williams, J. M. G. (2010). 'Effects of mindfulness on meta-awareness and specificity of describing prodromal symptoms in suicidal depression'. *Emotion,* 10(1), 34; Vago, D. R., and Silbersweig, D. A. (2012). 'Self-awareness, self-regulation, and self-transcendence (S-ART): a framework for understanding the neurobiological mechanisms of mindfulness'. *Frontiers in Human Neuroscience,* 6, 296; van der Velden, A. M., Kuyken, W., Wattar, U., Crane, C., Pallesen, K. J., Dahlgaard, J., . . . and Piet, J. (2015). 'A systematic review of mechanisms of change in mindfulness-based cognitive therapy in the treatment of recurrent major depressive disorder'. *Clinical Psychology Review,* 37, 26–39; Dunne, J. D., Thompson, E., and Schooler, J. (2019). 'Mindful meta-awareness: sustained and non-propositional'. *Current Opinion in Psychology,* 28, 307–311; Dunne, J. D., Thompson, E., and Schooler, J. (2019). 'Mindful meta-awareness: sustained and non-propositional'. *Current Opinion in Psychology,* 28, 307–311.

p. 78 **'mindfulness meditation has also been linked to improvements in':** For more, see: Bishop, S. R., Lau, M., Shapiro, S., Carlson, L., Anderson, N. D., Carmody, J., et al. (2004). 'Mindfulness: a proposed operational definition'. *Journal of Clinical Psychology.* 11, 230–241; Jha, A. P., Rogers, S. L., Schoomaker, E., and Cardon, E. (2019). 'Deploying mindfulness to gain cognitive advantage: Considerations for military effectiveness and well-being'. In *NATO Science and Technology Conference Proceedings.* (pp. 1–14).

p. 78 **'research has shown that practising mindfulness meditation can':** Zhang, D., Lee, E. K., Mak, E. C., Ho, C. Y., and Wong, S. Y. (2021). 'Mindfulness-based interventions: an overall review'. *British Medical Bulletin,* 138(1), 41–57.

p. 78 **'mindfulness meditation can support both performance and mental wellbeing':** Focusing on performance – Noetel, M., Ciarrochi, J., Van

NOTES

Zanden, B., and Lonsdale, C. (2019). 'Mindfulness and acceptance approaches to sporting performance enhancement: A systematic review'. *International Review of Sport and Exercise Psychology*, 12(1), 139–175.

Focusing on performance and wellbeing – Birrer, D., Röthlin, P., and Morgan, G. (2021). 'Helping athletes flourish using mindfulness and acceptance approaches: An introduction and mini review'. *Sport and Exercise Medicine Switzerland*, 69(2), 29–34.

Focusing on wellbeing: Zhang, C. Q., Li, X., Chung, P. K., Huang, Z., Bu, D., Wang, D., Gao, Y., Wang, X., and Si, G. (2021). 'The effects of mindfulness on athlete burnout, subjective well-being and flourishing among elite athletes: A test of multiple mediators'. *Mindfulness*, 12(4), 1899–1908.

p. 79 **'Meditation is the only intentional, systematic human activity':** Kabat-Zinn, J. (2009). *Wherever You Go, There You Are: Mindfulness Meditation in Everyday Life.* Piatkus Books.

p. 79 **'Amishi Jha's book *Peak Mind*':** Jha, A. (2021). *Peak Mind: Find Your Focus, Own Your Attention, Invest 12 Minutes a Day.* Piatkus Books.

p. 79 **'Apps such as Smiling Mind and Headspace':** Smiling Mind, https://www.smilingmind.com.au/; Headspace, https://www.headspace.com/

p. 79 **'Author and businesswoman Arianna Huffington':** Tate, G. (2020, 3 February). 'Arianna Huffington Talks Meditation, the Importance of Failure, and the Underrated Power of Sleep'. High Existence. https://www.highexistence.com/arianna-huffington-interview/

p. 79 **'three-time Super Bowl-winning MVP Patrick Mahomes':** McDowell, S. (2023, 12 February). '*Meditation and perfecting the mind: How Patrick Mahomes handles the Super Bowl stage*'. *Kansas City Star.* https://amp-kansascity-com.cdn.ampproject.org/c/s/amp.kansascity.com/sports/spt-columns-blogs/sam-mcdowell/article272408998.html

p. 79 **'Northern Irish golfer Rory McIlroy':** Cannizzaro, M. (2019, 10 April). '*Rory McIlroy taking mindfulness to the next level*'. *New York Post.* https://nypost.com/2019/04/10/rory-mcilroy-taking-mindfulness-to-the-next-level/

p. 79 **'tennis star Serena Williams':** Jade Scipioni (2020, 19 February). '*2 things Serena Williams does every day to be productive*'. CNBC Make It. https://www.cnbc.com/2020/02/19/what-serena-williams-does-every-day-to-be-productive.html

p. 81 **'In his book *McMindfulness*':** Purser, R. (2019). *McMindfulness: How Mindfulness Became the New Capitalist Spirituality*. Repeater.

p. 82 **'In a review of *McMindfulness*':** Wolf, J. (2019, August 6). *McMindfulness by Ronald Purser; Mindfulness by Christina Feldman and Willem Kuyken – review*. Guardian. https://www.theguardian.com/books/2019/aug/06/mcmindfulness-ronald-purser-mindfulness-christina-feldman-willem-kuyken-review

p. 82 **'Philosopher Amia Srinivasan's belief that':** Srinivasan, A. (2018). 'The aptness of anger'. *Journal of Political Philosophy*, 26(2), 123–144. (p.19).

p. 83 **'He spoke about these in a podcast interview':** High Performance Podcast (2021, 8 November). 'All Blacks DAN CARTER Interview on finding your personal purpose' [Video file]. YouTube https://www.thehigherperformancepodcast.com/podcast/dancarter

p. 85 **'Mumford is quoted as saying':** Marder, J. (2022, 8 Jan). 'Be Here Now: How to Exercise Mindfully: Bringing meditation into your movement can enrich your workout and help you feel clearheaded afterward'. *New York Times*. https://www.nytimes.com/2022/01/28/well/move/exercise-mindfulness.html

p. 86 **'In an article published in the *New Yorker* in November 2022, Hetfield talked about':** Petrusich, A. (2022, 28 November). 'The Enduring Metal Genius of Metallica: On the road with the band in its forty-first year'. *New Yorker*. https://www.newyorker.com/magazine/2022/12/05/the-enduring-metal-genius-of-metallica

p. 86 **'It's a sign of the times that when Metallica':** Petrusich, A. (2022, 28 November). 'The Enduring Metal Genius of Metallica: On the road with the band in its forty-first year'. *New Yorker*. https://www.newyorker.com/magazine/2022/12/05/the-enduring-metal-genius-of-metallica

p. 87 **'Research has shown that we tend to overestimate the levels of happiness':** Wilson, T. D., and Gilbert, D. T. (2003). 'Affective forecasting.' In M. Zanna (Ed.) *Advances in Experimental Social Psychology*. Elsevier. (pp. 345–411).

p. 87 **'*Happier: Learn the Secrets to Daily Joy and Lasting Fulfilment*':** Ben-Shahar, T. (2007). *Happier: Learn the Secrets to Daily Joy and Lasting Fulfilment*. McGraw-Hill.

p. 87 **'what the poet John Astin refers to as':** Astin, J. (2013). *This is Always Enough*. CreateSpace Independent Publishing Platform.

p. 87 **'During an interview in 2005, Tom Brady':** 60 minutes. (2019, 31 January). *'Tom Brady's favorite Super Bowl ring? "The next one"'* [Video file]. YouTube. https://www.youtube.com/watch?v=ypELsuR1MRM

p. 87 **'the term "mis-wanting"':** Gilbert, D. T., and Wilson, T. D. (2000). 'Miswanting: Some problems in the forecasting of future affective states'. In J. Forgas (ed.), *Thinking and Feeling: The Role of Affect in Social Cognition*, Cambridge University Press.

p. 88 **'Lou Holtz, the former Notre Dame football coach':** Snowden, J. (2009, 27 June). 'Lou Holtz Notre Dame WIN'. YouTube. https://youtu.be/KZu_rdmbFe4

p. 88 **'According to the American psychologist and author Rick Hanson':** Hanson, R. (n.d.). 'Take in the Good'. Dr Rick Hanson. https://www.rickhanson.net/take-in-the-good/

p. 88 **'bad events tend to register more than the good':** Baumeister, R. F., Bratslavsky, E., Finkenauer, C., and Vohs, K. D. (2001). 'Bad is stronger than good'. *Review of General Psychology*, 5(4), 323–370.

p. 89 **'Although definitions of savouring vary':** Bryant, F. B. (2021). 'Current progress and future directions for theory and research on savoring'. *Frontiers in Psychology*, 12, 771698.

p. 89 **'the Savouring Beliefs Inventory':** Bryant, F. B. (2003). 'Savoring beliefs inventory (SBI): A scale for measuring beliefs about savouring'. *Journal of Mental Health*, 12(2), 175–196.

p. 89 **'to help with solidifying our memories of those events':** Bryant, F.B.; Veroff, J. (2007). *Savoring: A New Model of Positive Experience*. Lawrence Erlbaum Associations.

p. 89 **'associated with increased levels of life satisfaction':** Smith, J. L., and Bryant, F. B. (2019). 'Enhancing positive perceptions of aging by savoring life lessons'. *Aging Mental Health*, 23, 762–770.

p. 89 **'savouring is associated with . . . positive psychological functioning':** Smith, J. L., and Bryant, F. B. (2017). 'Savoring and well-being: Mapping the cognitive-emotional terrain of the happy mind'. In M. D. Robinson and M. Eid (Eds.), *The Happy Mind: Cognitive Contributions to Well-Being Springer*. International Publishing/Springer Nature. (pp. 139–156).

p. 89 **'how often people subsequently report life events as being pleasurable':** Jose, P. E., Bryant, F. B., and Macaskill, E. (2020). 'Savor now and also reap the rewards later: Amplifying savoring predicts greater uplift frequency over time'. *Journal of Positive Psychology.* 2020:1805504.

p. 90 **'parents' patterns of savouring predict how well their offspring savour, both as children and adolescents':** Moran, K. M., Root, A. E., Vizy, B. K., Wilson, T. K., and Gentzler, A. L. (2019). 'Maternal socialization of children's positive affect regulation: Associations with children's savoring, dampening, and depressive symptoms'. *Social Development* 28, 306–322; Fredrick, J. W., Mancini, K. J., and Luebbe, A. M. (2019). 'Maternal enhancing responses to adolescents' positive affect: Associations with adolescents' positive affect regulation and depression'. *Social Development* 28, 290–305.

Chapter 4: Willing

p. 93 **'Through a process called thigmomorphogenesis':** Ehrenberg, R. (2020, 31 January). 'Bent into shape: The rules of tree form'. *Knowable Magazine.* https://knowablemagazine.org/content/article/living-world/2020/bent-shape-rules-tree-form; Hole, J. (2017, 26 June). 'Young trees need space to flex their "muscles"'. *St. Albert Gazette.* https://www.stalbertgazette.com/amp/lifestyle-news/young-trees-need-space-to-flex-their-muscles-2044637

p. 95 **'The pair travelled 29,000 miles in nineteen days and twenty-one hours':** National Air and Space Museum – Smithsonian Gondola (n.d.). 'Breitling Orbiter 3'. https://airandspace.si.edu/collection-objects/gondola-breitling-orbiter-3/nasm_A19990257000

p. 95 **'In an interview with the *New Yorker*':** Taub, B. (2022, 3 October). 'Close to the sun: The making of Bertrand Piccard's solar-powered air journey around the world'. *New Yorker.* https://www.newyorker.com/magazine/2022/10/10/bertrand-piccards-laps-around-the-world/amp

p. 96 **'Jonny Wilkinson, the World Cup-winning former England rugby star':** High Performance Podcast (2020, 26 September). 'Jonny Wilkinson – Full Extended Episode' [Video file]. YouTube https://www.youtube.com/watch?v=O80qs9OEadw

p. 98 **'billions of Portable Document Format files':** Johnson, D. (2018, 14 May). 'PDF statistics – the universe of electronic documents'. PDF Association https://pdfa.org/wp-content/uploads/2018/06/1330_Johnson.pdf

p. 99 **'the American author John Augustus Shedd once remarked':** Shedd, J.A. (1928). *Salt From My Attic.* The Mosher Press. (p. 20).

p. 104 **'Just like your memories, and how you want to remember them':** Google UK (2021, 9 December). 'Make photobombers disappear with Magic Eraser on Pixel 6' [Video file]. YouTube https://www.youtube.com/watch?v=K837CUgzhiE

p. 105 **'The so-called "rebound effect"':** Wegner, D. M., Schneider, D. J., Carter, S. and White, T. (1987). 'Paradoxical effects of thought suppression'. *Journal of Personality and Social Psychology*, 53, 5–13.

p. 105 **'Research has consistently shown that the wish not to':** Wang, D., Hagger, M.S., and Chatzisarantis, N.L.D. (2020). 'Ironic effects of thought suppression: a meta-analysis'. *Perspectives on Psychological Science*, 15(3), 778–793.

p. 105 **'Research led by Emily C. Willroth':** Willroth, E. C., Young, G., Tamir, M., and Mauss, I. B. (2023). 'Judging emotions as good or bad: Individual differences and associations with psychological health'. *Emotion*, 23(7), 1876–1890.

p. 108 **'by working with an Acceptance and Commitment Therapy trainer':** Dr Ray Owen has provided training and supervision in Acceptance and Commitment Therapy to Lydia Thompson.

p. 108 **'Speaking in an interview':** Harvey, J. (2022, 9 November). 'Lydia Thompson Exclusive – Red Roses wing talks Black Ferns redemption, self-doubt and gratitude'. Talking Rugby Union. https://www.talkingrugbyunion.co.uk/lydia-thompson-exclusive-red-roses-wing-talks-black-ferns-redemption-self-doubt-and-gratitude/34757.htm

p. 118 **'The late, great NBA star Kobe Bryant made this point brilliantly':** Jay Shetty Podcast (2020, 19 September). 'Kobe Bryant's Last Great Interview on How to Find Purpose in Life | Kobe Bryant and Jay Shetty' [Video file]. YouTube. https://www.youtube.com/watch?v=g2cQ2kD6lzs

p. 119 **'Dutch broadcaster and journalist Wilfred Genee':** Wilfred Genee (@wilfredgenee). (2015, 17 February). 'Andy Murray's note'. [Tweet]. X. https://twitter.com/wilfredgenee/status/567625102880436224?s=20andt=b1OGodOa2MDSGhjIA-vt_A

p. 119 **'There are two types of strategic self-talk':** Hatzigeorgiadis, A., Zourbanos, N., Galanis, E., and Theodorakis, Y. (2011). 'Self-talk and sports performance: A meta-analysis'. *Perspectives on Psychological Science*, 6(4), 348–356.

p. 119 **'Win the moment in front of your face':** Pendulum Summit (2020,

18 May). '21 Days Of Inspiration II | Day 1 with Paul O'Connell: Win The Moment That Is In Front of You' [Video file]. https://www.facebook.com/watch/?v=572249513690144

p. 119 **'Research conducted with athletes involved in a wide range of sports'**: Hatzigeorgiadis, A., Zourbanos, N., Galanis, E., and Theodorakis, Y. (2011). 'Self-talk and sports performance: A meta-analysis'. *Perspectives on Psychological Science*, 6(4), 348–356.

p. 120 **'A research study demonstrated that self-talk expressed'**: Hardy, J., Thomas, A. V., and Blanchfield, A. W. (2019). 'To me, to you: How you say things matters for endurance performance'. *Journal of Sports Sciences*, 37(18), 2122–2130.

Chapter 5: Empowered

p. 122 **'For every square yard of forest'**: Zimmermann, L.; Raspe, S.; Schulz, C.; Grimmeisen, W. (2008). 'Wasserverbrauch von Wäldern'. In: *LWF aktuell* (66), S. 16–20.

p. 122 **'Through a process called positive phototropism'**: Duchemin, L., Eloy, C., Badel, E., and Moulia, B. (2018). 'Tree crowns grow into self-similar shapes controlled by gravity and light sensing'. *Journal of the Royal Society Interface*, 15(142), 20170976.

p. 125 **'Woe to him who saw no more sense'**: Frankl, V. E. (1985). *Man's Search for Meaning*. Simon and Schuster.

p. 125 **'William Damon and his colleagues defined it'**: Damon, W., Menon, J., and Cotton Bronk, K. (2003). 'The development of purpose during adolescence'. *Applied Developmental Science*, 7(3), 119–128. (p. 120).

p. 125 **'Purpose allows us to see our lives as journeys'**: Rudd, M., Catapano, R., and Aaker, J. (2019). 'Making time matter: A review of research on time and meaning'. *Journal of Consumer Psychology*, 29(4), 680–702.

p. 125 **'from the Multidimensional Existential Meaning Scale'**: George, L. S., and Park, C. L. (2017). 'The Multidimensional Existential Meaning Scale: A tripartite approach to measuring meaning in life'. *Journal of Positive Psychology*, 12, 613–627.

For other questionnaires with subscales assessing purpose, see: The Three-Dimensional Meaning in Life Scale (Martela and Steger, 2023) – Martela, F., and Steger, M. F. (2023). 'The role of significance relative to the other dimensions of meaning in life – an examination utilizing the three-dimensional meaning in life scale (3DM)'. *Journal of Positive Psychology*, 18, 606–626.

The Psychological Well-Being Scale (Ryff, 1989) – Ryff, C.D. (1989). 'Happiness is everything, or is it? Explorations on the meaning of psychological well-being'. *Journal of Personality and Social Psychology*, 57, 1069–1081.

p. 126 **'A high level of purpose is predictive of'**: Hill, P.L, and Turiano, N.A. (2014). 'Purpose in life as a predictor of mortality across adulthood'. *Psychological Science*, 25(7), 1482–86; McKnight, P. E. and Kashdan, T. B. (2009). 'Purpose in life as a system that creates and sustains health and well-being: an integrative, testable theory'. *Review of General Psychology*, 13(3), 242–51; Steger, M. F. (2012). 'Experiencing meaning in life: optimal functioning at the nexus of spirituality, psychopathology, and well-being'. In P. T. P. Wong (Ed.), *The Human Quest for Meaning: Theories, Research, and Applications*. Routledge ; For more, see King, L. A., and Hicks, J. A. (2021). 'The science of meaning in life'. *Annual Review of Psychology*, 72, 561–584.

p. 126 **'we experience increases in self-esteem and pleasant emotions'**: Kashdan, T. B., and McKnight, P. E. (2013). 'Commitment to a purpose in life: An antidote to the suffering by individuals with social anxiety disorder'. *Emotion*, 13, 1150–1159.

p. 126 **'As Friedrich Nietzsche famously remarked'**: Nietzsche, F. (2018). *The Twilight of the Idols*. Jovian Press.

p. 128 **'Harvard Business Review Guide to Crafting Your Purpose'**: Coleman, J. (2022). *HBR Guide to Crafting Your Purpose*. Harvard Business Press.

p. 128 **'prompts that have been shown to help with cultivating purpose'**: King, L. A., and Hicks, J. A. (2021). 'The science of meaning in life'. *Annual Review of Psychology*, 72, 561–584.

p. 133 **'these were the values of the Enron Corporation'**: Lencioni, P.M. (2020, July). 'Make Your Values Mean Something: Your corporate values statement may be doing more harm than good. Here's how to fix it'. *Harvard Business Review*. https://hbr.org/2002/07/make-your-values-mean-something

p. 133 **'described as the "corporate crime of the century"'**: Independent Television Service (n.d.). *Enron: The Smartest Guys in the Room*. https://itvs.org/films/enron

p. 133 **'the value of Enron's share price'**: Beckett, J. (2023, 8 September). 'Enron Stock Chart – The History Of Enron'. MoneyStocker. https://www.tinyhigh.com/passive-investing/enron-stock-chart-the-history-of-enron/

p. 133 **'It's $63.4 billion of assets'**: Constable, S. (2021, 2 December). 'How the Enron Scandal Changed American Business Forever'. *Time*. https://time.com/6125253/enron-scandal-changed-american-business-forever/

p. 133 ***'Enron: The Smartest Guys in the Room'***: Independent Television Service (n.d.). *Enron: The Smartest Guys in the Room*. https://itvs.org/films/enron

p. 135 **'plenty of values' card-sorting tasks and online tools'**: Miller, W.R., C'de Baca, J., Matthews, D.B. and Wilbourne, P.L. (2011). 'Personal Values Card Sort' https://www.guilford.com/add/miller11_old/pers_val.pdf?t=1; Personal Values Free Online Test (n.d.). 'Here is a list of your most important values'. https://personalvalu.es/results/cead6752-90b9-4289-a0f4-e08c16c40531; Crace, R. K. and Brown, D. (n.d.). Life Values Inventory – online. https://www.lifevaluesinventory.org/the-process.html

p. 135 **'Questionnaires such as the Valuing Questionnaire'**: Smout, M., Davies, M., Burns, N., and Christie, A. (2014). 'Development of the valuing questionnaire (VQ)'. *Journal of Contextual Behavioral Science*, 3(3), 164–172.

p. 135 **'associated with higher levels of wellbeing'**: Christie, A. M., Atkins, P. W., and Donald, J. N. (2017). 'The meaning and doing of mindfulness: The role of values in the link between mindfulness and well-being'. *Mindfulness*, 8, 368–378.

p. 135 **'lower levels of depression, anxiety and stress'**: Carvalho, S.A., Palmeira, L., Pinto–Gouveia, J., Gillanders, D., Castilho, P. (2018). 'The utility of the Valuing Questionnaire in Chronic Pain'. *Journal of Contextual Behavioral Science*, 9, 21–29.

p. 135 **'the "Birthday Speech exercise"'**: This exercise is based on similar methods that have been developed by ACT therapists and trainers including the '80th Birthday' and 'Eulogy' exercises. Russ Harris and Steven C. Hayes amongst others have been instrumental in inspiring approaches I use with clients.

p. 139 **'If you always do what you've always done'**: Jessie Potter, then-director of the National Institute for Human Relationships in Oak Lawn, Ill., as quoted in: *Milwaukee Sentinel*. (1981, 24 October). 'Search For Quality Called Key To Life by Tom Ahern', page 5, column 5.

p. 139 **'All overnight success takes about ten years'**: The Good Life Mentor (2017, 18 November). 'Jeff Bezos discusses what made Amazon so successful, including his key principles' [Video file]. YouTube https://www.youtube.com/watch?v=FJ3jw6TkVmc

p. 140 **'As the actor Hugh Laurie reportedly notes'**: Bridges, F. (2015, 31 July). 'The Risk Of Waiting Until You're Ready'. *Forbes*. https://www.forbes.com/sites/francesbridges/2015/07/31/the-risk-of-waiting-until-youre-ready/

p. 141 **'commitment is healthiest when it is not without doubt'**: May, R. (1975). *The Courage to Create*. W. W. Norton and Company. (p. 21).

p. 142 **'Bandura himself stated that'**: Bandura, A. (1978). 'The self system in reciprocal determinism'. *American Psychologist*, 33, 344–358. (p. 357).

p. 143 **'our unique personality traits'**: Levin, I. P., Gaeth, G. J., Schreiber, J., and Lauriola, M. (2002). 'A new look at framing effects: Distribution of effect sizes, individual differences, and types of effects'. *Organizational Behavior and Human Decision Processes*, 88, 411–429.

p. 143 **'anticipate how others will respond'**: Sanfey, A. G. (2007). 'Social decision-making: Insights from game theory and neuroscience'. *Science*, 318(5850), 598–602.

p. 143 **'our decision-making style'**: Galotti, K. M. (2007). 'Decision structuring in important real-life choices'. *Psychological Science*, 18(4), 320–325.

p. 143 **'In his book *Thinking, Fast and Slow*'**: Kahneman, D. (2011). *Thinking, Fast and Slow*. Macmillan.

p. 143 **'Research has shown that we tend to use System 1 more'**: Savioni, L., Triberti, S., Durosini, I., and Pravettoni, G. (2022). 'How to make big decisions: A cross-sectional study on the decision making process in life choices'. *Current Psychology*, 1–14.

p. 144 **'research has shown that practising mindfulness meditation'**: Sun, S., Yao, Z., Wei, J., and Yu, R. (2015). 'Calm and smart? A selective review of meditation effects on decision making'. *Frontiers in Psychology*, 6, 1059.

p. 144 **'he asked if there were any one-armed economists'**: Buttonwood (2010, 7 June). 'One-armed economists: How is the humble investor to cope when expert opinion is divided?' *Economist*. https://www.economist.com/buttonwoods-notebook/2010/06/07/one-armed-economists

p. 145 **'Søren Kierkegaard, the Danish philosopher, described the dread'**:

Kierkegaard, S., and Lowrie, W. (1957). *The Concept of Dread*. Princeton University Press.

p. 145 '*The Paradox of Choice: Why More Can be Less*': Schwartz, B. (2004). *The Paradox of Choice: Why More Can be Less*. Harper Perennial.

p. 145 'A review of the research evidence': Chernev, A., Böckenholt, U., and Goodman, J. (2015). 'Choice overload: A conceptual review and meta-analysis'. *Journal of Consumer Psychology*, 25(2), 333–358.

p. 147 'the task unification technique': This is a technique derived from an approach called Systematic Inventive Thinking (SIT). See: Boyd, D., and Goldenberg, J. (2014). *Inside the Box: A Proven System of Creativity for Breakthrough Results*. Simon and Schuster.

For more on lateral thinking approaches, see: Sloane, P. (2023). *Lateral Thinking for Every Day: Extraordinary Solutions to Ordinary Problems*. Kogan Page Publishers.

p. 148 'more than 5 million have been sold': Baker, H. (2023; 6 February). 'Bristol *Dragons' Den* reject Trunki to be sold for millions of pounds'. *Bristol Live*. https://www.bristolpost.co.uk/news/business/bristol-dragons-den-reject-trunki-8115698

p. 148 'Chesky would later recall': Rhode Island School of Design (2027, 3 June). 'Brian Chesky RISD Commencement Address 2017' [Video file]. Vimeo. https://vimeo.com/220140027

p. 149 'Chesky alone accrued debt of $30,000 on his credit card': Kenja Explains (2020, 15 August). 'How Airbnb Founders Sold Cereal to Keep Their Dream Alive'. Medium. https://ehandbook.com/how-airbnb-founders-sold-cereal-to-keep-their-dream-alive-d44223a9bdab

p. 150 'these cereal boxes raised a staggering $30,000': Kenja Explains (2020, 15 August). 'How Airbnb Founders Sold Cereal to Keep Their Dream Alive'. Medium. https://ehandbook.com/how-airbnb-founders-sold-cereal-to-keep-their-dream-alive-d44223a9bdab

p. 150 'At the last count, Airbnb now advertises properties in': Airbnb (n.d.) 'About us'. https://news.airbnb.com/about-us/

p. 150 'market capitalization is valued at $107 billion': Forbes Profile. (2024, 21 March). 'Airbnb'. *Forbes*. (https://www.forbes.com/companies/airbnb/

p. 150 'the symbol for belonging': Design Studio (n.d.). 'Airbnb'. https://www.design.studio/work/air-bnb#:~:text=The%20'Belo'%20logo%20sat%20at,to%20be%20drawn%20by%20anyone.

p. 150 **'outlined in their mission statement'**: Airbnb (2019, 15 January). 'Airbnb 2019 Business Update' https://news.airbnb.com/airbnb-2019-business-update/

p. 150 **'the company has four core values'**: Airbnb (n.d.). 'Life at Airbnb'. https://careers.airbnb.com/life-at-airbnb/

Part III

p. 156 **'supported by contemporary psychological theory'**: Richardson, M., McEwan, K., Maratos, F., and Sheffield, D. (2016). 'Joy and calm: how an evolutionary functional model of affect regulation informs positive emotions in nature'. *Evolutionary Psychological Science*, 2(4), 308–320; Gilbert, P. (2009). *The Compassionate Mind*. Robinson; Depue R.A., Morrone-Strupinsky J.V. (2005). 'A neurobehavioral model of affiliative bonding: implications for conceptualizing a human trait of affiliation'. *Behavioral and Brain Sciences*, 28(3), 313–349.

Chapter 6: Get

p. 159 **'more light can penetrate its canopy to reach the bark'**: Kim, N., Makar, M., Osleger, A., and Shenouda, J. (2019). 'The adaptive value of leaf quaking in Populus tremuloides'. *CEC Research*, 3(2).

p. 160 **'dopamine has been identified as playing a prominent role in this mode'**: Lewis, R. G., Florio, E., Punzo, D., and Borrelli, E. (2021). 'The Brain's reward system in health and disease'. In Engmann, O., and Brancaccio, M. (Eds.). *Circadian Clock in Brain Health and Disease*. Springer International Publishing. (p. 57–69).

p. 160 **'an over-reliance on extrinsic forms of reward'**: Stone, D. N., Deci, E. L., and Ryan, R. M. (2009). 'Beyond talk: Creating autonomous motivation through self-determination theory'. *Journal of General Management*, 34(3), 75–91.

p. 161 **'deliver short-term gain and create long-term problems'**: Stone, D. N., Deci, E. L., and Ryan, R. M. (2009). 'Beyond talk: Creating autonomous motivation through self-determination theory'. *Journal of General Management*, 34(3), 75–91.

p. 161 'Self-Determination Theory': Deci, E. L. and Ryan, R.M. (1985). *Intrinsic Motivation and Self-Determination in Human Behavior*. Plenum.

p. 161 'identified across different cultural contexts': Chirkov, V., Ryan, R. M., Kim, Y., and Kaplan, U. (2003). 'Differentiating autonomy from individualism and independence: a self-determination theory perspective on internalization of cultural orientations and well-being'. *Journal of Personality and Social Psychology*, 84(1), 97.

p. 161 'Ryan and Deci have likened these yearnings to': Deci, E.L., and Ryan, R.M. (2000). 'The "what" and "why" of goal pursuits: Human needs and the self-determination of behavior'. *Psychological Inquiry*, 11, 227–268. (p. 229).

p. 161 'reviews of the research evidence have consistently shown': Stanley, P. J., Schutte, N. S., and Phillips, W. J. (2021). 'A meta-analytic investigation of the relationship between basic psychological need satisfaction and affect.' *Journal of Positive School Psychology*, 5(1), 1–16; Tang, M., Wang, D., and Guerrien, A. (2020). 'A systematic review and meta-analysis on basic psychological need satisfaction, motivation, and well-being in later life: Contributions of self-determination theory'. *PsyCh Journal*, 9, 5–33.

p. 162 'research has shown that focusing on money as a reward is linked with': Vohs, K. D., Mead, N. L., and Goode, M. R. (2006). 'The psychological consequences of money'. *Science*, 314(5802), 1154–1156.

p. 162 'less able to savour the richness of simpler everyday pleasures': Quoidbach, J., Dunn, E. W., Petrides, K. V., and Mikolajczak, M. (2010). 'Money giveth, money taketh away: The dual effect of wealth on happiness'. *Psychological Science*, 21(6), 759–763.

p. 164 'introduced the acronym SMART': Doran, G. T. (1981). 'There's a SMART way to write management's goals and objectives'. *Management Review*, 70(11), 35–36.

p. 167 'it [mental imagery] has also been used to boost': Vasquez, N. A., and Buehler, R. (2007). 'Seeing future success: Does imagery perspective influence achievement motivation?' *Personality and Social Psychology Bulletin*, 33(10), 1392–1405; Conroy, D., and Hagger, M. S. (2018). 'Imagery interventions in health behavior: A meta-analysis'. *Health Psychology*, 37(7), 668; Pearson, J., Naselaris, T., Holmes, E.A., and Kosslyn, S. M. (2015). 'Mental imagery: functional mechanisms and clinical applications'. *Trends in Cognitive Sciences*, 19(10), 590–602.

p. 167 'pioneered by Paul Holmes and Dave Collins': Holmes, P. S., and

Collins, D. J. (2001). 'The PETTLEP approach to motor imagery: A functional equivalence model for sport psychologists'. *Journal of Applied Sport Psychology*, 13(1), 60–83.

p. 168 '**Jonny Wilkinson, the former England rugby fly-half**': Wilkinson, J. (2006). *My World*. Headline Publishing Group. (p. 49).

p. 169 '**research evidence found that athletes' use of mental imagery**': Simonsmeier, B. A., Andronie, M., Buecker, S., and Frank, C. (2021). 'The effects of imagery interventions in sports: A meta-analysis'. *International Review of Sport and Exercise Psychology*, 14(1), 186–207

p. 169 '**One in every fifty of us is affected by . . . aphantasia**': Costandi, M. (2016, 4 June). 'If you can't imagine things, how can you learn?' *Guardian*. https://amp.theguardian.com/education/2016/jun/04/aphantasia-no-visual-imagination-impact-learning

p. 170 '**Although definitions of self-confidence vary widely**': Oney, E., and Oksuzoglu-Guven, G. (2015). 'Confidence: A critical review of the literature and an alternative perspective for general and specific self-confidence'. *Psychological Reports*, 116(1), 149–163.

p. 170 '**perceived ability to accomplish a certain level of performance**': Feltz, D.L. (2007). 'Self-confidence and sports performance'. In Smith, D., Bar-Eli, M., (Eds.). *Essential Readings in Sport and Exercise Psychology*. Human Kinetics. pp. 278–294. (p. 279).

p. 171 '**the concept of self-efficacy, which he defined as**': Bandura, A. (1977). 'Self-efficacy – toward a unifying theory of behavioral change'. *Psychology Review*, 84, 191–215.

p. 171 '**A major review of more than forty research papers**': Lochbaum, M., Sherburn, M., Sisneros, C., Cooper, S., Lane, A. M., and Terry, P. C. (2022). 'Revisiting the Self-Confidence and Sport Performance Relationship: A Systematic Review with Meta-Analysis'. *International Journal of Environmental Research and Public Health*, 19(11), 6381.

p. 176 '**David Bowie, the late, great musician, said**': Haddon C. (2023, 29 May). 'David Bowie on How to Create: "Never Play to the Gallery"'. Medium. https://medium.com/@cole.haddon/david-bowie-on-how-to-create-never-play-to-the-gallery-e958c9b5e3f7#:~:text=Always%20go%20a%20little%20further,place%20to%20do%20something%20exciting.%E2%80%9D

p. 177 '**Boardman's advice is to ask yourself**': Scott, G. (2014, 23 April). 'Chris Boardman's five top tips for your first ten-mile time trial'. Road Cycling

UK. https://roadcyclinguk.com/how-to/chris-boardmans-ten-mile-time-trial-tips.html/2

p. 177 **'the Inishowen 100':** Foyle Cycling Club (2022). 'Inishowen 100'. https://www.foylecycling.net/inishowen100

p. 180 **'Technical definitions of flow describe it':** Csikszentmihalyi, M., and LeFevre, J. (1989). 'Optimal experience in work and leisure'. *Journal of Personality and Social Psychology*, 56(5), 815.

p. 180 **'Research conducted with 500 families':** Isham, A., Gatersleben, B., and Jackson, T. (2019). 'Flow activities as a route to living well with less'. *Environment and Behavior*, 51(4), 431–461.

p. 182 **'the Long Flow State Scale':** Jackson, S. A., and Eklund, R. C. (2002). 'Assessing flow in physical activity: The flow state scale-2 and dispositional flow scale-2'. *Journal of Sport and Exercise Psychology*, 24(2), 133–150.

p. 182 **'the Flow Research Collective':** Flow Research Collective (n.d.). https://www.flowresearchcollective.com

p. 182 **'a further nineteen triggers of flow':** Kotler, S. (2021). *The Art of Impossible*. Harper Collins. (p. 233).

p. 182 **'balanced with periods of rest and recovery':** Kotler, S. (2021). *The Art of Impossible*. Harper Collins; Ignjatovic, C., Kern, M. L., and Oades, L. G. (2022). 'Values-Flow in Contextual Psychotherapy: The "What", "Why", and "How" of Sustainable Values-Based Behaviour'. In *Happiness and Wellness – Biopsychosocial and Anthropological Perspectives*. IntechOpen.

p. 182 **'Research has indicated that flow helps us to glow':** Wu, J., Xie, M., Lai, Y., Mao, Y., and Harmat, L. (2021). 'Flow as a key predictor of subjective well-being among Chinese university students: A chain mediating model'. *Frontiers in Psychology*, 12, 743906; Tse D. C., Nakamura J., Csikszentmihalyi M. (2021). 'Living well by "flowing" well: the indirect effect of autotelic personality on well-being through flow experience'. *Journal of Positive Psychology*, 16, 310–321.

p. 182 **'small but consistent positive relationship between flow and':** Harris, D. J., Allen, K. L., Vine, S. J., and Wilson, M. R. (2021). 'A systematic review and meta-analysis of the relationship between flow states and performance'. *International Review of Sport and Exercise Psychology*, 1–29.

p. 182 **'anxiety, which adversely impacts on our ability to perform skills':** Eysenck, M. W., and Wilson, M. R. (2016). 'Sporting performance, pressure and cognition: Introducing attentional control theory: Sport'. In D. Groome and M. Eysenck (Eds.), *An Introduction to Applied Cognitive Psychology*, Routledge. (pp. 329–350); Nieuwenhuys, A., and Oudejans, R. R. D. (2012). 'Anxiety and perceptual-motor performance: Toward an integrated model of concepts, mechanisms, and processes'. *Psychological Research*, 76(6), 747–759.

p. 182 '[anxiety is] conspicuously lacking when we experience flow': Harris, D. J., Allen, K. L., Vine, S. J., and Wilson, M. R. (2021). 'A systematic review and meta-analysis of the relationship between flow states and performance'. *International Review of Sport and Exercise Psychology*, 1–29.

p. 182 'focusing on outcomes might detract from our ability to experience flow': Csikszentmihalyi, M. (1990). *Flow: The Psychology of Optimal Experience*. Harper.

p. 183 'flow can have a "dark side"': Hogarth, B. (2020, 1 September). 'The Dark Side of Flow (1/2)'. Flow Research Collective. https://www.flowresearchcollective.com/blog/dark-side-of-flow

p. 183 'research that has linked flow with risk-taking and addictive behaviours': Schüler, J., and Nakamura, J. (2013). 'Does flow experience lead to risk? How and for whom'. *Applied Psychology: Health and Well-Being*, 5(3), 311–331; Thatcher, A., Wretschko, G., and Fridjhon, P. (2008). 'Online flow experiences, problematic internet use and internet procrastination'. *Computers in Human Behavior*, 24, 2236–54.

p. 183 'Kotler himself has warned of the risk': Kotler, S. (2014). *The Rise of Superman: Decoding the Science of Ultimate Human Performance*. Houghton Mifflin Harcourt.

p. 183 'A review of seventeen different research studies found': Schutte, N. S., and Malouff, J. M. (2023). 'The connection between mindfulness and flow: A meta-analysis'. *Personality and Individual Differences*, 200, 111871.

p. 183 'psychological flexibility were associated with their levels of flow': Carrança, B., Serpa, S., Rosado, A., Guerrero, J. P., and Magalhães, C. (2019). 'Mindful compassion training on elite soccer: effects, roles and associations on flow, psychological distress and thought suppression'. *Revista iberoamericana de psicología del ejercicio y el deporte*, 14(2), 141–149.

p. 186 'Thankfully, a solution is eventually found': Middleton, P. and Spinney, J. (Directors). (2021). *The Real Charlie Chaplin*. Showtime.

p. 186 'Reflecting on it years later, Chaplin said': Robinson, David (1985). *Chaplin: His Life and Art*. McGraw-Hill Books Company. (p. 399).

p. 186 'She said of Chaplin': Middleton, P. and Spinney, J. (Directors). (2021). *The Real Charlie Chaplin*. Showtime.

p. 187 'in a 2013 interview with the *Telegraph*': Hoby, H. (2013, 18 August). 'Margaret Atwood: interview'. *Telegraph*. https://www.telegraph.co.uk/culture/books/10246937/Margaret-Atwood-interview.html

p. 187 'Three distinct forms of perfectionism': Hewitt, P. L., and Flett, G. L. (1991). 'Perfectionism in the self and social contexts: conceptualization, assessment, and association with psychopathology'. *Journal of Personality and Social Psychology*, 60(3), 456.

p. 188 'most strongly related to a range of mental health difficulties': Limburg, K., Watson, H. J., Hagger, M. S., and Egan, S. J. (2017). 'The relationship between perfectionism and psychopathology: A meta-analysis'. *Journal of Clinical Psychology*, 73(10), 1301–1326.

p. 188 'harsh judgements directed at us during our childhood': Hewitt, P. L., Flett, G. L., and Mikail, S. F. (2017). *Perfectionism: A Relationship Approach to Conceptualization, Assessment, and Treatment*. Guildford Press.

p. 188 'A study led by two British psychologists': Curran T. and Hill A.P. (2019). 'Perfectionism is increasing over time: A meta-analysis of birth cohort differences from 1989 to 2016'. *Psychological Bulletin*, 145(4), 410–429.

p. 188 'Reflecting on the findings, Curran suggested': American Psychological Association (2018). 'Perfectionism Among Young People Significantly Increased Since 1980s, Study Finds'. https://www.apa.org/news/press/releases/2018/01/perfectionism-young-people

p. 188 'Apps such as Facetune and AirBrush': Facetune (n.d.). https://www.facetuneapp.com/; AirBrush (n.d.). https://airbrush.com/tools/app

p. 189 'Excellencism – defined by the Canadian psychologist Patrick Gaudreau': Gaudreau, P. (2019). 'On the distinction between personal standards perfectionism and excellencism: A theory elaboration and research agenda'. *Perspectives on Psychological Science*, 14(2), 197–215. (p. 200).

p. 189 'misguided assumption that perfectionism is "good for business"': Harari, D., Swider, B.W., Steed, L.B., and Breidenthal, A. P. (2018). 'Is perfect good? A meta-analysis of perfectionism in the workplace'. *Journal of Applied Psychology*, 103(10), 1121.

p. 190 'research conducted by Gaudreau and his colleagues': Gaudreau, P.,

Schellenberg, B.J., Gareau, A., Kljajic, K., and Manoni-Millar, S. (2022). 'Because excellencism is more than good enough: On the need to distinguish the pursuit of excellence from the pursuit of perfection'. *Journal of Personality and Social Psychology*, 122(6), 1117.

p. 190 **'a flexible mind can help with managing perfectionism':** Ong, C. W., Lee, E. B., Krafft, J., Terry, C. L., Barrett, T. S., Levin, M. E., and Twohig, M. P. (2019). 'A randomized controlled trial of acceptance and commitment therapy for clinical perfectionism'. *Journal of Obsessive-Compulsive and Related Disorders*, 22, 100444.

p. 192 **'an essay she wrote for *Marie Claire* in 2010':** Musk, J. (2010, 10 September). '"I Was a Starter Wife": Inside America's Messiest Divorce'. *Marie Claire*. https://www.marieclaire.com/sex-love/a5380/millionaire-starter-wife/

p. 193 **'Do I think hard work matters?':** Kale, S. (2022, 10 June). '"Insecurity was my biggest motivator": how *Dragons' Den*'s Steven Bartlett became a "happy sexy millionaire"'. *Guardian*. https://www.theguardian.com/life-andstyle/2022/jun/20/dragons-den-steven-bartlett-happy-sexy-millionaire

Chapter 7: Threat

p. 197 **'a force equivalent to 220 tons':** Wohlleben, P. (2016). *The Hidden Life of Trees: What They Feel, How They Communicate—Discoveries from a Secret World*. Greystone Books.

p. 197 **'an area equivalent to sixteen football pitches':** Harvey, F. (2022, 17 August). 'Tree loss due to fire is worst in far northern latitudes, data shows'. *Guardian*. https://www.theguardian.com/environment/2022/aug/17/tree-loss-due-to-fire-is-worst-in-far-northern-latitudes-data-shows#:~:text=The%20amount%20of%20tree%20cover,year%20or%2036%2C000%20additional%20hectares.

p. 197 **'more than 73,000 species of trees':** Wilson, C. (2023, 21 July). 'How many trees are there on earth?' Gardeners Dream. https://www.gardenersdream.co.uk/blog/2023/07/21/how-many-trees-on-earth-are-there/#:~:text=Of%20the%203%20trillion%20trees,73%2C300%20distinct%20species%20currently%20known.

p. 199 **'Researchers from Miguel Hernandez University':** Conrad, P. (2023, 25 June). 'Hell on earth – how a place of torture has haunted us culturally

over time'. *Guardian.* https://www.theguardian.com/culture/2023/jun/25/
hell-on-earth-how-a-place-of-torture-has-haunted-us-culturally-
over-time#:~:text=The%20panel%20on%20the%20left,detains%20
viewers%20for%2026%20seconds

p. 201 **'problems such as high blood pressure and heart disease':** Crawford,
A. A., Soderberg, S., Kirschbaum, C., Murphy, L., Eliasson, M., Ebrahim,
S.,... and Walker, B. R. (2019). 'Morning plasma cortisol as a cardiovascular
risk factor: findings from prospective cohort and Mendelian randomization
studies'. *European Journal of Endocrinology,* 181(4), 429–438.

p. 202 **'Freudenberger had been working as a psychoanalyst':** Lepore,
J. (2021, 17 May). 'Burnout: Modern Affliction or Human Condition?'
New Yorker. https://www.newyorker.com/magazine/2021/05/24/burnout-
modern-affliction-or-human-condition

p. 202 **'It is precisely because we are dedicated':** Malesic, J. (2022, 1 January). 'Burnout dominated 2021: The history of our burnout problem'.
Washington Post. https://www.washingtonpost.com/history/2022/01/01/
burnout-history-freudensberger-maslach/

p. 202 **'the Maslach Burnout Inventory':** Maslach, C., and Jackson, S. E.
(1981). *MBI: Maslach Burnout Inventory.* Palo Alto, CA, 1(2), 49–78.

p. 202 **'burnout was included in the World Health Organization's (WHO)
International Classification of Diseases':** World Health Organization
(2019/2021). *International Classification of Diseases, Eleventh Revision*
(ICD-11). Geneva, WHO.

p. 203 **'burnout was included as "an occupational phenomenon"':** CTV News
(2019, 28 May). 'Burn-out' is an "occupational phenomenon" not disease':
WHO'. https://www.ctvnews.ca/health/burnout-is-an-occupational-
phenomenon-not-disease-who-1.4438757

p. 203 **'A 2018 survey of 7,500 employees':** Wigert, B. and Agrawal, S. (2018,
12 July). 'Employee Burnout, Part 1: The 5 Main Causes'. Gallup. https://
www.gallup.com/workplace/237059/employee-burnout-part-main-causes.
aspx

p. 203 **'surveys conducted with more than 10,000 office workers':** Future
Forum Pulse (2023). 'Amid spiking burnout, workplace flexibility fuels
company culture and productivity: Winter Snapshot'. https://futureforum.
com/wp-content/uploads/2023/02/Future-Forum-Pulse-Report-Winter-
2022-2023.pdf

p. 204 **'A survey conducted in 2022 by ADP Research Institute':** ADP (2022). 'People at Work 2022: A Global Workforce View'. https://uk.adp. com/resources/insights/people-at-work-2022-a-global-workforce-view.aspx

p. 204 **'The intersection of life and work needs some work':** Newport, C. (2022, 3 January). 'It's time to embrace slow productivity: We need fewer things to work on starting now'. *New Yorker.* https://www.newyorker.com/ culture/office-space/its-time-to-embrace-slow-productivity

p. 204 **'small, inconsistent or partial effects on burnout':** Maricuțoiu, L. P., Sava, F. A., and Butta, O. (2016). 'The effectiveness of controlled interventions on employees' burnout: A meta-analysis'. *Journal of Occupational and Organizational Psychology,* 89(1), 1–27; Towey–Swift, K. D., Lauvrud, C., and Whittington, R. (2023). 'Acceptance and commitment therapy (ACT) for professional staff burnout: a systematic review and narrative synthesis of controlled trials'. *Journal of Mental Health,* 32(2), 452–464.

p. 205 **'Debbie Sorensen's excellent book *ACT for Burnout*':** Sorensen, D. (2024). *ACT for Burnout: Recharge, Reconnect, and Transform Burnout with Acceptance and Commitment Therapy.* Jessica Kingsley Publisher.

p. 205 **'failing to satisfy one or more of these yearnings':**
– Basic psychological needs satisfaction negatively associated with burnout of teachers: Slemp, G. R., Field, J. G., and Cho, A. S. H. (2020). 'A meta-analysis of autonomous and controlled forms of teacher motivation'. *Journal of Vocational Behavior,* 121, 103459.

– Basic psychological needs satisfaction negatively associated with burnout in the sports domain: Ryan, R. M., Duineveld, J. J., Di Domenico, S. I., Ryan, W. S., Steward, B. A., and Bradshaw, E. L. (2022). 'We know this much is (meta-analytically) true: A meta-review of meta-analytic findings evaluating self-determination theory'. *Psychological Bulletin,* 148(11–12), 813.

p. 206 **'our wellbeing is affected by the social, political and economic circumstances':** Willen, S. S., Williamson, A. F., Walsh, C. C., Hyman, M., and Tootle, W. (2022). 'Rethinking flourishing: Critical insights and qualitative perspectives from the US Midwest'. *SSM Mental Health,* 2, 100057; Willen, S. S., Selim, N., Mendenhall, E., Lopez, M. M., Chowdhury, S. A., and Dilger, H. (2021). 'Flourishing: migration and health in social context'. *BMJ Global Health,* 6(Suppl 1), e005108.

p. 206 **'dancers attending the prestigious Royal Ballet School and Elmhurst**

Ballet School': Mark, D. (2023, 11 September). 'Ex-dancers describe body-shaming at top ballet schools'. BBC News. https://www.bbc.co.uk/news/uk-66720433

p. 206 **'the then-Chief Executive of Swim England'**: Woods, R. (2023, 8 March). 'Swim England "truly sorry" over abuse and bullying claims'. BBC News. https://www.bbc.co.uk/news/uk-england-64826839

p. 207 **'The Whyte Report, published in June 2022'**: Whyte, A. (2022). 'The Whyte Report: An independent investigation commissioned by Sport England and UK Sport following allegations of mistreatment within the sport of gymnastics'. https://www.uksport.gov.uk/-/media/files/resources/the-whyte-review--final-report-of-anne-whyte-qc.ashx?la=enand-hash=9148BBE7D10D579B795B73E7590741CD

p. 207 **'Maggie Haney, an elite coach with USA Gymnastics'**: Allentuck, D. (2020, 19 April). 'Maggie Haney, Elite Gymnastics Coach, Is Suspended for 8 years'. *New York Times*. https://www.nytimes.com/2020/04/29/sports/gymnastics-coach-banned-maggie-haney.html

p. 207 **'Raab appeared unrepentant'**: *Guardian* (2023, 21 April). 'Threshold for bullying in danger of being too low, says Dominic Raab' [Video file]. https://www.theguardian.com/politics/video/2023/apr/21/threshold-for-bullying-in-danger-of-being-too-low-says-dominic-raab-video?CMP=Share_iOSApp_Other

p. 207 **'Todd B. Kashdan's book *The Art of Insubordination'***: Kashdan, T. B. (2022). *The Art of Insubordination: How to Dissent and Defy Effectively*. Penguin.

p. 209 **'social identity theory'**: Tajfel, H., Turner, J. C. (1979). 'An integrative theory of intergroup conflict'. In W.G. Austin, and S. Worchel (Eds.), *The Social Psychology of Intergroup Relations*. Brooks/Cole. (pp. 33–37).

p. 209 **'in-group favouritism has served some evolutionary advantages'**: Everett, J. A., Faber, N. S., and Crockett, M. (2015). 'Preferences and beliefs in in-group favoritism'. *Frontiers in Behavioral Neuroscience*, 9, 15.

p. 210 **'Tajfel and his colleagues highlighted'**: Tajfel, H. (1970). 'Experiments in intergroup discrimination'. *Scientific American*, 223(5), 96–103; Ryan, C. S., and Bogart, L. M. (1997).

 – Development of new group members' in-group and out-group stereotypes: 'Changes in perceived variability and ethnocentrism'. *Journal of Personality and Social Psychology*, 73(4), 719.

p. 210 'a process called identity foreclosure': See the work of James Marcia and 'Ego-identity Status': Marcia, J. E. (1966). 'Development and validation of ego-identity status'. *Journal of Personality and Social Psychology*, 3(5), 551.

p. 211 'They shoot horses, don't they': Moss, S. (2003, 25 August). 'I lost the seventies completely'. *Guardian*. https://www.theguardian.com/football/2003/aug/25/sport.comment4

p. 212 'In his book *The Ego and the Id*': Freud, S. (1927). *The Ego and the Id*. The Hogarth Press.

p. 214 'Of course, we need an ego to get out of bed': Nicholson, R. (2024, 7 January). '"I'm never bored': Willem Dafoe on art, yoga – and alpacas'. *The Guardian*. https://www.theguardian.com/film/2024/Jan/07/im-never-bored-willem-dafoe-on-art-yoga-and-alpacas

p. 214 'gathering traction in high-performance environments': Lewis, K. J., Walton, C. C., Slemp, G. R., and Osborne, M. S. (2022). 'Mindfulness and nonattachment-to-self in athletes: can letting go build well-being and self-actualization?' *Mindfulness*, 13(11), 2738–2750.

p. 214 'both the general population and in high-performance populations': Whitehead, R., Bates, G., Elphinstone, B., and Yang, Y. (2021). 'The relative benefits of nonattachment to self and self-compassion for psychological distress and psychological well-being for those with and without symptoms of depression'. *Psychology and Psychotherapy: Theory, Research and Practice*, 94(3), 573–586; Lewis, K. J., Walton, C. C., Slemp, G. R., and Osborne, M. S. (2022). 'Mindfulness and Nonattachment-To-Self in Athletes: Can Letting Go Build Well-being and Self-actualization?' *Mindfulness*, 13(11), 2738–2750.

p. 215 '*On Having No Head: Zen and the Rediscovery of the Obvious*': Harding, D. (2013). *On Having No Head: Zen and the Rediscovery of the Obvious*. The Shollund Trust.

p. 216 '*Waking Up: A Guide to Spirituality without Religion*': Harris, S. (2014). *Waking Up: A Guide to Spirituality without Religion*. Simon and Schuster.

p. 216 'also called *Waking Up*': *Waking Up* (n.d.). 'A new operating system for your mind'. https://www.wakingup.com/

p. 217 'Eckhart Tolle noted in his book *A New Earth*': Tolle, E. (2009). *A New Earth: Create a Better Life*. Penguin.

p. 217 'Theodor Geisel won a Pulitzer Prize': Fishman, R. (2019, 14 July).

'An Enduring Lesson From Dr. Seuss on Self-Doubt and Belonging'. My Meadow Report: The Juice is in the Journey. https://mymeadowreport.com/reneefishman/2019/dr-seuss-self-doubt-belonging/; The Art of Dr Seuss Collections. (n.d.). 'Accolades and honours'. https://www.drseussart.com/bioaccolades

p. 217 **'It's estimated that more than 700 million copies'**: Alter, A. and Harris, E.A. (2021, 20 October). 'Dr. Seuss Books Are Pulled, and a "Cancel Culture" Controversy Erupts.' *New York Times.* https://www.nytimes.com/2021/03/04/books/dr-seuss-books.html#:~:text=He%20went%20on%20to%20publish,enduringly%20popular%20children's%20book%20authors.

p. 218 **'What's this little boy doing here?'**: Klein, C. (2023, 14 August). '10 Things You May Not Know About Dr. Seuss'. The History Channel. https://www.history.com/news/9-things-you-may-not-know-about-dr-seuss

p. 218 **'In an interview conducted sixty-eight years later'**: *San Diego Magazine*, May 1986, 'Dr. Seuss from Then to Now' by Don Freeman. Cited in: Smith, C. M. (2012). *Dr. Seuss: The Cat Behind the Hat: The Art of Dr. Seuss.* Andrews McMeel Publishing.

p. 218 **'Oh, the Places You'll Go!'**: Seuss, Dr. (1990). *Oh, the Places You'll Go!* Random House.

p. 218 **'first introduced in 1978 by Pauline Clance and Suzanne Imes'**: Clance, P. R., and Imes, S. A. (1978). 'The imposter phenomenon in high achieving women: Dynamics and therapeutic intervention'. *Psychotherapy: Theory, Research and Practice*, 15(3), 241–247.

p. 225 **'losses are twice as powerful as gains'**: Tversky, A., and Kahneman, D. (2000). 'Advances in Prospect Theory: Cumulative Representation of Uncertainty'. In A. Tversky and D. Kahneman (Eds.). *Choices, Values, and Frames.* Cambridge University Press. (pp. 44–66).

p. 226 **'A research study that analysed 2.5 million putts'**: Pope, D. G., and Schweitzer, M. E. (2011). 'Is Tiger Woods Loss Averse? Persistent Bias in the Face of Experience, Competition, and High Stakes'. *American Economic Review*, 101 (1): 129–57.

p. 226 **'You don't ever want to drop a shot'**: Associated Press (2007, 23 March). 'Woods on course for third straight victory at Doral'. ESPN https://www.espn.co.uk/golf/news/story?id=2810111

p. 227 **'As Nelson Mandela once remarked'**: Herron, A. (2024, 29 March).

'Remembering Nelson Mandela: "I never lose. I either win or learn"'. *Indianapolis Recorder*. https://indianapolisrecorder.com/remembering-nelson-mandela-i-never-lose-i-either-win-or-learn/

p. 229 **'Djokovic has won just over half'**: ATP Tour (2023, 12 August). 'Novak Djokovic'. https://www.atptour.com/en/players/novak-djokovic/d643/player-stats?year=allandsurface=all

p. 229 **'In an interview with the BBC, Djokovic'**: Bevan, C. (2023, 2 July). 'Wimbledon 2023: Brain games and conscious breathing – the secrets of Djokovic's success'. BBC Sport. https://www.bbc.co.uk/sport/tennis/66077815

p. 230 **'godfather of modern mindfulness'**: Booth, R. (2017, 22 October). 'Master of mindfulness, Jon Kabat-Zinn: "People are losing their minds. That is what we need to wake up to"'. *Guardian*. https://www.theguardian.com/lifeandstyle/2017/oct/22/mindfulness-jon-kabat-zinn-depression-trump-grenfell

p. 230 **'If your mind wanders away from the breath'**: Kabat-Zinn, J. (1996). *Full Catastrophe Living: How to Cope with Stress, Pain and Illness Using Mindfulness Meditation*. Bantam Doubleday Dell Publishing Group.

p. 231 **'We've got to show our disapproval'**: Bieler, D. (2020, 27 August). 'Bill Russell, who led a 1961 NBA boycott, salutes "getting in good trouble"'. *Washington Post*. https://www.washingtonpost.com/sports/2020/08/27/bill-russell-nba-boycott/

Chapter 8: Reset

p. 235 **'In a cartoon by Emily Flake in the New Yorker'**: *New Yorker* (2022, 3 October). 'Cartoons from the 10 October 2022 issue – Cartoon by Emily Flake'. https://www.newyorker.com/cartoons/issue-cartoons/cartoons-from-the-october-10-2022-issue

p. 235 **'activated when we express compassion'**: Stellar, J. E., Cohen, A., Oveis, C., and Keltner, D. (2015). 'Affective and physiological responses to the suffering of others: compassion and vagal activity'. *Journal of Personality and Social Psychology*, 108(4), 572; Stellar, J. E., and Keltner, D. (2017). 'Compassion in the autonomic nervous system: The role of the vagus nerve'. In P. Gilbert (Ed.), *Compassion: Concepts, Research and Applications*. Routledge/Taylor and Francis Group. (pp. 120–134).

p. 237 **'referred to as "self-transcendent emotions"'**: Fogarty, C. T. (2020). 'Compassion, gratitude and awe: The role of pro-social emotions in training physicians for relational competence'. *The International Journal of Psychiatry in Medicine*, 55(5), 314–320; Stellar, J. E., Gordon, A. M., Piff, P. K., Cordaro, D., Anderson, C. L., Bai, Y., . . . and Keltner, D. (2017). 'Self-transcendent emotions and their social functions: Compassion, gratitude, and awe bind us to others through prosociality'. *Emotion Review*, 9(3), 200–207.

p. 238 **'overwhelming sense of oneness and connectedness'**: Quotes. (n.d.). 'In the Shadow of the Moon'. https://www.quotes.net/movies/in_the_shadow_of_the_moon_126849

p. 238 **'author Ralph Waldo Emerson wrote'**: Emerson R. W. (1836). *Nature.* Reprinted in *Ralph Waldo Emerson, Nature and Other Essays* (2009). Dover.

p. 238 **'In 1982, Tomohide Akiyama'**: An Darach (2022, 2 February). 'What Are The Differences Between Shinrin Yoku And Forest Bathing?'. https://silvotherapy.co.uk/articles/differences-between-shinrin-yoku-and-forest-bathing#:~:text=Japan%20is%20very%20heavily%20forested,and%20wellbeing%20through%20connection%20with

p. 239 **'90 per cent of the Japanese population live in urban areas'**: World Bank (n.d.). 'Urban population (% of total population) – Japan'. https://data.worldbank.org/indicator/SP.URB.TOTL.IN.ZS?locations=JP (accessed 30 March 2024).

p. 239 **'two-thirds of the country is covered in forest'**: Trading Economics (n.d.). 'Japan – Forest Area (% Of Land Area)' https://tradingeconomics.com/japan/forest-area-percent-of-land-area-wb-data.html (accessed 30 March 2024).

p. 239 **'Shinrin-Yoku: The Art and Science of Forest Bathing'**: Li, Q. (2018). *Shinrin-Yoku: The Art and Science of Forest Bathing.* Penguin UK.

p. 239 **'Research studies have shown that forest-bathing'**: Wen, Y., Yan, Q., Pan, Y., Gu, X., and Liu, Y. (2019). 'Medical empirical research on forest bathing (Shinrin-yoku): A systematic review'. *Environmental Health and Preventive Medicine*, 24(1), 1–21; Kotera, Y., Richardson, M., and Sheffield, D. (2020). 'Effects of shinrin-yoku (forest bathing) and nature therapy on mental health: A systematic review and meta-analysis'. *International Journal of Mental Health and Addiction*, 1–25.

p. 240 **'Evidence collected in studies conducted in eighteen different** countries': White, M. P., Elliott, L. R., Grellier, J., Economou, T., Bell, S., Bratman, G. N., . . . and Fleming, L. E. (2021). 'Associations between green/ blue spaces and mental health across 18 countries'. *Scientific Reports*, 11(1), 8903.

p. 240 '**Attention Restoration Theory**': Kaplan, R. and Kaplan, S. (1989). *The Experience of Nature: A Psychological Perspective*. Cambridge University Press.

p. 240 '**activities with other people can also do the trick**': For an overview of relevant research see: Monroy, M., and Keltner, D. (2023). 'Awe as a pathway to mental and physical health'. *Perspectives on Psychological Science*, 18(2), 309–320.

p. 241 '**Research conducted at the Booth School of Business**': Kumar, A., and Epley, N. (2018). 'Undervaluing gratitude: Expressers misunderstand the consequences of showing appreciation'. *Psychological Science*, 29(9), 1423–1435.

p. 242 '**a book about it entitled: *365 Thank Yous***': Kralik, J. (2010). *365 Thank Yous: The Year a Simple Act of Daily Gratitude Changed My Life*. Hyperion.

p. 243 '**Kralik said in a 2017 interview**': Hawk, R. (Host). (2017, 9 April). 'John Kralik – The Power of Gratitude (A Simple Act of Gratitude) – Episode 199' [Audio podcast]. *The Learning Leader*. https://learningleader.com/episode-199-john-kralik-power-gratitude-simple-act-gratitude/

p. 243 '**Seligman and his colleagues in 2005**': Seligman, M. E., Steen, T. A., Park, N., and Peterson, C. (2005). 'Positive psychology progress: Empirical validation of interventions'. *American Psychologist*, 60(5), 410–421.

p. 243 '**researchers from the University of New England in Australia**': Kirca, A., M. Malouff, J., and Meynadier, J. (2023). 'The Effect of Expressed Gratitude Interventions on Psychological Wellbeing: A Meta-Analysis of Randomised Controlled Studies'. *International Journal of Applied Positive Psychology*, 8(1), 63–86.

p. 244 '**Another review, this time conducted by a team of researchers based in Japan**': Komase, Y., Watanabe, K., Hori, D., Nozawa, K., Hidaka, Y., Iida, M., . . . and Kawakami, N. (2021). 'Effects of gratitude intervention on mental health and well-being among workers: A systematic review'. *Journal of Occupational Health*, 63(1), e12290.

p. 244 '**While gratitude interventions may not be vastly superior**': Davis,

D. E., Choe, E., Meyers, J., Wade, N., Varjas, K., Gifford, A., . . . and Worthington Jr, E. L. (2016). 'Thankful for the little things: A meta-analysis of gratitude interventions'. *Journal of Counseling Psychology*, 63(1), 20; Dickens, L. R. (2017). 'Using gratitude to promote positive change: A series of meta-analyses investigating the effectiveness of gratitude interventions'. *Basic and Applied Social Psychology*, 39(4), 193–208.

p. 244 **'the more often gratitude lists are completed'**: Komase, Y., Watanabe, K., Hori, D., Nozawa, K., Hidaka, Y., Iida, M., . . . and Kawakami, N. (2021). 'Effects of gratitude intervention on mental health and well-being among workers: A systematic review'. *Journal of Occupational Health*, 63(1), e12290.

p. 245 **'gratitude may conjure up undertones of indebtedness'**: Gulliford, L., and Morgan, B. (2017). 'The Meaning and Valence of Gratitude in Positive Psychology'. In N. Brown, T. Lomas, and F. J. Eiroa-Orosa (Eds.), *The Routledge International Handbook of Critical Positive Psychology*. Routledge. (pp. 53–69).

p. 247 **'Yes, elephants express compassion too!'**: PBS (2010, 11 October). 'Nature: Elephant Emotions'. https://www.pbs.org/wnet/nature/echo-an-elephant-to-remember-elephant-emotions/4489/

p. 248 **'research findings from sixteen different studies'**: McIntyre, R., Smith, P., and Rimes, K. A. (2018). 'The role of self-criticism in common mental health difficulties in students: A systematic review of prospective studies'. *Mental Health and Prevention*, 10, 13–27.

p. 248 **'self-compassion has three components'**: Neff, K. D. (2003). 'Self-compassion: An alternative conceptualization of a healthy attitude toward oneself'. *Self and Identity*, 2, 85–102.

p. 249 **'low levels of self-compassion strongly predict'**: MacBeth, A., and Gumley, A. (2012). 'Exploring compassion: A meta-analysis of the association between self-compassion and psychopathology'. *Clinical Psychology Review*, 32(6), 545–552; Mackintosh, K., Power, K., Schwannauer, M., and Chan, S. W. (2018). 'The relationships between self-compassion, attachment and interpersonal problems in clinical patients with mixed anxiety and depression and emotional distress'. *Mindfulness*, 9, 961–971; Millard, L. A., Wan, M. W., Smith, D. M., and Wittkowski, A. (2023). 'The effectiveness of compassion focused therapy with clinical populations: A systematic review and meta-analysis'. *Journal of Affective Disorders*, 326, 168–192.

p. 249 '**Psychological theories have proposed that the care we receive**': Gillath, O., Shaver, P.R., Mikulincer, M. (2005). 'An attachment-theoretical approach to compassion and altruism'. In: Gilbert P, (Ed.), *Compassion: Conceptualizations, Research, and Use in Psychotherapy.* Brunner-Routledge; Gilbert P. (2010). 'An introduction to compassion focused therapy in cognitive behavior therapy'. *International Journal of Cognitive Therapy,* 3(2), 97–112.

p. 249 '**study that followed 1,090 adults living in San Diego County**': Lee, E. E., Govind, T., Ramsey, M., Wu, T. C., Daly, R., Liu, J., . . . and Jeste, D. V. (2021). 'Compassion toward others and self-compassion predict mental and physical well-being: a 5-year longitudinal study of 1090 community-dwelling adults across the lifespan'. *Translational Psychiatry,* 11(1), 397.

p. 249 '**Psychological interventions aimed at boosting self-compassion**': Ferrari, M., Hunt, C., Harrysunker, A., Abbott, M. J., Beath, A. P., and Einstein, D. A. (2019). 'Self-compassion interventions and psychosocial outcomes: a meta-analysis of RCTs'. *Mindfulness,* 10(8), 1455–1473; Gilbert, P. (2014). 'The origins and nature of compassion focused therapy'. *British Journal of Clinical Psychology,* 53(1), 6–41; Neff, K. D. (2003). 'Self-compassion: an alternative conceptualization of a healthy attitude toward oneself'. *Self and Identity,* 2(2), 85–101; Kirby, J. N., Tellegen, C. L., and Steindl, S. R. (2017). 'A meta-analysis of compassion-based interventions: Current state of knowledge and future directions'. *Behavior Therapy,* 48(6), 778–792.

p. 250 '**fearful about the consequences that being self-compassionate might bring**': P. Gilbert (2009). 'Evolved minds and compassion-focused imagery in depression'. In L. Stopa (Ed.), *Imagery and the Threatened Self in Cognitive Therapy,* Routledge. (pp. 206–231); Kirby, J. N., Day, J., and Sagar, V. (2019). 'The "Flow" of compassion: A meta-analysis of the fears of compassion scales and psychological functioning'. *Clinical Psychology Review,* 70, 26–39.

p. 250 '**In a post on [Boone's] blog in 2019**': Boone, A. (2019, 8 July). 'The recovery I needed'. Race Ipsa Loquitur. http://www.ameliabooneracing.com/blog/uncategorized/therecoveryineeded/

p. 251 '**In a 2021 interview, Boone spoke**': Pompliano, P. (2021, 6 April). 'Four-Time Obstacle Race Champion Amelia Boone on Mastering the Art of Suffering: "I'm not the strongest. I'm not the fastest. But I'm really good at suffering."' The Profile. https://theprofile.substack.com/p/amelia-boone

p. 251 'increase people's levels of self-compassion': Lv, J., Jiang, Y., Li, R., Chen, Y., Gu, X., Zhou, J., ... and Zeng, X. (2023). 'Effects of loving-kindness and compassion meditations on self-compassion: A systematic review and meta-analysis'. *Clinical Psychology: Science and Practice*, 31(1), 19–35.

p. 251 'and compassion towards others': Chio, F. H., Mak, W. W., Cheng, R. H., Hsu, A. Y., and Kwan, H. H. (2022). 'Can compassion to the self be extended to others: the association of self-compassion and other-focused concern'. *Journal of Positive Psychology*, 17(5), 679–689.

p. 252 'effective at reducing symptoms of anxiety and depression': Zheng, Y., Yan, L., Chen, Y., Zhang, X., Sun, W., Lv, J., ... and Zeng, X. (2023). 'Effects of Loving-Kindness and Compassion Meditation on Anxiety: A Systematic Review and Meta-Analysis'. *Mindfulness*, 1–17; Lv, J., Liu, Q., Zeng, X., Oei, T. P., Liu, Y., Xu, K., ... and Liu, J. (2020). 'The effect of four Immeasurables meditations on depressive symptoms: A systematic review and meta-analysis'. *Clinical Psychology Review*, 76, 101814.

p. 252 'lead to structural changes in how our brains function': Goleman, D., and Davidson, R. J. (2017). *Altered Traits: Science Reveals How Meditation Changes Your Mind, Brain, and Body*. Avery.

p. 253 'Holding on to anger is like grasping a hot coal': Buddhaghosha (circa fifth century CE). *Visuddhimagga* IX, 23.

p. 253 'the Compassionate Colour exercise': Gilbert, P. (2010). 'Training Our Minds in, with and for Compassion: An Introduction to Concepts and Compassion-Focused Exercises'. https://www.getselfhelp.co.uk/docs/GILBERT-COMPASSION-HANDOUT.pdf

p. 254 'brief practice known as a "self-compassion break"': Neff, K. (n.d.). 'Exercise 2: Self-Compassion Break'. Self-Compassion. https://self-compassion.org/exercises/exercise-2-self-compassion-break/

p. 254 'The Benefits of Not Being a Jerk to Yourself': TED (2022, 10 October). 'The Benefits of Not Being a Jerk to Yourself | Dan Harris | TED' [Video file]. YouTube. https://www.youtube.com/watch?v=NuhIzO57HVk

p. 256 Centre for Disease Control and Prevention in the USA recommends': Centre for Disease Control and Prevention (n.d.). 'How Much Sleep Do I Need?' https://www.cdc.gov/sleep/about_sleep/how_much_sleep.html; 'How much physical activity do adults need?' https://www.cdc.gov/phys-icalactivity/basics/adults/; 'Healthy Eating for a Healthy Weight' https://www.cdc.gov/healthyweight/healthy_eating/index.html

p. 256 **'Outlive: *The Science and Art of Longevity*':** Attia, P. (2023). *Outlive: The Science and Art of Longevity*. Harmony.

p. 257 **'the World's 50 Best Restaurants Awards for 2021':** The World's 50 Best Restaurants 2021 (n.d.). 'The World's 50 Best Restaurants 2021'. https://www.theworlds50best.com/previous-list/2021

p. 258 **'In an article in *The New York Times*, Redzepi described':** Moskin, J. (2023, 9 January). 'Noma, Rated the World's Best Restaurant, Is Closing Its Doors'. *New York Times*. https://www.nytimes.com/2023/01/09/dining/noma-closing-rene-redzepi.html#:~:text=In%20the%20past%20two%20years,it%20ineligible%20for%20future%20wins.

p. 258 **'news conference announcing her decision, Ardern said':** McClure, T. (2023, 19 January). 'Jacinda Ardern resigns as prime minister of New Zealand'. *Guardian*. https://www.theguardian.com/world/2023/jan/19/jacinda-ardern-resigns-as-prime-minister-of-new-zealand

p. 258 **'interviewed on ABC's *Good Morning America*':** Kindelan, K. (2023, 20 September). 'Former New Zealand Prime Minister Jacinda Ardern says it wasn't burnout that led her to step down'. ABC NEWS. https://abcnews.go.com/GMA/News/former-new-zealand-prime-minister-jacinda-ardern-burnout/story?id=103337531

p. 259 **'A 2023 report published by the PwC accounting firm':** PWC (2023, 20 June). 'One in four workers looking for new jobs as cost-of-living concerns bite: PwC Global Workforce Hopes and Fears Survey'. https://www.pwc.com/gx/en/news-room/press-releases/2023/pwc-global-workforce-hopes-and-fears-survey-2023.html

p. 259 **'PwC also highlight "(p)urpose, company culture and inclusion"':** PWC (2023, 20 June). 'One in four workers looking for new jobs as cost-of-living concerns bite: PwC Global Workforce Hopes and Fears Survey'. https://www.pwc.com/gx/en/news-room/press-releases/2023/pwc-global-workforce-hopes-and-fears-survey-2023.html

p. 260 **'How hard is it to slow down':** Apatow, J. (Director and Producer). (2018). *The Zen Diaries of Garry Shandling – Part II* [Film]. Apatow Productions and Radical Media. https://www.imdb.com/title/tt7860890/

p. 261 **'Research evidence indicates that contrary to what we might think':** Bruk, A., Scholl, S. G., and Bless, H. (2018). 'Beautiful mess effect: Self-other differences in evaluation of showing vulnerability'. *Journal of Personality and Social Psychology*, 115(2), 192.

p. 262 **'construal level theory'**: Trope, Y., and Liberman, N. (2010). 'Construal-level theory of psychological distance'. *Psychological Review*, 117(2), 440.

p. 262 **'Nick Cox, Director of Manchester United Football Club's Academy alluded to'**: Humphrey, J. and Hughes, D. (Hosts). (2022, 15 August). 'Nick Cox: Why the future IS bright at Manchester United (No. 137)' [Video podcast episode]. *The High Performance Podcast*. https://www.thehighper-formancepodcast.com/podcast/nickcox

p. 263 **'Research has shown that people with higher levels of self-compassion'**: Bruk, A., Scholl, S. G., and Bless, H. (2022). 'You and I both: Self-compassion reduces self-other differences in evaluation of showing vulnerability'. *Personality and Social Psychology Bulletin*, 48(7), 1054–1067.

p. 267 **'refer to this process as "mental contrasting"'**: Oettingen, G., Mayer, D., and Brinkmann, B. (2010). 'Mental contrasting of future and reality'. *Journal of Personnel Psychology*, 9(3), 138–144.

p. 267 **'Research has shown that engaging in mental contrasting'**: Oettingen, G. (2012). 'Future thought and behaviour change'. *European Review of Social Psychology*, 23, 1–63; Cross, A., and Sheffield, D. (2019). 'Mental contrasting for health behaviour change: a systematic review and meta-analysis of effects and moderator variables'. *Health Psychology Review*, 13, 209–225.

Conclusion: Thrive

p. 280 **'It is not the strongest species that survive'**: Megginson, L. C. (1963). 'Lessons from Europe for American Business'. *The Southwestern Social Science Quarterly*, 44(1), 3–13.

p. 283 **'Our ability to connect with others is important'**: In his book *Bowling Alone*, the American political scientist Robert D. Putnam highlights the health benefits that connecting with others brings. It makes for startling reading. 'As a rough rule of thumb, if you belong to no group but decide to join one, you cut your risk of dying over the next year in half' he writes – Putnam, R. D. (2020). *Bowling Alone: The Collapse and Revival of American Community*. Simon and Schuster. (p. 298).

Appendices

p. 293 'It was Aristotle who warned that': Aristotle (circa fourth century BCE). *Nicomachean Ethics*, Book 2, 1108b.

p. 293 'research has shown that when fear starts to dominate': Roest, A. M., de Jonge, P., Lim, C. W. W., Stein, D. J., Al-Hamzawi, A., Alonso, J., . . . and Scott, K. M. (2017). 'Fear and distress disorders as predictors of heart disease: a temporal perspective'. *Journal of Psychosomatic Research*, 96, 67–75.

p. 294 'expressions of sadness can act as a stimulus to encourage others': Huron, D. (2018). 'On the functions of sadness and grief'. In H.C. Lench (Ed.), *Function of Emotions*. Springer. (pp. 59–91).

p. 295 'If you suddenly and unexpectedly feel joy': Oliver, M. (2010). *Swan: Poems and Prose Poems*. Beacon Press (p. 42).

p. 295 'The artist and naturalist John Muir Laws suggests': Laws, J. M., and Lygren, E. (2016). *The Laws Guide to Nature Drawing and Journaling*. Heyday.

p. 296 'Stephen R. Covey, the American educator, said that': Covey, S. R., and Merrill, R. R. (2006). *The Speed of Trust: The One Thing that Changes Everything*. Simon and Schuster.

p. 311 'Bringing other people with us': This approach draws on: Kashdan, T. B. (2022). *The Art of Insubordination: How to Dissent and Defy Effectively*. Penguin.

p. 313 'Compassionate colour exercise': Adapted from: Gilbert, P. (2010). 'Training Our Minds in, with and for Compassion: An Introduction to Concepts and Compassion-Focused Exercises'. https://www.getselfhelp.co.uk/docs/GILBERT-COMPASSION-HANDOUT.pdf

p. 314 'Self-compassion break' : Adapted from: Neff, K. (n.d.). 'Exercise 2: Self-Compassion Break'. Self-Compassion. https://self-compassion.org/exercises/exercise-2-self-compassion-break/

p. 320 'a book by forest scientist and author Peter Wohlleben': Wohlleben, P. (2016). *The Hidden Life of Trees: What They Feel, How They Communicate – Discoveries From a Secret World*. Greystone Books.

Index

Entries in **bold** refer to key themes.

INDEX

INDEX